The Gift of Worship

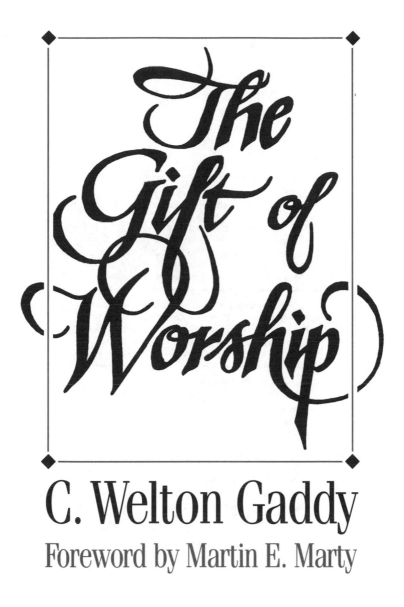

The Gift of Worship

C. Welton Gaddy

Foreword by Martin E. Marty

BROADMAN PRESS
NASHVILLE, TENNESSEE

Unless otherwise noted, all Scripture quotations are from the *Revised Standard Version of the Bible*, copyrighted 1946, 1952 © 1971, 1973 by the National Council of the Churches of Christ in the U.S.A., and used by permission.

**Library of Congress
Cataloging-in-Publication Data**

Gaddy, C. Welton.
    The gift of worship / C. Welton Gaddy ; foreword by Martin E. Marty.
        p.   cm.
    Includes bibliographical references and index.
    IBSN 0-8054-6053-5
    1. Public worship. 2. Public worship—Baptists. 3. Baptists—Liturgy. I. Title.
BV15.G33   1992
264—dc20   92-4362
                                                       CIP

To the Glory of God
and
In memory of
John W. Carlton
and
Franklin M. Segler

Other books by C. Welton Gaddy

Easter Proclamation: Remembrance and Renewal
Profile of a Christian Citizen
Proclaim Liberty
In Awe of the Ordinary: Reflections on the Christian Life
Beginning at the End
Discovering Hebrews
God's Clowns
Tuning the Heart: University Sermons
A Soul Under Siege: Surviving Clergy Depression

Contents

Foreword

Let's call the two parties "higher church" and "lower church," because they are not pure, never merely "high church" or "low church." They face off against each other consistently, but never with more passion than in matters of Christian worship.

"Higher:" Catholic, Orthodox, Lutheran, Anglican, and the like, have their own ideas about biblical traditions of worship as they get worked out in contemporary life. There is to be a sense of awe, of what Paul Tillich called a "revelatory constellation," enhanced by the divine elemental roar of the pipe organ, the sunlight prismed through dark yet vivid stained glass, the air sometimes redolent of incense, the bodies given to kneeling, with hands making the sign of the cross. "Paganism!" snort the "lower church" people.

"Lower:" this means free churches, Baptists, mainstream Protestants, evangelicals, who have their counter ideas about biblical traditions of worship as these get worked out in contemporary life. There is to be a sense of awe, of what Paul Tillich called a "revelatory constellation," enhanced by the intimacy of electronic organ or guitar, the sunlight direct through plain or simply colored glass, the air fresh and the breeze blowing, the bodies naturally standing or sitting, with hands folded in quiet prayer. "Vulgar!" sneer the "higher church" people.

Neither side would satisfy C. Welton Gaddy. In *The Gift of Worship* he displays no sense of the yearning some Free Church folk show of a need to "upgrade their status," as the airlines would have it, by turning aesthetically formal or aesthetically anything in worship. On the other hand he disdains the "aw, shucks!" approach to worship in which a slangy band of believers claims intimacy with a chummy God. He knows that when informalists say, "We don't have a liturgy, the way high church people do," they will go on to describe as predictable and routinized an order of worship as the Divinity Liturgy of Saint John Chrysostom for the Orthodox or the *Book of Common Prayer* as used by high Anglicans.

Gaddy's interest is in finding a path, or shall we say an aisle, not between but beyond the concerns of the partisans. The peculiar virtue of his book lies in his intention to induce the leader and other participants in worship to think "from scratch," as it were. Is he not asking here, "Who is the God who would be worshiped? What is the character of the worship which would flow from the answers we would supply to such a question?"

Gaddy's God is one who inspires awe and whose Godness is trivialized by chumminess, casual and inept worship, inertness, nondescriptness. The God he would worship is appropriately addressed by God-centered language and not mere reports on the passing feel-bad or feel-good emotions of the devotees. This deity or *theos*ness is thought of with awe, with concentrated and thought-through worship, worship which turns out to be "ert" and "descript."

Never is it the purpose of a foreword writer to give away the plot. Suffice it to say that the strength of the book, which derives from its central virtue, lies in the stick-to-itiveness of an author who never forgets he is talking about worship as gift. Thus conceived, worship is at heart devoted to praise, and praising is the one distinctive thing a Christian congregation does. (Anyone else can have fund drives, committees, programs, good works; but only the congregation praises.)

No reader will expect to find a complete match with the picture of worship here presented, as Gaddy works it out from a particular church tradition, particular as they all are. This Lutheran would like to have heard even more about baptism than this Baptist gives us, and would not have waited 141 pages to bring up the Lord's Supper, from which the keynotes of worship derive. For us. But my type reads his kind of book for compensation, only to find that this one is itself not an extreme corrective but a balanced work: biblical, thought through indeed, nuanced, provocative. As worship itself should be.

Martin E. Marty
The University of Chicago

Preface

Worship is a gift.—A capacity to worship and the responsibility to worship inherent in that ability are gifts from God to all people. The attitudes, activities, words, and commitments of worship, as well as the sincerity with which they occur, are gifts from people to God.

Worship is a gift between lovers.—In the New Testament a writer named John declares, "We love, because he [God] first loved us" (1 John 4:19). Christian worship participates in and is pervaded by that love—from its beginning as an act of which people are capable and for which people are responsible (because of the gift from God who loves the world) to its expression through adoration, praise, and service, which is the gift of people who love God. Within all people the most appropriate response to a realization of being loved by God is a resolution to live lovingly toward God. Worship is a love gift to the love-giving God.

Worship is a gift between lovers who keep on giving to each other.—God showers creation with good gifts. In worship with gratitude and devotion, people give back to God what has been received from God. For example, God gives faith. Recipients of that faith return it to God as confessions of redemption and acts of submission in worship. God gives material goods. Worshipers, in turn, lay before God their tithes and other offerings made possible by an accumulation of material things. God gives music. In worship, persons blessed with this gift demonstrate their stewardship of it as music becomes a medium of praise to God. God gives friendship and fellowship. People who receive those gifts form a community whose central purpose is to worship God. Giving and receiving form a circular pattern between God and the people of God, which defies comprehension and lasts forever.

My highest hopes for this book will be realized if it can share in the nature of the subject it addresses. I offer my work as *a gift.*

It is a gift to Baptists. My life has benefited immensely from the generosity of Baptist people. As a child, I was taught the central truths of the Bible and introduced to Christ in a Baptist church. In that fellowship, I sensed the call of God to ministry and received affirmation and support when I responded to that call. My college and seminary education was financed in part by Baptist funds.

Among Baptists I learned about the relationship that exists between faith and reason, prayer and politics, unity and diversity, freedom and discipline. As a result of biblically based lectures and the personal examples of countless numbers of Baptist individuals, I have come to understand the significance of worship and the ingredients that make worship most meaningful. Many of the most memorable worship experiences of my life have occurred in Baptist congregations around the world.

Baptists have important contributions to make to conversations on worship within the Christian community. Regrettably, though, Baptist monographs on worship have been relatively scarce. This work is intended as a gift to aid Baptists to think about, discuss, and plan worship. It is offered with a hope of encouraging other Baptists to address the subject, not only among themselves but also within the larger Christian family. Therefore, I am profoundly grateful to Broadman Press for the opportunity to write about the importance of congregational worship.

I have received blessings from the goodness of Baptist people. This book is one gift of response. But any treatment of the subject of worship has a much broader application than the members of one denomination. My work in this volume is offered as a gift to all people who seek a better understanding of worship in order to be more faithful and joyful participants in worship.

Perhaps individuals in the Free Church tradition will identify most readily with my sentiments and interact most energetically with my suggestions because of our common heritage. However, the basic themes of the book are compatible with the worship interests of the entire Christian community.

I have tried to blend academic insights and personal experiences, practical suggestions and ideological considerations. Notes at the conclusion of the text point to valuable resources on worship that address at length and in detail aspects of worship treated only briefly here. I must confess, however, that I offer this volume not as an expert on worship but as a devotee of worship.

At every point in this writing project, I have tried to consider the needs of different people—people seeking a better understanding of worship, people charged with the responsibility of planning experiences of public worship and people desiring more meaningful personal participation in worship. The work is an offering to all such folk.

More basic than all of that, the book is *a gift to God.* A sincere effort has been made to produce this volume with an attitude, motivations, intentions, and hopes acceptable to God. My prayer is that this affirmation of the importance of congregational worship will honor God and enhance the worship experiences of others so that God will be glorified.

Obviously, no book is ever the work of one person alone. While working on this volume, I have realized again my indebtedness to far more people than I can remember (literally). So many people whetted my interest in the subject of corporate worship, contributed to my ideas about its nature, and helped me to find courage enough to put something in print about worship.

What follows is not nearly so much a report on research as the confession of a pilgrim. In my first pastorate (Beechwood Baptist Church in Louisville, Kentucky) after graduate studies at Southern Seminary, I was encouraged to make congregational worship a high priority in my ministry. I continue to be grateful for the support of my ministerial colleagues there—Gary and Judy Crow, Cleamon Downs, Gary Evans, Joe Paul Pruett, and Hugh and Ruth McElrath. Fortunately, people committed to the primacy of worship have been present in every church I have pastored.

This volume is dedicated to the memory of two men and their ministries. John Carlton and Franklin Segler were my mentors, colleagues, and friends.

At The Southern Baptist Theological Seminary, John Carlton helped me, as no one had before, to understand the nature of worship, the scope of responsibilities related to worship leadership, and the importance of both. My admiration for John Carlton first developed in a classroom. However, my love and appreciation for him grew as I enjoyed his company in other settings. Shortly before his death, John and I had an opportunity to spend several hours together talking about church, faith, values, and the manner in which all of those concerns are caught up in the worship of God. I miss him. I thank God for him.

Franklin Segler was a pioneering advocate of public worship among Southern Baptists. His book *Christian Worship: Its Theology and Practice* continues to be a valuable resource in studies of worship. Prior to becoming senior minister at the Broadway Baptist Church in Fort Worth, Texas, I had known Franklin Segler only through his writings. However, Franklin was a member of the ministerial staff in the Broadway congregation. In that context we became good friends. Though Franklin was then well over seventy years of age, in many ways he was the youngest member of our ministry team. We planned together, exchanged ideas from our readings, shared meals together with our wives, played touch football together on staff retreats, and worked on worship together. What a great encourager as well as an excellent teacher and an exemplary minister!

Sojourners with me throughout much of my pilgrimage related to worship have been Judy, my wife, and James and John Paul, our two sons. None of the three hesitates to share personal opinions. More than once, on their way out of a sanctuary after a worship service, our sons have handed me an order of worship covered with handwritten notes critiquing the service and making suggestions for improvements in future services. Usually, Judy has been more patient before sharing her comments about a worship experience. As I write these words, I am smiling and not at all complaining. I have learned much from these three individuals. Their continued companionship is a source of great gratitude. Their love and support are reasons for thanksgiving.

The old Westminister Shorter Catechism declares that the chief end of every person is to praise God and to enjoy God forever. What follows are an unconditional affirmation of that assertion and materials offered with the hope of increasing that enjoyment.

—C. Welton Gaddy

Introduction
"Something for Thee"

Worship is the most important work of the church. The people of God exist to serve God. No higher service to God is possible than the worship of God.

Numerous books address various dimensions of worship. One more volume like many others is unnecessary. My reason for risking this venture is to state unequivocally that worship is the highest priority in the lives of God's people. An examination of the relationship between this biblically mandated responsibility of the church and the very practical, ministry-related concerns of a local congregation supports this affirmation. This book also seeks to clarify the nature and importance of the total act of corporate worship and each of the essential parts which make up that experience.

Christian worship is about offerings or gifts—from God and to God. The opportunity (privilege) to worship God is itself a gift from God and specific acts of worship are prompted by other gifts from God—spiritual and material. Conversely, the worship of God consists of offering gifts to God. Since worship is a gift from God to us and since worship involves gifts from us to God, the focus of this volume is on the gifts of Christian worship.

For us to study worship, we must share a common understanding of the meaning of that word. From the Anglo-Saxon *weorthscipe*, worship emerged as an English word denoting an ascription of worth, a recognition of the merit of another. Essentially, worship is a verb. To worship is to express appreciation, to adore, to love, and to praise. Thus, in relation to God, worship is our total response in praise and commitment to the Divine, Holy Presence (our gifts responding to God's gift). We dedicate all that we are and have to all that God is.

The German word for worship, *Gottesdienst,* is much richer and more descriptive than the English term. The German term captures the dialogical nature of worship in a manner impossible for a single English word. *Gottesdienst* conveys both of the major movements of worship—God's service and people's service to God. *Gottesdienst* reflects the union of what God has done for all persons and the services that congregations offer to God as worship.[1]

In the New Testament two different words are translated *worship*. Each contributes to a more comprehensive understanding of the act. *Proskuneo* means literally "to kiss toward" or "to bow down." Immediately obvious is the sense of humble adoration so important in each worshiper and so vital in a worshiping congregation. *Latreuo* means rendering honor or paying homage. Again, the appropriateness of such gestures in relation to God is readily apparent. Notice that in each instance the idea of making an offering is central to the idea of worshiping. To worship is to make an offering (our gifts as responses to God's gift).

To worship God is to give glory and honor to God, to adore God, to exalt God. A. S. Herbert describes worship as "the recognition and acknowledgement at every level of human nature of the absolute worth of God."[2] Similarly, William Temple writes of worship in terms of joyful submission to God. Of all the definitions of Christian worship which I have read, Temple's is by far the most comprehensive as well as beautiful:

> Worship is the submission of all our nature to God. It is the quickening of the conscience by His holiness; the nourishment of the mind with His truth; the purifying of imagination by His beauty; the opening of the heart to His love; the surrender of will to His purpose—and all of this gathered up in adoration, the most selfless emotion of which our nature is capable.[3]

Worship is an offering of love to the God of love.

But worship is not a one-way experience—monologue rather than dialogue. Even as we approach God, we discover that God already has been approaching us. [And still is. In fact, in a genuine experience of worship we realize that the entire matter was started by God rather than by us. We seek God because God has sought us. We love God because God has loved us. We give to God because God has given to us. In no sense must we storm the gates of heaven in order to attract God's attention and demand that God listen to our orations. God has entered our history. God has sought us personally. God has provided a foundation for divine-human communication and extended an invitation for us to enjoy it. Worship is a conversation between the God of revelation and people in need of redemption—each of whom has been (and is) seeking the other.]

Christian worship embraces and celebrates the incarnation of God in Jesus Christ. We know best who God is, all that God does, and the content of God's desires through the life and ministry of Jesus. Christ is the foundation of Christian worship as well its facilitator. Christian worship is participation in the worship of God made possible by the person of Christ.

In His compassionate act of complete self-giving on the cross, Jesus demonstrates the basic nature of worship. As the great High Priest, Jesus invites us to participate in worship made possible by God's gift to us and challenges us toward a dedication of ourselves and our gifts as acts of worship to God. Complete obedience to God marks the authentic worship of God. J. G. Davies highlights this truth helpfully in his assertion that worship is a response to the total work of Christ in one's total existence.[4]

The presence of the Holy Spirit prompts and guides true worship as well as empowers the obedience born in worship. Being "in the Spirit" is inevitably related to participating in worship. Ralph Martin captures the significant role of the Holy Spirit in worship as he describes our worship of the Trinitarian God: "Christian worship is the adoration and service of God the Father through the mediation of the Son and prompted by the Holy Spirit."[5]

Human expressions of the worship of God vary considerably, even dramatically—formal and informal, orderly and chaotic, emotional and rational. Notice that no one mood of worship or form of worship is dictated by any of the definitions of worship. However, the worship of God is to be consistent with the nature of God as revealed both in Jesus Christ and in the Bible.

Worship always must be understood theologically rather than functionally. Worship is an end in itself. To attempt the worship of God for any other purpose than glorifying God compromises worship. Worship is not meant to promote an institution, to publicize a program, or to elevate any person but to exalt God. Worship is not a self-serving experience but a God-serving endeavor.]

Biblical Foundations

Worship is a necessity for the people of God. The Bible assumes a recognition of the absolute priority of worship rather than asserting or arguing it. Indeed, the Scriptures are filled with statements which record God's invitation to worship and God's expectations of a worshiping congregation.

Often the psalmist seems to function as the worship leader in a cosmic service of praise. Many of his words have the sound of a call to worship extended to a congregation made up of the whole creation. Psalm 29:2 enjoins, "Ascribe to the Lord the glory of his name; worship the Lord in holy array." Psalm 95:6-7a says, "O come, let us worship and bow down, let us kneel before the Lord, our Maker! For he is our God."

The centrality of worship in the Psalter is appropriate since each of the psalms is an instrument of worship. But the priority of the worship of God was established in the Old Testament long before any of the psalms took shape. The first mandate of the Decalogue was the command to worship only the one true God. Prohibition and admonition were intertwined. False gods were to be avoided entirely so Yahweh, the only true God, could be worshiped sincerely and unreservedly.

Often the prophets are depicted as divinely appointed itinerants clearly positioned against the established religion and its leaders, interested only in spontaneous expressions of devotion to God, and thus self-acclaimed opponents of corporate, public worship. Not so. To be critical of the abuses of worship is not to be antagonistic toward authentic worship. God's prophets offered fiery denunciations of worship practices in which show had replaced substance; words were spoken apart from significant meaning; rituals were repeated without regard for righteousness; and formality had been confused with spirituality. But the authentic worship of God was highly revered.

Isaiah, a prophet whose insights into the nature of worship are among the best in all of the Bible, received his call from God in the midst of worship. Jeremiah repeatedly went to the temple to offer prophetic discourses. Even a rugged, seemingly independent prophet like Amos valued the hymns of praise prevalent in corporate worship. Anticipation of the restoration of the true worship of God was an integral component in the prophetic vision of a better future: "All flesh shall come to worship before me, says the Lord" (Isa. 66:23); "It shall come to pass in the latter days that the mountain of the house of the Lord shall be established as the highest of the mountains,... and peoples shall flow to it,... and say: 'Come, let us go up to the mountain of the Lord,... that he may teach us his ways and we may walk in his paths'" (Mic. 4:1-2).

The sweep of the Old Testament reflects the importance, indeed the centrality, of corporate worship in the life of the people of God. By way of prayers, special festivals, holy days, hymns, sermons, and many other means, Israel incorporated into worship its most cherished traditions of sacred history, creation, covenant, and law.[6] Old Testament worship centered on Almighty God, author of the gifts of grace and glory and recipient of the gifts of worship and glory, and found its greatest fulfillment in the worshipers' complete obedience to God.[7]

Jesus identified with the best of the worship tradition in the Old Testament. He participated in synagogue services and joined worship-based, festival-related pilgrimages to Jerusalem. Jesus encouraged His followers in the discipline of worship, looking toward the time "when the true worshipers will worship the Father in spirit and truth, for such the Father seeks to worship him" (John 4:23).

Most of the early Christians were converted Jews who saw no need for a complete break with the worship practices of Judaism. Thus, the New Testament describes Christians continuing to participate in temple and synagogue services. With the passing of time, Christians changed their places of worship. However, except for sacrificial rites, most of the primary elements of worship found in the Old Testament were retained in the New Testament community of faith.

A distinctive element in Christian worship was the celebration of the incarnation. The messianic promises that had been present in worship were now a fulfillment worthy of the highest praise. Even the primary day of worship was changed to reflect this all-important distinctive. The Lord's Day, the first day of the week, replaced the Sabbath, the seventh day of the week, as the appropriate time for corporate worship. Each Sunday was considered a renewal of the Easter festival—a day of rejoicing because of the resurrection of Jesus.

Service and worship became almost synonymous within the primitive community of faith. Worship was an act of service in itself, but worship also was an act meant to assure a lifetime of service. Nowhere is this truth more obvious than in a portion of Paul's words to the Christians in Rome. Raymond Bailey is correct in likening Romans 12:1 to the ancient Israelite call to worship: "I appeal to you therefore, brethren, by the mercies of God, to present your bodies as a living sacrifice, holy and acceptable to God, which is your spiritual worship."[8] God's gifts in love invite people's gifts in worship and service.

Worship is so integral to the life of faith as described in the New Testament that one without the other is unthinkable. Gerhard Delling presents this truth, powerfully asserting that, "there is no possibility of being a Christian in the New Testament without worship."[9] Worship stood at the center of the lives of believers. All of the ministries of the early church developed out of this center and remained in constant contact with it. Little wonder, then, that nearing the end of his words in the Apocalypse, the author of Revelation passes on to his immediate readers, as well as to people in all times, the angelic message declared to him: "Worship God" (Rev. 22:9).

Keep in mind that the Scriptures from which these truths about worship have been drawn were (and are) themselves essential ingredients in worship practices. Much of the material in both the Old Testament and the New Testament developed in and was preserved by a worshiping community of faith. Worship of the creating and redeeming God preceded both theology and Scripture.

Historical Perspective

Most historians agree that early Christian worship embraced three basic services: the Word-of-God service, the Lord's Supper, and baptism. Though a neat division of these emphases is questionable (usually a celebration of the Lord's Supper was combined with proclamation of the Word), the importance of the three is without significant debate.

The Word-of-God service was influenced by synagogue worship. This service began with a Scripture reading by a well-educated person in the congregation. By the second century, both the Old Testament and the New Testament were read. Preaching followed. Prayers dominated by praise and thanks concluded the service as all of the worshipers said, "Amen."

Early Christian documents mention two different types of Lord's Supper observances. One, usually viewed as pre-Pauline, focused on the "breaking of bread" and omitted references to "the cup" or the last supper of Jesus. The emphasis of this meal, oriented more to Easter than to Good Friday, was the Presence of Christ, not His death. Sometimes this meal was referred to as a "love feast."

The second type of Lord's Supper observance received direction from the writings of Paul and looked back to the last supper of Jesus. Early on, this celebration was held in conjunction with a fellowship meal. However, by the end of the second century, the Lord's Supper stood alone, unless combined with a Word-of-God service.

Most students of early Christian worship conclude that the celebration of the Lord's Supper was the central act of Christian worship at that time. The meal evoked communion and thanksgiving. Worshipers were caused to look back to the sacrificial suffering of Jesus and to look ahead to the glories of the age to come.

In the second century, baptism was always preceded by a period of preparation and instruction. Each new disciple of Christ was led into the water without clothes, shed to symbolize the renunciation of evil, and immersed three times. Usually, baptism was followed by a celebration of the Lord's Supper.

One historian has observed that the most striking characteristic of Christian worship during the first three centuries was related to fellowship. Worship emanated from a strong fellowship among believers and was offered to God through corporate action.[10]

Over the next several hundred years, though worship generally retained an important place in the church, the significance of typical services deteriorated tragically. Preaching fell to a low level of importance. By the sixteenth century Scripture selections in public readings were replaced by passages chosen from both the historical and legendary words of the Church's saints. Formality and ritual were woven into a straitjacket which was forced onto worshipers, thus preventing their meaningful involvement in worship. Even the Lord's Supper, for years a meal of celebration and proclamation, became a spectacle full of superstition.

Congregational worship benefited greatly from the Protestant Reformation. In Martin Luther's mind, the purpose of worship was to glorify God as the Giver (as opposed to the more Catholic intent of winning God's favor). Members of the congregation were not to be spectators. Each Christian was a priest who should offer a sacrifice of praise and openly confess belief in God. The Word of God occupied the primary place in worship for Luther. He believed that the preached Word reveals God, conveys Christ's presence, and invites faith as the needed response.

Latin had become the official language of the church. Luther stressed the importance of people being able to worship God and hear God's Word in their own language. To this end, he introduced congregational singing into services, encouraged priests to use the language of the people rather than Latin, and translated the Bible into German.

John Calvin also understood worship in terms of a gift. He thought that everyone in a community of faith should participate in offering confession, homage, and thanksgiving to God. Calvin insisted on stark simplicity in worship, rejecting material attractions and encouraging the involvement of each worshiper's heart. Calvin's reforms were more radical than Luther's. While Luther stressed the joy and peace of believing, Calvin emphasized the necessity of obedience. Calvin did allow congregational singing in worship services, but, unlike Luther, he limited such music to the metrical psalms.

Reform in worship practices took place also among the Independents, Separatists, Puritans, and Anabaptists, people usually considered together under the designation of "Free Churches."[11] These believers rejected the idea of a fixed liturgy. They emphasized the ministry of the Word of God. Long sermons based on various biblical texts formed the heart of their worship. Fixed orders of services were rejected. Set prayers were replaced by extemporary prayers by the preacher. The Free Churches intended to be free in worship as well as in all other dimensions of their work.

From the Reformation came a new spirit, a new power, and new forms in worship. Congregational involvement in worship was restored. Simplicity and understanding replaced a mysterious (often meaningless) formality. Christian worship was reshaped to conform more closely with its original biblical pattern.

In Colonial days, when Christians in the New World had no houses of worship, ordained ministers, or material resources,

thcy gathered together and decided to put worship first, confident that if such action was taken other needs would be
attended and ministries added. What wisdom! And, what a warn-
ing. No number of other "important" church-related concerns
should ever be allowed to crowd out the priority of worship.

History underscores the truth about worship contained in the
Holy Scriptures. Worship is God's gift to the church, which
invites the church's best gifts in a response of worship before
God. Worship is the key to understanding how a church pleases
God and the church's power to do God's work in the world.

Contemporary Thought

Staggering changes in worship practices have occurred in the
Roman Catholic Church in recent years. The Second Vatican
Council (1962-65) and its *Constitution on the Sacred Liturgy*
brought sweeping reforms. The changes increased the laity's
understanding of each component of worship to involve all of
the people. Latin was discarded as the official language of worship. Priests were instructed to speak the language of the people. Great prominence was assigned to the Bible. Church
leaders were told to open the Scriptures more fully to all people. Biblically based sermons became vital components in corporate experiences of worship.

Non-Roman churches—the "mainline" denominations and
congregations in the Free Church tradition—also have given
themselves to a serious rethinking and reshaping of worship
practices. Some historians have observed that the recent concern for reforms and renewal in worship have no parallels since
the Reformation and the Counter-Reformation of the sixteenth
century.[12] A statement issued by United Methodists after their
extensive study of worship expresses both the spirit and the
conviction of many Christians: "The reform and renewal of our
Sunday worship is...nothing less than the recovery of Christ in
the life of the church and its mission in the world."[13]

Given the incredible diversity within Christianity, an amazing
amount of unity exists about the importance of worship. From
Karl Barth, a leading spokesman for the movement known as
neoorthodoxy, comes the statement, "Christian worship is the
most momentous, the most urgent, the most glorious action
that can take place in human life."[14] More recently, even

Orlando Costas, a Third World theologian dedicated to human liberation, confesses, "Worship is not a mere function of the church, it is her *ultimate* purpose."[15] Similarly, amid his global efforts aimed at racial equality and freedom, the world-renowned South African Bishop Desmond Tutu writes, "The church exists primarily to worship and adore God."[16]

John McArthur, Jr., observes that the testimony of a worshiping church usually has a greater impact for good on the lost than do most sermons.[17] Though occupying a different position along the theological spectrum, William Nicholls's sentiment about worship is much the same as McArthur's. Nicholls says, "Worship is the supreme and only indispensable activity of the Christian church."[18] Insightfully, this writer underscores the truth that the worship of the church is the only work of the church that will endure into eternity. Toward the end of his influential life, I heard the great Southern Baptist teacher and leader Gaines S. Dobbins reflect on his ministry. He said that if he had the opportunity to begin again, the only thing he would do differently would be to give more importance to worship.

Truthfully, though, agreements about the importance of worship are not unanimous. Contemporary critics of worship often point to the great cathedrals of Europe, now populated by only a small number of the faithful, as the result of making worship a primary concern. I have heard some Christian leaders say that worshiping churches are dying churches. Each time my soul shudders. What are the alternatives? If the people of God do not exist to offer worship to God, what is their raison d'etre? Are the witness of the Bible and the message of church history regarding the significance of worship without meaning?

While I was writing this book, a colleague commented, "Don't you know that Southern Baptists are not a worshiping people?" I found his words devastating. All Christians, Southern Baptists and others alike, live to worship. People of the Book know that incontrovertible truth of the Book. As churches, if we do not worship God, we do not live.

I think that criticisms of worship stem mostly from serious misunderstandings of worship. Obviously, some public disparagers of worship equate a commitment to worship with an endorsement of one specific style of worship. Not liking that particular form of worship, they direct their negative judgments toward worship generally. From that kind of thought come such often-heard comments as: "That congregation majors on worship; it's 'high church.' " "Formality in worship kills spirituality within a church." "Advanced planning for worship has a deadening effect on the service."

Actually, affirming the primacy of worship in the life of a church can no more be identified exclusively with highly organized services than with free-flowing, even chaotic ones. The high priority of the corporate worship of God can be acclaimed apart from any stereotyped reference to formality or informality, emotionalism or rationalism, predictability or spontaneity.

Personal Pilgrimage

Worship was a word I hardly ever heard as a child. As an adult, I rarely think that any activity is more important than worship—the worship of God.

On a Sunday morning just days after my birth, my parents took me to their church. This pattern would be repeated throughout my growing-up years and commended for all of my life. Sunday was a day for "going to church." It still is. But notice the terminology—"going to church."

Attending a Sunday service was synonymous with "going to church." Neighbors asked each other, "Are you going to church this Sunday?" Visitors in the community were told, "We would love to have you in church Sunday." Absentee members of the congregation from one weekend asked someone who was present, "How was church last Sunday?" Students in Sunday School classes polled each other regarding the day's activities, "How many are staying for church?" "Who is coming to church tonight?"

When conversations about Sunday services became more specific, usually preaching was the subject. The corporate meeting place was referred to most commonly as "the auditorium"— a place for listening, listening to preaching. Often Sunday School teachers encouraged their class members to "stay for preaching." Every part of the service prior to the sermon was considered a "preliminary." When there were too many "preliminaries," people complained. Except for an occasional comment about the "special music" in a service or the numerical response to "the invitation," reviews of the Sunday morning hour of gathering were restricted to evaluations of the sermon.

Precisely how and when I began to think and feel differently about all of this, I am not certain. Perhaps the opening assemblies in the annual sessions of Vacation Bible School were the earliest catalysts for change. I still recall the thrill of walking in the processionals attempting to muster as much dignity as I could, carefully listening to worship promptings (instrumentally led and individually led) regarding when to stand and when to sit, when to listen and when to speak; the pleasure of participating in the service in ways in addition to singing; a feeling of accomplishment in joining in responsive readings; the sense of satisfaction that accompanied memorized statements of important Bible passages recited in unison; the excitement of hearing new music and learning to sing a new anthem; the use and appreciation of visual symbols of faith commitments; and the eagerness which preceded voicing a prayer aloud. I was far more impressed with the joy of participating in the service than with the absence of a sermon (though minimessages often were presented). Significantly, all of these activities were associated with worship. I actually had a sense of doing more than "going to church" or "attending preaching." Each day of VBS started with a "morning worship service." In that time I began to learn how to worship God. And I worshiped God.

Informality in Sunday services was greatly prized in the church where I grew up. From time to time self-congratulatory comments about our casual style in congregational gatherings revealed an attitude akin to hostility toward more formal approaches. Yet, ironically, each service developed with routine sameness. The actions of the hour and the sequence of their appearance were as rigidly entrenched as the procedures prescribed in the most narrow of liturgical traditions.

Each week the pastor's office prepared a "bulletin" in which the hymn numbers and sermon titles for the Sunday services were printed. No one really needed a printed "order of service." The procedure of our carefully structured informality remained the same Sunday after Sunday. Nothing was read except the Bible, and that but briefly. Reading anything—a call to worship, a prayer, a sermon—was an undesired formality and a "quenching of the Spirit."

Most of the music in our services consisted of gospel songs. "Holy, Holy, Holy"—then and now one of my favorites—was one of the few majestic hymns sung with regularity. I was always glad it was number 1 in our hymnal. Instrumental accompaniment for congregational singing was limited to a piano. Guitars, brass, and the like were suspect. Eventually a second piano was moved into the sanctuary—primarily for preservice music and piano duets during the passing of the "collection plates." Personally, I liked the use of two instruments in the services. Honestly, though, at times any hint of harmony gave way to an amateurish presention of "dueling pianos."

Please do not confuse accurate descriptions with disparagement. Within that context of worship, I grew spiritually. Oh, early on, Sunday mornings and evenings were filled with pinches from my dad and stares from my mother in the choir in front of me intended to stop my wiggling and quiet my whispering. Reverence was pretended if not practiced. Later, though, my attitude was altered. I found myself addressed by the Word of God and invited into Christian discipleship by way of my repentance and faith and God's forgiveness and grace. I knew that my positive decision in that regard was nothing less than a response of devotion to Almighty God. But outside of that gift of my life and a periodic reaffirmation of that gift before God, most of the other aspects of a typical worship service seemed more like a response to the musicians, the pastor, or the church itself than to God.

Between those moments remembered gratefully and the time in which I write, convictions about corporate worship have been born, tested, questioned, sharpened, discussed, and expressed in actions. A wide variety of experiences has enhanced my appreciation for diversity in forms of worship and created within me an insatiable hunger for unity regarding the meaning and importance of worship.

Influential Images

In addition to the impact of biblical teachings, theological principles, and historical insights, the content of the chapters which make up this book has been influenced by and taken form against the backdrop of a collage of cherished pictures from personal experiences:

• Attending a Christian meeting on a sweltering summer evening in West Tennessee in an outside "tabernacle" with no walls. Rough-hewn poles supported a makeshift ceiling created by leaf-bearing tree limbs and green brush branches thrown over a modicum of lattice work. Homemade benches made of unsanded lumber faced a rickety platform adorned only by two folding chairs and an unstable lectern, which leaned from one side to the other when touched. The cardboard fans provided by a local funeral home were used as much for swatting mosquitoes and scattering other insects as for stirring a slightly cooling breeze. A portable piano accompanied the singing of songs printed on the dog-eared pages of well-worn, paperback booklets. The sermon was long and loud. After the closing prayer, some people said, "It was a good service."

• Standing around a campfire one late-summer evening in the Great Smoky Mountains singing familiar choruses and contemplating God's will. Though very much aware of the presence of a large number of other people, each element of the service seemed to facilitate a private, personal encounter with God.

• Staring with intense interest and smiling with immense joy as quick-moving dancers sought to express the exuberance of their life in Christ. The rhythmic beating of tribal drums provided the background against which the songs, chants, and shouts of the dancers were offered to the glory of God. On this midsummer morning in Nairobi, Kenya, these African Christians were celebrating the unity of a fellowship formed by faith in Christ.

• Shivering in a massive expanse of unheated space in St. Mary's Cathedral during an early morning service on a chilly Sunday in Munich, Germany. Solemnity and reverence were inspired by a sense of God's transcendence. Much was strange. Only the opening words of the Lord's Prayer and several "hallelujahs" were recognized since the service was done in German and Latin. But that was more than enough to assure a happy identification and union with strangers in singing and praying together. Not understanding most of the words and movements of the hour did not preclude a meaningful experience of worship, which concluded fittingly with more "hallelujahs" and an "Amen."

• Gathering at sunrise atop Mount Nebo in Jordan and watching the early morning mist dissolve while quickly changing shafts of light shifted shadows across that rocky terrain which Moses had seen as "the promised land." Scriptures were read, Scriptures which told of the ancient patriarch's visit to this very place. Remembering that thousands of years earlier Moses had been confronted and directed by God gave way to realizing that a similar experience was being repeated. The worship of God occurred in that significant place.

• Receiving a wafer of bread and a small container of grape juice from a close friend who pastored the First Baptist Church of Ipanema just outside of Rio de Janeiro, Brazil, and realizing the unrivaled power of worship shared with others in the name of Christ. Evil lessons of prejudice that I learned in my childhood were discredited, shattered, and transcended by the soundless language of love which permeated the room and rendered people's race and color inconsequential around a table set for the Lord's Supper.

• Walking into the cathedral-like worship center of Broadway Baptist Church in Fort Worth, Texas, and exulting in the beauty of a sanctuary in which spring flowers filled virtually every space not occupied by people. Listening to members of the congregation—first one at a time sporadically, then enthusiastically altogether—declaring aloud, "He is risen!" Thrilling to the sound of the pipe organ swelling with the music of high praise, and later walking away with the triumphant choral presentation of Handel's "Hallelujah Chorus" reverberating in my heart and thinking, *He is risen indeed. Hallelujah!*

Images. Important images of experiences of corporate worship. These are a vital part of the reservoir from which I draw as I write. Of course, there are others, too many to mention. A mental scrapbook is bulging with glimpses of experiences which are retrained like precious snapshots.

What I know experientially confirms what I confess theologically. No substitute exists for corporate worship. Here, as nowhere else, I know the meaning of living by dying, receiving by giving, and finding by losing. Worship provides an avenue of devotion unlike any other expression of love to God. Subsequently, worship results in a renewal of the spirit unattainable in any other manner.

How many times during a prelude of praise to God have I felt burdens lifted. In a prayer of confession I have touched or been touched by forgiveness. In the reading of the Word of God I have found my humanity accepted and maturity encouraged. My spirit has soared. Tears have flowed. Laughs have emerged. Prayers of my own have been whispered. Convictions have been declared. Decisions have been reached which prompted specific actions offered to God as worship continued beyond the sanctuary and into the world.

Worship is the most important work of the church. The people of God exist to serve God. No higher service to God is possible than the worship of God.

Part I
Priority: The Church and Worship

1
The Primacy of Worship in the Fellowship of the Church
"Blest Be the Tie"

The worship of God is an absolute necessity for the people of God. Worship is a gift of response to the invitation of God, who, from the time of creation, judged it not good for a person to be alone. God provided the possibility of fellowship with each other, then God offered individuals an opportunity for fellowship with Him. Throughout history, God has consistently called people together and joined their communion. In fact, when a person responds to God in faith, that response includes a commitment to be involved in community. The God of creation is committed to fellowship. God invites fellowship in worship.

Worship is a gift of response to the invitation of God, who, in the act of redemption, demonstrated that every disciple should live as a member of a community of faith. God established the church as a fellowship in which all followers of Christ can beneficially participate. To live "in Christ" is to join with others who also are "in Christ." Inherent in the priesthood of an individual, made possible by Christ, is a constant give-and-take with other believers. Disciples of Christ are priests to each other, with each other, and for each other.[1] The God of redemption is committed to fellowship. God invites fellowship in worship.

To worship God is to respond to the God veiled by the mystery of creation and revealed in the redemptive mission of Jesus. For an individual, such worship means participating in divinely directed praises, confessions, and offerings with others—members of a community of faith and worship brought into existence by the Christ who makes faith possible and the God who is worshiped.

Congregational worship can be enhanced by private worship. However, corporate worship can never be replaced by private worship. Correctly understood, the two are complementary to each other, not unrelated competitors. Each supports, contributes to, and draws from the other. But the push of Christian discipleship is always toward fellowship rather than away from it. Authentic worship on the part of an individual inevitably moves that person toward compassionate involvement in a community and conscientious participation in public worship. Within Christianity, congregational worship is primary.

Prominent amid terms for worship in the Bible are *synago, synerchomai, synerchesthai,* and *synagesthai,* words that document a relentless movement inspired by God. Individual believers seek an assembly of believers. God's Spirit shapes a congregation of the faithful. So strong was this conviction in ancient Israel that some Old Testament writers apparently viewed dispersion as a horrible consequence of disobedience to God. Solitude was interpreted as a result of divine judgment.[2] Conversely, redemption was understood as an activity in which God brings people together (Isa. 11:12; Ps. 106:47). Similar sentiments pervade the New Testament as well. A major dimension of the ministry of the Holy Spirit is the nurture of a family of faith.

Biblically and historically, worship and fellowship are inseparable. A fellowship of believers cannot exist apart from regular experiences of corporate worship. In like manner, forms of worship that do not contribute to the realization of community are inadequate. Divine worship strengthens human fellowship. Authentic fellowship shapes obedient worship.

Any attempt to separate the worship of God and the fellowship of the people of God is nothing less than a lethal assault on the nature of the church. Far more than theoretical speculation, this truth has a specific local application. In every place, contemporary disciples of Christ are called into fellowship with each other. The worship of God forms the center of this fellowship. Efforts to build a fellowship of God's people around a center other than the worship of God—education, witness, social service (regardless of how noble and virtuous)—can build an important, respected institution, but not a Christian church.

The Purpose of Congregational Worship

Congregational worship has only one purpose—to give glory to God. The apostle Paul states this truth unequivocally, "Do all to the glory of God" (1 Cor. 10:31). In the middle of holy history, worshipers gather with a lively hope and a vibrant memory. God's redemptive actions are recalled. Fulfillment of divine promises is anticipated. Praise, adoration, and thankfulness are declared to God. The presence of God is celebrated.

A Model

Concerned about attitudes toward worship and practices in worship in the churches of his time, Søren Kierkegaard, a nineteenth-century Danish philosopher/theologian, compared what was taking place in the theater and what was happening in Christian worship. In a theater, actors, prompted by people offstage, perform for their audiences. To his dismay, Kierkegaard found that this theatrical model dominated the worship practices of many churches. A minister was viewed as the on-stage actor, God as the offstage prompter, and the congregation as the audience. Unfortunately, that understanding of worship remains as prevalent as it is wrong.

Each ingredient of the theatrical model mentioned by Kierkegaard is an essential component in Christian worship. Crucial, though, is a proper identification of the role of each one. In authentic worship, the actor is, in fact, many actors and actresses—the members of the congregation. The prompter is the minister, if singular, or, if plural, all of the people who lead in worship (choir members, instrumentalists, soloists, readers, prayers, preachers). The audience is God. Always, without exception, the audience is God!

If God is not the audience in any given service, Christian worship does not take place. If worship does occur and God is not the audience, all present participate in the sin of idolatry.

The purpose of every gathering for Christian worship is to offer to God that which will be pleasing to God. Worship experiences are inappropriately constructed (and spiritually dangerous) if their aim is congregationally directed. A major distinction exists between worship in which people seek to please God and entertainment in which people, with God's help, seek to please other people. Both activities have a proper place among God's people and can be beneficial as well as enjoyable. But to confuse the two is to risk doing great harm to the spirituality of all the people involved.

All who gather for worship as God's people have the responsibility of addressing God. Prompters can help, but everyone is expected to participate. No one person can do worship or put on worship for another person. Every Christian is an actor or actress in the drama of worship humbly presented to God, who is its only audience and who offers the only judgment about it that matters.

A Liturgy

The word *liturgy* is derived from the Greek *leitourgia,* a term which is made up of *ergon,* meaning work, and *laos,* meaning people. Thus, literally, liturgy is the work of the people. Early on, the term "liturgy" was used to translate the Old Testament word *sharath,* which carried the idea of ministering on behalf of a community. (That seems to be the idea behind Paul's use of the term in Rom. 13:6 and 15:16.) Eventually, though, the word *liturgy* was associated most closely with the act of people worshiping God. (Such is the sense of the word in Acts 13:2 where it is employed to describe the efforts of Christians in Antioch.)

For many Christians, especially those within the Free Church tradition, *liturgy* is a bad word and an unwelcome ingredient in public worship. Numerous stereotypes are mistakenly associated with the concept of liturgy. In reality, liturgy cannot be stereotyped. Liturgy is not related to any one form of worship alone.[3] To describe a service as liturgical has nothing to do with whether or not the worship experience is formal or informal, cold or warm, inviting or repelling, joyous or somber.

Liturgy makes congregational worship possible. For Christian worship to be acceptable to God, it must be an authentic expression of the sentiments of a congregation. Such authenticity requires worshipers' agreement on the meaning of those words and actions which form the content of the service they offer to God. Those commonly understood declarations and enactments constitute a liturgy. Repetition of a liturgy tends to intensify participation in it, strengthen the meaning of it, and thus enrich the total worship experience of a congregation.

In some churches the liturgy is written down and distributed to all who worship there. Other churches preserve their liturgies only by common consent and corporate memory. However, an unwritten liturgical tradition is every bit as powerful as one that has been published. A local church with a printed order of worship that changes to some extent week by week may not be nearly as bound to a single preferred liturgy as a congregation that takes pride in its lack of printed materials and its devotion to informality. In this latter situation, the informal actions and spontaneous expressions of both the worship leaders and members of the congregation may occur in exactly the same sequence each time the church meets for worship.

Stephen Winward explains that "a pattern of words is a rite, a pattern of actions a ceremony, and a combination of both a ritual."[4] Every church has its own *rites, ceremonies,* and *rituals,* though the use of these particular words may be vigorously resisted by its members. Properly used, rites, ceremonies, and rituals are valuable enhancements to the worship of God.

Dangers do exist, however. Certain aspects of a church's liturgy can become deadened because of the congregation's overfamiliarity with them. When any act of worship becomes so routine that it can be carried out thoughtlessly and effortlessly, that part of the church's liturgy requires renewed attention and perhaps major revision.

Biblical worship was liturgical worship. This is most apparent in the worship practices described in the Old Testament. However, the statement is equally applicable to the patterns of congregational worship that developed within the early communities of faith.

Students of the New Testament have identified evidence of several common liturgies used in the worship services of early believers. Praise was primary. Common expressions of conviction, exultation, and joy were "Marana-tha," "Abba," and "Amen." Psalms were sung by congregations even as were other kinds of songs and hymns. Various members of the fellowships offered different kinds of prayers aloud. Sometimes a congregation prayed in unison. (Acts 4:24-30 may be a model of one of the congregational prayers regularly incorporated into public worship.) The church's fundamental declaration of faith (arguably the earliest Christian confession of faith) was spoken both spontaneously and at times according to a prescribed order of service, "Jesus Christ is Lord!"[5]

Labeling a worship service as liturgical indicates that the service was conceived in a manner intended to involve all of the people present in a meaningful experience of divine worship. Liturgy is a prized possession among people who value the public worship of God. A liturgy is never an end in itself. Liturgy is always a tool in the hands of a congregation, a means by which a significant service of worship can be constructed. But not even the finished product of a given service is the goal of liturgy. The praise of God, the unconditional opening of all of life to God, an adoration of God that finds expression in unquestionable devotion to God—that is the goal of it all, the end to which liturgy offers itself as a means of attainment.

An antiliturgical bias pervaded the church in which I grew up. Of course, that posture was much more a matter of pretense and profession than actual practice. Symbols, rites, ceremonies, and rituals were denounced verbally. Everyone enthusiastically agreed with the negation. But, within that tradition, each observance of the Lord's Supper and every baptism was accompanied by lengthy comments on the meaning of these symbols. Ceremonies surrounded the church's treatment of tithes and offerings, reactions to public conversions, and affirmation of new members within services of worship. Though there were no printed litanies to be read or prescribed acts of worship to be followed, the entire Sunday morning service was a ritual. In fact, as one new minister discovered when he attempted to make some minor alterations in the regular sequence of informal acts of worship, it was a cherished ritual. Members of this church had a shared understanding of the terms used in each service and a uniform sense of what each worship-based action meant. This antiliturgical fellowship in reality maintained a full and fixed liturgy.

I learned the value of liturgy experientially. As I visited worshiping congregations around the world I developed a passion for shared understanding in worship. Frustration developed when I longed to feel a part of a worshiping congregation, but had no idea why at certain times people were standing or sitting around me and no perception at all of what was being said. (I sought to emulate the actions of other members of the congregation, but what I was doing had no spiritual meaning for me whatsoever. I was motivated by a desire for conformity and a fear of looking odd.) But when something happened that I understood and could participate in, like singing the Doxology or the Gloria Patri, reciting the Lord's Prayer, or standing to voice a "hallelujah" or an "amen," joy swelled within me.

Liturgy enables persons to address God corporately. Aided by a liturgy, every member of a congregation can serve God through worship that is characterized by understanding, confidence, and commitment.

An Offering

Worship is an offering to God. The centrality of sacrifice in Old Testament worship left no doubt regarding the necessity of giving. Though expressed through different forms and acts, offering remained the central activity in New Testament worship as well.

At some point in the past, something went wrong. People began attending worship to receive a blessing rather than to make an offering. This destructive change most likely developed as congregations were relegated to a passive role in worship. Worshipers sensed no demand upon them beyond that of their presence in a service. Thus, people gathered for worship with no expectations of having to give anything of themselves, except perhaps a monetary offering. Rightly or wrongly, members of congregations felt much more like observers in an audience witnessing worship than actors and actresses corporately involved in the actual drama of worship. All anticipation related to worship came to center on what could be received from an experience (whether or not the music was inspiring, the lessons were edifying, and the sermon was exciting) rather than on what should be expended during a service.

Every act of Christian worship is to be an extension of a congregation's offering to God—a complement to each individual's gift of the self. Any action that does not meet with that qualification does not deserve to be a part of a worship experience.

From the prelude to the postlude of a service, instrumentalists give their musical talents to God, producing sounds that please God and serve the purpose of helping people to worship God. Words of thanksgiving and gratitude are gifts to God from all of the worshipers. Individually in silence and corporately aloud, prayers of confession and intercession are presented to God. The sermon is an offering to God in which members of a congregation participate along with a preacher. Choral gifts are contributed to God by both the congregation and the choir.

Special moments in worship highlight the importance of an offering to God. Worshipers are encouraged to give their finances, talents, time, and commitments to God. Actually, though, involvement in one part of a service cannot take the place of participation in the whole event. The entire act of Christian worship is a gift to God of the entirety of the worshipers' lives. Christian worship is an offering of unconditional love to the God of love.

Any potential confusion or alteration in the purpose of Christian worship must be addressed and avoided. A constant temptation toward utilitarianism has to be rejected. To use Christian worship for any purpose other than the glorification of God is to abuse it.[6]

God expects a church to meet for divine worship without ulterior motives. Thus, worship is not convened so that church budgets can be pledged, volunteers for ministry enlisted, programs promoted, attendance goals met, or personal problems solved. Authentic worship takes place only in order to honor God. People gather to worship God in order to give everything to God.

Even a presentation of the story of redemption—whether through proclamation from a pulpit, the text of an anthem sung from a choir loft, or a drama enacted by members of a congregation—is to be seen as an offering to God. Every recital of the mighty works of God delights God. When the good news of the gospel of Jesus is shared, God is pleased. God is honored and exalted as the reality of divine love for every person is declared through different media and as an invitation to experience the gift of salvation is announced.

Several years ago, at the conclusion of a lecture I gave on the purpose of Christian worship, the religion editor of the local newspaper requested an interview, which I agreed to do. "What kind of God is it who desires such constant praise and adoration?" The reporter's inquiry was a good one with which to begin, a perceptive question worthy of careful attention. What does the divinely mandated necessity of worship among the people of God indicate about the nature of God?

An uncritical person easily could imagine the existence of an extremely narcissistic divinity always eager to hear exalting praise. After all, God desires constant worship. God is pleased as the divine works in creation are praised and the divine work of redemption is extolled. Why?

God is revealed in the Scriptures and in Christ as a Divine Being whose essence is self-giving. Is a desire to be worshiped indicative of an aberration in or an exception to the divine nature? No. Emphatically not. Even God's desire for worship is oriented to the benefit of God's creation. God instructs people to do what they need to do in order to be whole persons. God is God. God will be God regardless of the nature of human responses. Neither is the nature of God adversely affected nor the power of God diminished by a lack of worship from people. But a similar comment cannot be made about people. Human fulfillment and wholeness require participation in the worship of God by every individual.

The audience of authentic Christian worship is God. Liturgy is the means by which all the members of a community can join in such worship together. Giving is the essence of worshiping. The purpose of Christian worship is to make an offering to God that will ascribe to God power, honor, and glory in such a manner as to cause divine pleasure.

The Consequences of Congregational Worship

To participate in congregational worship in order to receive a blessing is self-serving. Christian worship is God-serving. All attempts at worship motivated by self-interests are likely to fall far short of fulfillment. The singular purpose of worship is to glorify God.

Positive consequences of congregational worship are realities. But receiving benefits (individual or institutional) from the worship of God is like discovering happiness. The benefits are by-products of the pursuit of something else. Happiness is never the result of a search for happiness so much as a derivative from a variety of meaningful involvements in life. Similarly, benefits from the worship of God arise, at first almost without notice, nudging their way into the consciousness of a person whose focus is centered on God alone.

Malcolm Muggeridge warns that an individual who declares, "I must get near God in order to be happy," should be prepared for failure in both intents.[7] True. Happiness is not a goal to be sought by worship but an experience which fills a person who worshipfully realizes the presence of God. All the benefits of worship are realized in this same manner.

Though the purpose of worship is not to know the positive consequences which result from it, worship is filled with benefits. The consequences of worship can be positive factors in the individual lives of non-Christians and Christians as well as in the corporate life of the church.

Consequences for Non-Christians

A conversation with a recent medical school graduate was a revelation for me. By his own admission, the young doctor with whom I spoke was not a Christian. Until shortly before our conversation, he had never even attended a service of Christian worship. A Sunday morning visit to a local church had prompted observations and questions, which he eagerly shared with me. Many of his unfortunate but accurate perceptions of the worship service that he attended spawned negative impressions within him that troubled and saddened me. Thinking about that discussion, though, has helped me to understand the potential of public worship to make a powerful impact on a non-Christian. My doctor friend's experience was negative. But this does not have to happen.

No guarantees exist regarding a non-Christian's involvement in a worship service. The sensitivity and receptivity of each individual are crucial factors in a determination of reactions. Three non-Christians who have observed the same corporate experience of worship can walk away from it with three very different reactions to what they saw, heard, and felt (positive, negative, and apathetic). However, a potential for good exists any time a non-Christian encounters a congregation devoted to the authentic worship of God.

A confrontation with reality.—For a non-Christian, a recognition of Christian worship can be like an unexpected slap in the face. First comes shock, then sensitivity. As personal awareness is heightened, an individual suddenly sees what has been missed until the present moment. "God *is.* God is here! God is reality, not merely a projection of optimistic ideology or an invention of noble fantasy. God is real."

From this profound discovery, personal beliefs and behavior, priorities and sources of security, are subjected to serious questions by a nonbelieving worship attender. "What does this recognition of God say about how I have organized my life? How does it challenge my interests and the experiences, primarily professional and pleasurable, to which I have assigned the highest values?"

Even a complete stranger in a worship service can sense adoration, profound conviction, honest confession, and intense joy that form a powerful witness to the reality of God. While one individual may be struck by regret mixed with fear—"What have I done? What have I missed? How could I have been so blind to the power of God? What must I do now?"—another may be attracted to future possibilities—"I want to be able to speak with such love and to give myself in such exultation."

These developments do not always emerge as a result of a non-Christian's presence in a worshiping congregation. Hindrances may exist within the person. Or problems can be caused by members of the congregation. But reality can break through, an insight which shakes the foundations of an individual's life.

A glimpse of grace.—Attending a service of Christian worship can result in non-Christians catching a glimpse of grace. Though in most instances, non-Christians will not know the meaning, maybe not even the identity, of what they see, they can begin to form some impressions about the nature of redemption.

Many hymns serve not only as a medium through which worshipers express their love for God but also as declarations of the truth of God's love for all people. So do Scripture readings and sermons. Careful listening can prompt someone to think, *God loves me. Could that really be? Am I actually acceptable in the sight of God?*

In Christian worship, confessions of sin are always (that is correct, *always*) set within a context of an assurance of God's forgiveness. Paying attention to the penitent confessions of worshipers—whether in a prayer, a reading, or a piece of music—a non-Christian may begin to say, *These people know my kind of life. I am not alone in my sinfulness. Mistakes, sins, and failures are not reasons for avoiding church and an encounter with God.* Then, hearing an announcement of the assurance of God's pardon—whether by way of a human explanation or a recitation of the promise of Scripture—a non-Christian may experience the happy realization, *God can forgive me. I am not outside the reach of the Divine Being. I am not beyond help!*

Unrestrained expressions of joy and praise convey the truth that ordinary moments and common activities can be filled with significant meaning. Perhaps a non-Christian will conclude, *Evidently, God can bring happiness to people whose lives are no more special than my own.*

Christian worship dramatizes the gospel for non-Christians.

That portrayal is implicit in any worship service with its variety of emphases and diversity of participants. Nowhere is the story of Christian salvation more explicit, though, than in those services which include the witness of Christian baptism and communion through an observance of the Lord's Supper. No words are necessary. The truth of the good news of God's grace is enacted for all to see. A worshiping congregation can have a greater impact for good on non-Christians than most sermons or other spoken presentations.

A tug at the heart.—A lively fellowship of worshipers attracts people who are searching for meaning, purpose, and joy in their lives. Not uncommon is a confession, especially among seekers, *"I want that. I need such experiences in my life."*

Persons unfamiliar with Christianity may conclude that identifying with the worshiping people themselves is the key to finding satisfaction. Social dynamics can seem much more important than spiritual realities. A person may see the fellowship of worshipers as a club rather than as a church (since the observers have no basis for understanding a church). This is unacceptable as a conclusion about a body of worshipers, but it is totally acceptable as a place to begin. A person who is interested in a worshiping congregation can be pointed to the God who makes such a fellowship possible and to the Christ who authors redemption and gives people the praise with which to worship.

Mystery is also involved. God's Spirit can (and does) minister to persons through the words, deeds, emotions, and attitudes of God's people. A non-Christian can depart from a service of Christian worship, scratching her head and saying to herself, *I don't know what happened there. I felt something I have not felt before. I have to give more attention to the spiritual side of my life.*

Consequences for Christians

Though we may be uncertain about the positive consequences of a non-Christian attending a service of public worship, such is not the case with Christians. Benefits are inherent in the experience. But more is involved than attendance. Christians are people who have seen the glory of God revealed in Jesus, devoted themselves to His lordship, and resolved regularly to gather in His name for the worship of God. For Christians, worship is not so much an event to be attended as a service to be performed. Worship is an activity to be known by personal participation rather than by detached observation.

Why the certainty about positive benefits for worshiping Christians? Authentic worship requires an attitude of openness toward God and a spirit responsive to God. Each of those attributes, which contributes to worship that is pleasing to God, also creates within worshipers a hypersensitivity to the presence of God and a radical vulnerability which allows them to receive all that God has to offer. That sequence is sacred. If a desire to receive the benefits of worship ever replaces a commitment to the purpose of worship as the basic motivation behind worship, selfishness supersedes the adoration of God and the possibility of worship is destroyed. True worship can never be second in any order of importance. The more Christians lose themselves in the worship of God, the more that experience becomes an occasion in which they find themselves as beneficiaries of the grace and goodness of God.

Nurtures a healthy self-esteem.—In worship, as nowhere else, an individual is struck by both the largeness and the smallness, the infinite worth and the finite nature, the sinful tendencies and the glorious possibilities of a person's life. As God is recognized and praised, the depth of divine compassion and the vastness of divine redemption can overwhelm an individual. Sensing the transcendence and holiness of the Divine Being, a worshiper might conclude, *I feel so small and insignificant as well as unclean. Who am I to seek attention from God? I have far more weaknesses than strengths. My needs outnumber my abilities. God's kingdom will be better off without me in it, as if I could be a part of it anyway.* Plagued by such feelings, the prophet Isaiah declares, "Woe is me! For I am lost" (Isa. 6:5).

At this moment the vision of God central to worship begins to instruct a person with a better understanding of the self. *God loves me! Not only am I created in God's image, I am invited to be a beneficiary of God's fellowship.*

As the drama of redemption is played out and Christ is confronted, new insights are born. The God who seemed distant is seen as the God who draws near. Recognizing God's transcendence gives way to knowing God's presence. God's awe-producing holiness is complemented by Christ's personal call for servants of righteousness.

I am somebody, a worshiper realizes as he contemplates God as revealed in Jesus. *My life has significance. I have gifts which God desires to use. With God's help, I can make a contribution to God's kingdom.* Then a sensitive worshiper can address God as the psalmist did, "thou, O Lord, art,...the lifter of my head" (Ps. 3:3).

Picture the self-esteem possible for an individual whose life is committed to the worship of God. Possessing a proper sense of humility and a basic concept of personal worth and dignity, the individual resolves to live as a contributing member of the human family and as a loyal citizen of the kingdom of God.

Strengthens spiritual muscles.—Worshiping God is to a person's spiritual muscles what lifting weights is to a body builder. Engaging in the work of worship strengthens an individual's spirituality and establishes the discipline necessary for its maintenance and improvement. Spiritual maturity is an impossibility apart from regular experiences of congregational worship.

A person's faith is informed, encouraged, and strengthened by participation in the worship activities of a community of faith. No one can be strong all of the time. Doubts and questions stir everyone at one time or another. In a worshiping community acceptance and an understanding of weakness lead to nurture and compassionate support. Stating with others what is believed and singing with a congregation the great hymns of faith can bring renewed confidence to personal beliefs and create the boldness necessary for speaking about them and acting on them. Responsible worship prohibits a stagnation in faith and provokes a person of faith to take the risks of grace.

Memory gives birth to hope in worship. Worshipers are able to look to the future with assurance because of what they have discovered about the past. Every service of Christian worship is "a recapitulation of the history of salvation."[8] Discovering what God has done leads to looking closely to see what God is doing as well as anticipating what God will do. As the mighty acts of God are recited, praised, and celebrated, people realize that God is a promise keeper as well as a promise maker. When Christ is exalted, worshipers conclude with the apostle Paul that Christ is our hope (Col. 1:27).

Love is another of the spiritual muscles regularly flexed and eventually strengthened in worship. Confronted by the love of God as revealed in Jesus, worshipers are ushered past imposters of love, cheap cultural counterfeits of sheer sentimentality and good feelings. The "weight" of glory is shouldered and the meaning of tough love is learned. Love is embraced by the will as well as expressed through emotions. Adoring the God of love expands a worshiper's spiritual muscles to the point that forgiveness can be offered to the worst of offenders and love extended even to one's enemies.

None of that happens quickly or easily. Weight lifting is a useful analogy. Achieving the full potential of one's strength does not happen in a single session. Discipline is required. Changing the imagery, C. S. Lewis's comment about prayer is applicable to all of worship, "I must say my prayers...[participate in worship] whether I feel devout or not; but that is only as I must learn my grammar if I am ever to read the poets."[9]

Variety in worship is helpful. Different forms of worship have different benefits. Growth in appreciating new ways to worship God creates growth in the spiritual muscles required to serve God and people in need. Wanting to grow spiritually and working toward that end are essential. The alternative is sad—an adult whose communion with God never gets beyond the childhood petition that begins, "Now I lay me down to sleep..."; or, altering the metaphor, a musician who spends a lifetime tapping his foot to a musical warm-up exercise when he could be singing an aria or playing a trumpet with a choir performing the works of Handel.

Cares for the soul.—Worshiping congregations are composed of individuals with numerous and diverse needs. Inevitably, these needs are met as people devote themselves to worship activities. God therapeutically touches a soul that is intensely focused on worship.[10]

Virtually no aspect of a corporate worship experience is without healing significance for dis-eased persons. Readings from the Bible address the dominant needs of persons with the authoritative Word of God. The ancient writer Tertullian explained what happens: "With these holy words we feed our faith, we lift up our hope, we confirm our confidence; and no less we reinforce our teaching by inculcation of God's precepts."[11]

Penitent confession in the context of a worshiping community brings a sense of lifting the burden of guilt and cleansing the filth of sin. Words of assurance about the certainty of God's forgiveness are grasped with the joyful relief of a person who suddenly finds something to hold on to just before being swept down a torrent of raging waters. Almost panting aloud because of the panic produced by close scrapes with tragedy, a worshiper speaks words of repentance. The soul sighs with relief.

Prayer is crucial to the care of a soul. Since no dimension of life is excluded from prayerful communion with God, every care of the soul is brought into contact with the redemptive action of God by means of prayer in worship.

Worship music, so vital in conveying people's unspeakable sentiments to God, also ministers to the souls of worshipers—comforting, inspiring, exulting, calming. Drawing upon an excellent analogy, Athanasius declared, "As in music the pluck is used to strike the string, so the human soul may in music become like a stringed instrument completely devoted to the Spirit, so that in all one's members and emotions one is thoroughly responsive to the will of God."[12]

Virtually no aspect of the life of a soul is untouched by the gift of worship. Persons plagued by grief and anxieties find comfort and security in reminders of the promises of God. Lethargic individuals who well nigh have given up on life can be reawakened to new beginnings and even feel the stirrings of creative energies within themselves. People smug about the slyness and safety with which they persist in undetected sins can be shaken to the core by a confrontation with the horrendous consequences of continuing on an unaltered course.

Care for the soul is inherent in the worship of God. However, worship cannot legitimately be viewed as a technique for ministry or as a tool of psychology. The very activity of worship is therapy for the soul.

Informs a moral conscience.—To worship God who is holy is to learn the meaning of holiness and to develop a desire to live by what is known. Worship whets a person's appetite to feed on Christian values and creates a resolve to embody Christian character. Personal interest receives spiritual instruction. Desire finds direction. The content of Christian worship becomes the substance of a Christian conscience. A community of worship is the context in which Christian character is shaped. Augustine stated the truth succinctly, "We become what we adore."[13]

A common consequence of a vision of God is guilt. Pondering the perfect holiness of God, an individual becomes aware of personal imperfections and sinfulness. Guilt can be a healthy reality if it is a transitional experience. If guilt is terminal, however, it is not Christian, much less healthy. The insights of worship which may cause guilt in a worshiper also convey the reality of forgiveness and the possibility of an open future. The holy God is the God of grace.

Every element in an experience of Christian worship can contribute to enlightening a Christian conscience and developing Christian character. Scripture readings bring God's Word to bear upon personal dilemmas in moral decision making. Reflecting upon divine oracles from the past nurtures a passion for personal humility and social justice. Giving thanks for God's love stirs the will to share that love. Proclamation about the reality of the kingdom of God creates a sensitivity to the values and priorities that are present when God reigns. Righteousness is rescued from generalities and defined with specifics drawn from the ministry of Jesus. Receiving from the table of the Lord leads to offering gifts to others.

Paul's counsel to his Philippian readers is commendable. After encouraging people to "rejoice in the Lord" (Phil. 4:4), he wrote, "Whatever is true, whatever is honorable, whatever is just, whatever is pure, whatever is lovely, whatever is gracious, if there is any excellence, if there is anything worthy of praise, think about these things" (v. 8). That's it. That is what happens in worship. Such is the manner by which a service of worship to God instructs a person's conscience.

An important reminder is in order again. The purpose of worship is not moral education. Worship is for God. To participate in worship to be instructed and changed for the better is to set up oneself for failure. That purpose is self-centered. Moral instruction is a result of worship not a reason for worship.

Inspires compassionate service.—Elton Trueblood discovered a printed order of worship which concluded with these words: "The End of Worship—The Beginning of Service."[14] The explicit spirit of this statement is good and commendable. The division of action implicit in this statement is wrong and objectionable.

In the language of the Jews, the word for worship was derived from *abad,* a root term meaning "to serve." Then and now the worship of God and service in the community are two dimensions of one experience, not anthithetical, competitive actions.

Remember that liturgy means the work of the people. No restrictions applied. Actions in the marketplace, the home, the government, and the coliseum constituted liturgy every bit as much as what was said and done in a place of worship. Only with the passing of time was liturgy equated exclusively with the activity of worship (people's work in worship).[15]

To worship God is to realize the will to serve God in the world. To catch a vision of Christ is to be moved to a commitment to ministry in Christ's name. Worshipers discover that "God is a worldly God,"[16] who delights in worship that causes service-oriented engagements with the world, not a selfish disengagement from the world. When discontinuity exists between people's work in a sanctuary and their work in the world, the worship of those people is fraught with great problems.

True adoration of God involves a recognition of God as the Creator and Redeemer of *all* people. Thus, no person can be considered unimportant. Every person's needs are worthy of careful attention. Prayers of intercession to God prompt actions of compassion inspired by God. Authentic praying involves the one offering the prayer in a willingness to be used by God as at least a partial answer to the prayer. Praying for peace and the poor means working to eliminate hostilities and seeking to eradicate poverty. Earnest prayers for homeless people and abused children result in efforts to build permanent housing as well as to provide temporary shelters.

Voicing the Model Prayer of Jesus sends people scurrying to conform to the ministry of Jesus and to live as His servants. To request from God *"our* daily bread" (Matt. 6:11, emphasis added) is to accept responsibility for seeing that this prayer is answered among all people. Placing before God the petition "Thy kingdom come, Thy will be done" (v. 10) means offering oneself to God as an agent of such redemptive action.

To imagine that the worship of God causes a worshiper to be unconcerned, or less concerned, about the world is to flirt with heresy. The more a person understands about God, the more that individual will care for all people—the world in which they live and the needs with which they live. Such understanding is always a prelude to action.

Cultivates a sense of wonder.—Anyone who claims to have everything figured out about anything obviously has never really engaged in worship. Whatever else happens in true worship, a worshiper is confronted by mystery, often called the *mysterium tremendum.* Kneeling before Almighty God, figuratively or literally, a person realizes as nowhere else the inability of any individual to "know it all." Worshipers get off their knees with spirits pervaded by awe and minds filled with wonder.

People who are infatuated with objectivity and saturated with scientific data can be helped by a discovery of realities that are unmeasurable and inexplicable. Computers are useless instruments at an altar. The ways of God are unfathomable. At times even the obedience required by God seems impractical if not unreasonable.

True worship cultivates within persons a spontaneity and festivity much too uncommon in contemporary society.[17] Worship is filled with surprises that keep worshipers on the tiptoes of their souls. At the darkest moment amid a confession of sins comes a sudden burst of light generated by the reality of divine forgiveness. Repentance seems like such drudgery. Not so. Actually, repentance is "a flight to freedom, a human response to the R.S.V.P. on God's invitation to joy."[18] While pondering the prophetic picture of a valley of dry bones, a depressing conclusion to a dismal story, and considering the devastation of spiritual famine, one senses a movement of God's Spirit. Thoughts of death dissolve in the face of an emerging enthusiasm for life. Over and over again in worship, scenes that look to all the world like tragic endings are transformed into new beginnings.

A wise writer observes that "the soul must learn to abandon, at least in prayer, the restlessness of purposeful activity, it must learn to waste time for the sake of God."[19] That is not easy. Culture pushes us in another direction. In Christian worship, though, the constant social pressure for thinking, doing, producing, and achieving is superseded by a summons to enjoy the primacy of being.

Worshipers of God are sensitized to the glory and beauty of God's creation. God is praised for high blue skies filled with puffy white clouds that look like sailing ships and the unexpected appearance of a full-colored rainbow in the fine mist of a waterfall. Thanksgiving is offered to God because of a passionate kiss between two people who have been married for seventy-five years and in response to a baby's outburst that someone interprets as the sound of "mama." Given time in worship, requests for the joy of watching a sunrise can become more prominent than pleas for increased knowledge about computers.

Because of long-term conditioning, many people will seek to "catch" themselves in self-transcending moments, mumbling, "I must be realistic. I am a practical person." Guards will go up and serendipity will be stopped short. Worship shouts, "Let go!"

According to Jesus, finding oneself depends upon losing oneself. A similar principle applies to worship as well. Really enjoying God requires forgetting oneself. Surely that is the sense of the conclusion of one of Charles Wesley's great hymns: "Lost in wonder, love, and praise."[20]

This can happen in the worship of God.

Consequences for the Church

Christian worship is essentially a corporate act. No surprise, then, is the realization of positive corporate consequences derived from worship. The worship of the people of God benefits worshipers communally and individually. When a church offers the gift of worship to God, that church receives through worship gifts from God—gifts unavailable in any other context or through any other medium, gifts crucial to the life of a Christian congregation.

Shapes identity.—The true identity of the church is never in question. But it is almost always in danger of revision. From both within and outside, constant pressures push and pull at the church, favoring directions which, if followed, will alter its nature. Only in the worship of God can a church keep in touch with its divinely ordained identity and the strength needed to maintain it. Persuasive arguments aimed at redefining the nature of the church are plentiful. Powerful forces are bent on establishing a new orientation for the church. The confidence in and commitment to the identity of the church which come from Christian worship are essential to the successful resistance of such influences.

Numerous images are espoused as worthy likenesses of the church's identity: 1) *A spiritual garage.* Activists sometimes see the church as "a filling station" to which people go periodically to recharge their batteries and tune-up their engines. 2) *A Bible school.* Some congregations advertise their existence as that of a Bible fellowship. The church is considered primarily as a place for people to gather to study the Scriptures. 3) *A social service agency.* Many persons properly sensitive to widespread hurts and needs in society improperly seek to shape the church into little more than a community center for distributing food, rehabilitating addicts, housing street people, providing a clothes closet, and seeking work for the unemployed. 4) *A political bloc.* In recent years, political strategists have manipulated well-intentioned people to associate spiritual discipleship almost exclusively with a highly partisan national citizenship and to establish their churches as political bases for that point of view. 5) *An evangelistic organization.* Arguing that the winning of the world to Christ is the church's only reason for existence, some persons seek to subordinate within a church any aspect of its life which is not focused on "soul winning." 6) *A preaching station.* Devotees of religious rhetoric, especially preaching, insist that the real church gathers around a pulpit and acts according to the proclamation of the Word of God which comes from behind it.

Less noble portraits of the church also vie for attention: 7) *An ecclesiastical business.* Modeled after major for-profit corporations, the church, for some folks, is a business whose product is faith and whose needs are identical with those of any other successful sales-oriented institution. 8) *A nonprofit, charitable organization.* Even more secular in nature is the image of the church as an important community agency worthy of the support of socially minded people. Often, this particular concept of the church is difficult to distinguish from a description of a civic club.

Excluding the last two images, almost every one of these other concepts of the church contains at least a particle of truth that is noble and commendable. Of course, a church is interested in personal evangelism and social ministries, preaching and Bible study, offering inspiration and maintaining itself as an institution. However, if one part of the whole is allowed to replace the whole, everything changes. The church loses its basic identity and retains little hope of recovering it. Fidelity in the worship of God with integrity is the church's best means of retaining its true identity.

In worship the church is identified as the people of God committed to the lordship of Christ. Shaped by experiences of worship, the church exists as an extension of the ministry of Jesus, a communion that is a contradiction to society. In its worship, the church realizes the resourcefulness of its corporate life and thus acknowledges its promise as a community of giftedness.

According to Richard John Neuhaus, for many years most of the printed materials from St. John's Church in Brooklyn carried the statement, "God's People Are at God's Altar Every Week."[21] The words are intended to be both descriptive and prescriptive. That is the identity of a church shaped by Christian worship.

Creates community.—Fellowship and worship are inseparable within a church. Members of a church unify themselves to worship God properly. Every experience of worship contributes to the unity of the people involved. Worship creates community and strengthens it.

Corporate worship forges unity out of diversity within a church. Efforts to establish congregational unity on any other basis are likely to fail. Churches consist of persons who represent a radical degree of diversity in backgrounds, interests, professions, accomplishments, politics, economic statuses, education, and levels of spiritual maturity. Most Christian congregations are made up of persons who would never even cross paths with each other, much less assemble together, were it not for their membership in the same church. Public discussions of church business, ministry opportunities, and denominational beliefs highlight the diversity within a congregation. However, the diversity of a church is transcended (as it is molded into a unity) by the worship of God.

Worship is always an integrating activity among God's people. Always! Different interest groups, study units, and partnerships for ministry are normal in any church's fellowship. But, because of the unity in a church created by that church's worship, all of the various segments of a congregation are complementary, not competitive, aspects of its community.

A fellowship that fails to worship God together is not a church. The worship of a congregation that does not result in a sense of community among the worshipers is not Christian worship. Christian unity is a remote possibility apart from worship. But Christian worship that does not create such unity is an impossibility. "Christian worship is a way in which God gives of himself for the good the community through the community."[22]

In his Philippian correspondence, the apostle Paul paints a word picture of a community of people unified in and by worship. They are individuals "of the same mind, having the same love, being in full accord and of one mind" (Phil. 2:2).

"Edifies" the body.—Throughout his writings, Paul insists that worship edify the church. In a letter to the Corinthian Christians, Paul addresses the subject of their worship saying, "Let all things be done for edification" (1 Cor. 14:26). In his correspondence with Christians in Rome, Paul encourages worship practices in which people can edify each other (Rom. 14:19). Translations of the term *edify* vary: "upbuilding" (Rom. 14:19),

"help" (1 Cor. 14:26, GNB), and "strengthen" (Rom. 14:19, GNB). Regardless of the precise word employed in a specific text, the apostle's intent is conveyed—worship strengthens the church, helps the church, and builds up the body of Christ.

The words *edify* and *edifice* emerge from the same root. To edify is to build. Worship that edifies is worship that builds a community of faith that finds fulfillment in the worship of God. One writer has even referred to worship as the "School of Faith."[23]

By way of its traditions of worship, a church is constantly confronted by affirmation and criticism, encouragement and challenge. The content of a church's worship can help keep that church on a correct course of ministry. Specifically, worship is the medium through which congregations are given the best insights, instructions, and wisdom of their predecessors in the faith. In worship, Christians are continually called back to the foundation of their faith in Christ and to an exploration of their place in God's plan of redemption.

Abraham Heschel once commented on some of the complaints voiced by members of the synagogue that he served. According to Heschel, the people were displeased because the liturgy (worship) of the synagogue did not allow them to say what they meant. The rabbi wisely responded, "The goal is not that the liturgy say what you mean but that you mean what the liturgy says."[24]

Empowers mission.—"Get out!" *"Ite missa est."* Those are the final words of the old Roman Mass.[25] By means of this phrase, at the conclusion of God-directed activities in a sanctuary, worshipers are encouraged (maybe "mandated" or "set on fire" is better) to get on with their God-honoring mission in the world. That is the spirit of authentic worship.

A Christian church is mission. Worship is at the center of every Christian congregation. Worship leads to mission—providing its motivation and shaping its direction. The church's mission is empowered by the church's worship. Worship is mission. In a church, worship and mission are inseparable. A Christian church devoid of either worship or mission is impossible.

It is imperative for people to gather to worship God with adoration. It is also imperative for people to leave worship to serve God on mission. A church which exists for the glory of God also exists for the sake of the world. What God loves cannot legitimately be abandoned by the people of God. And no doubt is possible regarding God's love for the world. "For God so loved the world that he gave his only Son" (John 3:16).

Participating in worship, work which takes place in a worship center, can never be a substitute for doing God's work in the world. A call to worship is no rationale for perpetual retreat. Just the opposite. Corporate worship is the context in which Christians are confronted by the divinely given vision of their mission in the world and summoned to commit themselves to the faithful execution of it. K. E. Kirk accurately describes what happens among members of a worshiping congregation, "To look towards God, and from that 'look' to acquire insight both into the follies of one's own heart and the needs of one's neighbors, with power to correct the one no less than to serve the other."[26]

In the life of a church, increased fidelity to its mission is directly related to greater integrity in its worship.[27] Gathered for worship, members of a church celebrate God's redemptive revelation and hear the decree of the incarnate divinity, "Go therefore and make disciples of all nations" (Matt. 28:19). Also, while offering worship to God, people receive as a gift from God the power which they need to be obedient to Christ's great commission.

An intangible.—In the final analysis, worship's impact on the life of the church generally or one congregation specifically cannot be fully explained. An experience from John Killenger's past magnifies that truth beautifully.

A guest was preaching in a chapel service at the American Baptist Theological Seminary in Nashville, Tennessee. John Killenger attended the service to hear the visiting preacher. The president of the seminary, who doubled as the director of the choir, was presiding. When time came for the choir to present an anthem, the president spoke instead. He explained to those present that because he had been out of town the choir had not rehearsed. He apologized for the lack of music from the choir during this hour. The rest of the order of worship was followed as planned until near the end of the service. The guest preacher engaged the congregation in a powerful presentation of the gospel. According to Killenger, all present were caught up in a high and holy moment. When the preacher finished and took his seat, the president/choir director jumped to his feet, motioned for members of the choir to stand, and said, "Let's sing it now!" "They did," Killenger observed, as he recorded what happened, "The song rolled up to the roof and got thicker and thicker and louder and louder and more and more joyous until you almost couldn't breathe in the room. And when it was over the director smiled meekly and said, 'We couldn't have done that before.' "[28]

No amount of comparison can dramatize the difference for good that worship makes in the life of a church. A congregation faithful in its worship of God can accomplish regularly for God's glory what other fellowships will never even attempt.

2
The Centrality of Worship in the Ministry of the Church
"Stir Your Church"

The worship of God is the most important activity of the people of God. Worship is the source of the church's power to carry out its mission in the world. Worship is the only activity of the church that will persist beyond history. Worship can exist apart from a church, but a church cannot exist apart from worship.

Scholars have composed a variety of lists that identify the major functions of a church. Some tasks are common to most descriptions of the church's responsibilities. With near unanimity, writers conclude that the church exists for worship, evangelism (some use the term "outreach"), education (this may be designated "nurture" or "discipling"), and ministry (both pastoral care for individuals and service within society). Missions is on many lists, though some writers relate missions to evangelism while others assume its inclusion in ministry. Persons with experience among larger congregations often also identify administration as a basic function of a church.

However the functions of a church are enumerated, a tendency to give them equal importance must be resisted. Worship is more important than all of the rest or any one of the rest. Worship is fundamental. Worship is the foundation of everything else the church is doing. When a church's worship of God is right, all of its other endeavors will reflect that strength. If, however, a church's worship is out of kilter, every other activity of that church is susceptible to sickness and weakness, ineffectiveness and incompetence.

That is not to suggest that worship is the only means by which a church is enabled to accomplish its other purposes. The worship of God is always an end in itself, never a means to some other end.

Congregations become churches in the corporate worship of God. As God is served in worship, people develop the maturity which characterizes a church. In the worship of God, a church develops the kind of communal life in which its other functions are correctly understood, and it discovers the power to carry out those functions compassionately.

Paul Hoon offers a helpful reminder that the word *orthodoxy* (derived from *orthos* and *doxa*) means "right worship." Most crucial in a concern for orthodoxy is not correct doctrine or a proper understanding of a belief but right worship. An orthodox view of the church develops not by reading, talking, and writing about the nature of the church but by worshiping God. In Hoon's words, "When our worship is true, our thought about the Church is likely to be true."[1] That is why the worship of God must exist at the center of a church's life and impact all else that the church is about.

The Bible gives a model for the movement which is crucial in the life of a church. In the beginning was creation. In the end was worship. A church is to be moving constantly toward greater maturity in its worship of God. Not only does the Bible point the way for the development of a church, Scripture writers also provide resources of inestimable worth for the nurture of proper worship. "The Bible, from cover to cover, is the story of worship."[2]

History, too, is a good teacher. No ambiguity exists. In every age, attempts at reform and renewal in the church have begun with the worship practices of the church. Martin Luther sought to purify the worship of the church in the sixteenth century in order to restore the true nature of the church. During the same period of time, Thomas Cranmer focused on liturgical changes as he brought reformation to the English church. In the eighteenth century, John Wesley attempted to renew Anglicanism by altering patterns of Anglican worship. In the twentieth century, Roman Catholics have brought about monumental changes in the life of their church as a result of major reforms in the patterns of Catholic worship.

What has happened historically verifies what is true theologically.[3] Worship occupies the central place in a Christian church. To think seriously about the church requires a study of the church's worship. If a church changes its worship, other changes will invariably follow throughout that church's life.

A number of denominational bodies, each of which retains

obvious distinctives in worship, reveal a surprising number of common affirmations about the centrality of worship in the life of a church. From United Methodists comes the declaration, "Worship is central to the church as a whole ... if you don't have congregational worship, you don't have a church."[4] Similar support for the central place of public worship comes the Reformed tradition. "Worship is the life-giving center of the congregation,"[5] and "Worship is the supreme and only indispensable activity of the Christian church."[6]

Widely divergent schools of theological thought find common ground in supporting the centrality of worship. Robert Webber, a professor at Wheaton College in Chicago writes, "The church is first a worshiping community. Evangelism and other functions of ministry flow from the worship of the church."[7] In a shared writing project, Webber joins with Rodney Clapp, an associate editor of *Christianity Today* to declare, "Worship is the fullest, most concentrated enactment of what the church is and will be."[8] Responding to a question about why anyone should worship God today, Hans Kung, the controversial theologian from the German University of Tubingen, says, "It is through the religious service that a congregation is formed and convinced of Christ's cause and prepared to be his disciples."[9]

At Union Theological Seminary in New York City, Geoffrey Wainwright bases an entire volume of systematic theology upon the centrality of worship in the life of the church.[10] Frank Stagg, an internationally respected biblical scholar among Baptists, includes in his book on New Testament theology a statement asserting, "If it be the church, worship is not only proper but indispensable."[11] Using the term "liturgy" as a synonym for "worship," Roman Catholic theologians declare, "The liturgy is the summit toward which the activity of the church is directed; it is also the fount from which all her powers flows."[12]

Even special emphasis volumes for churches give attention to worship as foundational for ministry. Preoccupied with the needs of an inner-city parish and consumed by the challenges facing all churches in urban areas, George Webber writes, "Corporate worship brings together all the elements in a congregation to celebrate the gospel."[13] Similarly focused on churches in metropolitan settings, two British ministers who run a London-based research center for urban churches write, "Worship ... is the native soil of Christian existence. Christian identity, cohesive community, and spiritual sensitivity will wither and die without it."[14] Dedicated to the elaboration of a theology of liberation, Orlando Costas declares, "Worship is not a mere function of the church, it is her *ultimate* purpose."[15]

What about the Free Churches? Specifically, where are Baptists on this matter of the centrality of worship? After a review of the various functions of a church, W. M. S. West, a British Baptist, wrote, "The motive power for all these activities and for the life of the church stems . . . from the Sunday worship."[16] Almost fifty years ago, a highly esteemed Southern Baptist patriarch, W. T. Conner, wrote, "The first business, then, of a church is not evangelism, nor missions, nor benevolence, it is worship."[17]

Both of the men to whom this book is dedicated strongly advocated the centrality of worship in the church. In seminary classrooms, John Carlton lectured on worship within a spirit of worship. In one of his many published essays, he referred to the church at worship as that experience "which should gather and greaten its soul."[18] In his early work advocating the importance of worship among Southern Baptists, Franklin Segler asserted, "Worship is the fountainhead of all the ministries of the church— indeed, the 'life of the church.' "[19] The passing of time strengthened rather than eroded that conviction for Segler. In one of the last years of his life, Segler wrote in the newsletter of the church of which he was a member, "Worship is the church's first and most basic function."[20]

These unified affirmations of the centrality of worship in the life of the church strike a strong positive response within me, but it has not always been that way. In the church of my childhood and youth, two emphases were dominant. First was the responsibility "to go to church." Second was the necessity to witness to other people about Christ, always seeking to bring them to salvation. Both emphases "took" with me. Much of the time I did not find worship meaningful. I did not even know worship would be or should be meaningful. I thought getting through a service was part of the discipline of growing up as a religious person, and absence from worship was terrible, probably because of the guilt. I was so impressed by the duty to witness that I talked to numerous people about accepting Jesus as their Savior and being baptized before I had done either one myself. Worship was not a factor in any assessment of my early religious experience.

That changed. A combination of formal studies and personal experiences brought about the change. I came to understand that if any activity in a church is more important than worship, that church is in danger of idolatry. I watched people's spiritual lives shrivel because of a lack of good experiences of corporate worship.

A church musician friend of mine became disgusted with the pressure to perform and to please congregations. He quit. Another friend, a preacher, ran out of power—will power and spiritual power. He also quit. Eventually, I came to understand that apart from regular experiences of corporate worship, choirs forget why they are singing, ministers lose sight of why they are ministering, teachers cannot remember why they are teaching, and social activists forget the motivation for their helpful services. When reasons and motivations depart, meaning, discipline, and joy follow closely behind.

More positively, I was captivated by biblical injunctions about worship. I concluded that worship comes first for the people of God. Personal experiences sealed the truth discovered in scriptural studies. I found participation in the corporate worship of God to be an enriching experience like no other. In worship, strength and assurance came together. I confronted challenges to change certain aspects of my life. I found inspiration and direction.

In his apology for the centrality of preaching in the work of the ministry, John Killenger wrote words that capture my sentiments on worship. Killenger's narrative about what is crucial in pastoral ministry is for me a confessional statment about the centrality of worship: "In the end, it is the miracle of [worship]... that dispels the gloom again from this much-miracled, time-wearied Camelot of ours, and sets its knights and ladies all adance again. Nothing else can out-Merlin it; it is the supreme gift of God to this soul-spent, jag-jaded age we live in."[21]

Worship and Evangelism

Putting evangelism and worship at opposite ends of ministry is sheer mythology—a dangerous heresy—or pure malarky. That cannot be! People who decry worshiping chruches as dying churches and extol evangelistic congregations as lively and growing threaten the integrity of the church. Obviously, such folks do not understand the nature of worship, evangelism, or the church.

People not committed to worship fail in forming a church. Similarly, a congregation whose worship does not glorify Christ— retelling the story of salvation and inviting Christian disciple- ship—is not a church. Worship leads to and participates in evangelism. Evangelism leads to and participates in worship. Gaines Dobbins likens worship and evangelism to "breathing and heartbeat; nerve stimulus and muscle response; light and sight; sound and hearing."[22] Within the church, each is essential to the other.

At one point in my life, I thought a decision had to be made to set aside either worship or evangelism in order to give adequate attention to the other one. God forgive me. However, I did not achieve this plateau of misperception without assistance. With few exceptions, books on worship did not discuss evangelism, and authors who wrote on evangelism did not seriously address the subject of worship.

The doctrine of the incarnation saved me from such folly. Studying Jesus as the model for ministry as well as the reason for ministry, I realized the melding of liturgical interests and evan- gelical efforts in His life. In an evangelistic conversation with a Samaritan woman (John 4:7-30), Jesus clearly points to the importance of worship in God's plan of redemption. Through- out His ministry, Jesus demonstrates that the call to worship is a call to discipleship and vice versa.

The church of Jesus Christ exists to worship God. Evangelism is a vital dimension of that worship. The author of 1 Peter 2:4-9 details the indissoluble union between these two foci in the life of the church. People are redeemed in order to worship God. People who worship God speak, think, and act redemptively toward others.

Worship Precedes Evangelism

Luke's account of the Day of Pentecost in Acts 2 is a powerful aid to understanding the relationship between worship and evangelism. Worship is prior to evangelism. In first-century Jerusalem, people committed to an evangelistic witness came out of people gathered to worship God. They were the same people. To discover God in worship is to desire to bear witness to the power and presence of God among folks who have not met God in worship. A vision of Christ amid a congregation of worshipers inevitably results in joining Christ's mission of re- demption in the world.

Worship is primary not merely because it is a means by which evangelism is well served. Worship is an activity strictly intended for serving God. But what people experience in worship is essential for evangelism. "Men and women released into authentic worship will be vehicles of God's love and their lives will speak of the power and presence of the God they have come to know and love in worship."[23] Take away worship and you take away the worship-nurtured preparation so crucial to evangelism.

Without worship, evangelism would be devoid of any content. The good news of the salvation made possible by God's revelation in Jesus has been passed from generation to generation by means of worshiping congregations. Undoubtedly, the Gospel narratives which convey the story of divine redemption were first told, then recited over and over as oral discourses in services of worship. Then God inspired certain writers to preserve accurate accounts of these stories on parchment. Since that time, the Gospel narratives have been read as Scriptures.

Evangelism involves sharing a personal experience. However, no person can shape the evangelistic story according to individual interests. The normative content of evangelism is the narrative of the Gospels. The good news of Jesus has been best preserved, most accurately understood, and most convincingly shared, past and present, amid persons gathered to worship God.

Worship Pervades Evangelism

Evangelism is much more a matter of being than of doing. Persons do not *do* evangelism; they *become* evangelists.[24] Worship is the action and a worshiping congregation is the fellowship in which a person's being is shaped most holistically. James White makes a sobering observation about the influence of worship, "Until we become formed so as to see Christ in our neighbor, it will be hard for our neighbor to see Christ in our life."[25]

People live out day by day who (or what) they become in worship. Thus, the praise of God which dominates the worship of God pervades evangelists who are called and inspired by God. Evangelism exudes an enthusiasm and intensity born only in authentic worship. Evangelism is an act of worship.

Worship is every bit as insistent on making Jesus known as is evangelism. Within a church, the gospel story is told time and time again to persons gathered in worship as well as to nonbelievers who are nonparticipants in worship. Hans Kung sees an important relationship between these two functions. The German theologian believes that in order to be a credible witness to Jesus, a church must tell and retell the story of Jesus to itself. That happens in worship. Regarding the church's engagement in evangelism, Kung concludes, "Its credibility—and no amount of energetic and busy activity can replace that vital factor— depends on its remaining faithful to the message of Jesus."[26]

Worship Preserves Evangelism

Viewing evangelism from the perspective of divine worship preserves evangelism by protecting it from abuse and misuse. Unfortunately, people's evangelical zeal sometimes causes them to race ahead of spiritual wisdom. Eager to win new converts to Christ, people substitute rational arguments and emotional pleadings for the convicting ministry of God's Spirit. Though the enthusiasm involved is commendable, a self-reliance which ignores God's power is deplorable. Certainly, God uses the words and deeds of human witnesses to Christ. But no person, regardless of how filled with passion and good intentions, can do the evangelistic work that can be done by God alone. In the worship of God, people are continually reminded that ultimately evangelism is the work of God.

New Testament evangelism is never a matter of clever techniques. An intellectually, emotionally, and spiritually honest retelling of one's experience with Jesus is the essence of evangelistic witness. God will do the rest. People are saved by the power of God revealed in Christ, not by human ingenuity. The worship of God keeps that unmistakably clear.

Analogies between evangelists and salespersons can leave an impression that sharing the gospel with an individual is just another form of passing along a piece of propaganda or practicing the fine art of persuasion. Not so. Successes in evangelism have their source in the working of God's Spirit, not in the selling power of human rhetoric. Propagandists focus as much upon themselves as upon their hearers. They rely more upon their own skills of persuasion than upon the value and integrity of that which they are selling. When that attitude is employed in evangelism, serious consequences are likely. The emotional or psychological manipulation of nonbelievers can be substituted for the power of the gospel.

When evangelism grows out of worship, it is protected from

and preserved in the face of such dangers. An experience of divine worship creates a proper humility in all people. Worship nurtures a profound respect for the differences between individuals and God. Worshipers are filled with awe and appreciation for that which can be done by God alone.

Worship keeps people's vision focused on God, a vision essential in the preservation of evangelism. Temptations are strong to turn evangelism into a program aimed at an increase in a church's membership. Also to be resisted are predictable tendencies to use evangelism to bring glory to the evangelist.

While teaching a seminary class on preaching, I encountered a young man who epitomized an approach to evangelism desperately in need of the correction available in worship. I returned a sermon which he had written and I had graded. When he saw my low estimate of the quality of his work, the young man was highly offended. His voice quivered and rose in inflection as he defended his sermon: "You can't grade my preaching. I have used this sermon many times in different churches. Every time I preach it, I hang skins on the wall!" (I am confident the reference was to people whom *he* had won to Christ.)

The worship of God protects its participants from an infatuation with their own evangelistic skills. Worship confronts such an attitude with the need for repentance. As God is encountered in worship, worshipers are reminded that the purpose of serving God, whether in evangelistic efforts or in some other manner, is not personal enhancement or institutional development but the glorification of God.

Worship Participates in Evangelism

The very presence of people gathered to worship God is a form of evangelistic witness. The capacity of worship to advance the gospel is striking. In corporate worship, people are brought before God and led to consider their destinies under God. Christian salvation is declared, described, commended, and invited as well as celebrated.

An irony is apparent at this point. Generally, those churches which give the most emphasis to evangelism have the least appreciation for worship services that embrace the great themes of the Christian year.[27] Yet worship themes noted on the Christian calendar are among the most potent evangelistic statements available to the church. The Christian year is a plan by which the complete story of Jesus' life and ministry is retold annually. The dates on the Christian calendar introduce persons to the major events in the life of Jesus and dramatize the story of divine redemption which invites all people to become disciples of Jesus. A wonderful demonstration of evangelism can occur as God uses for the good of faith the worship-based emphases of the Christian calendar to bring people to a commitment to Jesus.

Amid all of the talk about world evangelization, worship can make an important contribution. "God's work in Christ is the focus of worship."[28] Everything done in worship participates in salvation history.[29] Worship is a substantive form of evangelism. Worship is the center from which such an evangelistic mission must spring and to which it must constantly return. James White says, "The roots of evangelism in our time lie in new understandings of worship."[30]

Worship and Education

Worship and education are formative experiences. In the life of faith, neither can exist without the other. "Becoming the persons God calls us to be is a lifelong process of *turning* and *returning* to God."[31] Among Christians, education takes place in worship, by worship, and for worship.

The presence of people gathered to worship God is an important didactic statement: "We belong to God. God deserves to be worshiped. Life is most meaningful when it exists for the glory of God." These crucial truths can be communicated in other ways but not with the same forcefulness.

In worship, faith is affirmed and celebrated holistically. Jesus draws from the Old Testament in describing the kind of divine-human relationship intended by God: "You shall love the Lord your God with all your heart, and with all your soul, and with all your mind, and with all your strength" (Mark 12:30).[32]

Apart from worship, education is susceptible to the allure of intellectualism or emotionalism. Educating the mind alone offers no assurance that people will act on what is known. Training the emotions exclusively encourages a faith without substance. In worship a helpful corrective is available. God is to be loved and honored by all of one's being. Thus, Christian education can never legitimately focus on only one part of personhood. Growing in Christ means developing intellectually, emotionally, and spiritually. A hymn text captures this truth:

> We praise you with our minds, O Lord. . . .
> . . . .
> We praise you thro' our bodies, Lord. . . .
> . . . .
> We praise you in our hearts, O King. . . . [33]

Education is accomplished *by worship*. Through the centuries, theologians have debated the priority of the rule of prayer (*lex orandi*) vis à vis the rule of faith (*lex credendi*). The weight of the argument favors the rule of prayer. "Worship is basic to doctrine and to instruction in doctrine. . . . Without worship 'Christian education has no heart.' "[34] William Willimon declares categorically, "Liturgy *is* education."[35]

From congregational praise through proclamation to personal commitment, corporate worship raises questions about the fundamental issues of life and points to biblically based answers. Praise is a good instructor in gratitude and humility. Confession teaches the reality of human sinfulness, the availability of God's grace, and the possibilities of forgiveness. From the Bible comes inspired insights which nurture beliefs and build character. Intercessory prayers sensitize worshipers to the reality of interdependence. The offering teaches about stewardship. By means of worship, persons learn both why and how life is best integrated around God.

Few elements in worship, if any, contribute to Christian education more than music. People eventually believe what they repeatedly sing. A singable truth tends to develop into a durable conviction. That is why children are taught to sing "Jesus Loves Me."

Special services of worship often carry an exceptional educational impact. A Christian funeral conveys essential statements of the meaning of life and death. Persons burdened by grief find understanding and encouragement in the truths dramatized in worship.[36] In like manner, a Christian wedding makes use of music, words, symbols, and dramatic actions to insist that the union of a man and a woman is of profound spiritual significance. At stake as well, is an opportunity for people to learn about the importance of promises, covenants, and fidelity.[37] In addition to worship experiences associated with life changes, the biblically based celebrations of baptism and the Lord's Supper abound with fruitful lessons.[38]

Occasionally, by participation in worship a person is prepared for difficult circumstances which occur later. The person may not be aware of learning, but in a moment of great need, a hymn, the sermon, a Scripture reading, or a prayer from that service comes to mind and is used by the Holy Spirit in a ministry of care. "The liturgy is a seed planted in the soul that grows in secret and reaches fruition as a miracle of God's grace (see Mark 4:26-29)."[39]

One writer calls worship a "rehearsal for life."[40] Exactly. By their involvement in worship people can be prepared for all of life. "Worship grooms a people to think theologically and to act doxologically."[41]

The educational value of worship is not the whole story, though. Worship is important as the goal of education—education *for worship.*

Divorced from worship, education can become an end in itself. Study serves learning, and learning is praised for the sake of learning. In those circumstances, people can know a lot of facts but little truth. Individuals can become very smart but lack wisdom.

Christian education nurtures whole persons who please God by all that they think, say, and do. The goal is not a celebration of learning but a way of living. The fruits of Christian education include a learned faith and the festive worship of the one God whose incarnate Son was Himself truth.

Baptist churches and other groups who resist the use of creeds oppose the idea of a catechism and thus protest catechetical instruction.[42] However, education in the faith is important for each new generation. Within noncatechetical traditions, worship is the source of a body of truth to be received with congregational gratitude and personally internalized with freedom. Similarities do exist between the value of education for Christian worship and the instructional importance of a catechism.

A memorable story from D. L. Moody's visit to Edinburgh illustrates the point. One Sunday morning, the great evangelist was scheduled to speak to a large congregation of very young boys and girls. Moody began his message with a rhetorical question. Not expecting an answer, he asked, "What is prayer?" To Moody's amazement, though, no sooner were the words out of his mouth than hands went up all over the hall. The evangelist decided to test this remarkable response. He picked out a little boy and asked for his answer. Without the slightest hesitation, the young child said, "Prayer is an offering up of our desires unto God, for things agreeable to His will, in the name of Christ, with confession of our sins and thankful acknowledgement of His mercies." The words were from the Shorter Catechism. Every child had been taught that description of prayer and memorized it verbatim. Moody declared, "Thank God, my boy, that you were born in Scotland."

Remember that orthodoxy, usually posited as the goal of Christian education, is a matter of worship, not of belief alone. To be orthodox is to be correct in praise, authentic in worship.

Worship and Preaching

Preaching is the central act of corporate worship within the Free Church tradition. Pastors tend to spend more time on the preparation of sermons than on any other of their worship-related responsibilities. Some preaching ministers even assign worship planning to someone else with the instruction, "I don't care what you do within reason. Just be sure I have a minimum of thirty minutes preaching time in every service." Often the title of the sermon determines all of the hymn selections, Scripture readings, and other ingredients of that service. Laypeople speak of "going to preaching" rather than of "participating in worship." Conversations about a worship experience usually consist of reactions to the sermon. One Sunday morning after a worship service, a well-meaning woman complained to her pastor, "You have got to talk to those music people. Too much time was spent on preliminaries this morning. We need more time for the sermon. That's what we come to hear."

Preaching is an important act of worship. Indeed, preaching is a significant form of worship. The sermon is no less a gift to God than words of praise or prayers of gratitude. But one part of an experience of worship must not be equated with the total event.

Worship is the most natural setting for the presentation of a Christian sermon. However, the substance of any worship experience involves much more than the content of a sermon presented as a part of it. Worship can no more legitimately be made subservient to preaching than to any other activity without risking an idolatry which is as harmful as it is sinful. Only when the centrality of worship in the church is recognized, appreciated, and protected is preaching truest to its nature and best positioned to achieve its God-given potential.

Preaching is God revealing through human proclamation the divine intention for persons in their private and social relationships.[43] By definition, preaching is an act in which an individual personality becomes a medium for divine activity. The promise of preaching carries with it a potential for peril.

In preaching, as in no other act of worship, there is danger of a worship leader receiving more attention than the experience of worship or the God to be worshiped. Far too easily the magnetism of a particular preacher can be confused with the power of the Word of God. Personal charisma can be identified as spiritual power. Church members may even gather to hear the preacher rather than to worship God.

The problem is not a new one. In the New Testament, Luke records at least two experiences in which people sought to assign to some of the early preachers the divinity which belongs exclusively to God. (Acts 10:25; 14:8-15). A guest preacher had been scheduled to fill the pulpit of Plymouth Church in Brooklyn one Sunday morning. Henry Ward Beecher usually delivered the sermon there. When the visiting preacher stepped to the pulpit, numerous people in the congregation rushed to the exits disappointed that their hero preacher was absent. Witnessing this rapid flight from the sanctuary, the guest preacher raised his hand and said, "All those who came here to worship Henry Ward Beecher may now withdraw—all who came to worship God may remain."[44]

The people of God gather around the Word of God—the Word revealed in Scripture and the Word incarnate in Christ—to worship God. If people assemble only around preaching or a preacher, worship will not occur and that fellowship will not endure as a Christian church. As an act of worship, preaching contributes immensely to both the meaning of worship and the growth of a church. But preaching cannot singularly carry the burden of sustaining either worship or a church of worshipers.

When Charles Haddon Spurgeon was preaching regularly at the Metropolitan Tabernacle in London, England, crowds gathered to hear him. Each Sunday Spurgeon preached to an average of ten thousand people. Few ministers have filled a pulpit with such power. Not long ago, a friend of mine sought out the fellowship of the Metropolitan Tabernacle in order to worship with them. Only a very small group of people was present. One long-time member of that Baptist congregation explained that only a few years earlier the church had nearly disbanded. He indicated that in more recent days the membership of the church had climbed back to a figure of more than two hundred.

In no sense is that contemporary situation a negative judgment on the earlier preaching of Spurgeon or the subsequent ministering of the congregation. However, it is a rather dramatic example of the fact that preaching alone, even great preaching, cannot build a church and assure it of endurance with strength. Shortly after Spurgeon's death, the Tabernacle burned to the ground. In its place, a new church building was erected with a greatly reduced seating capacity—a decision of an insightful congregation and a portent of the future.

Preachers come and go, succeed and fail, encourage and disappoint, minister and mess up, move and die. When attempts are made to build worship services and churches around human personalities, trouble is inevitable. No human being can assume that responsibility alone. Worship must be convened to please God. Churches must assemble around and upon the Word of God.

Maintaining the centrality of worship in the life of the church is crucial to sustaining integrity in preaching. When worship is central, preaching takes on characteristics that make it an effective means of communicating the gospel.

Preaching Is Dialogical

Preaching is a congregational act of worship, not just a monologue from one individual. The sermon, like the Word of God upon which it is based, belongs to the whole church. Preaching is not the exclusive possession of the preacher.[45]

Preaching facilitates dialogue between people and God as well as between the preacher and other members of a church. When sermons are delivered by preachers whose purposes are oriented to the glory of God, hearers of the sermons are engaged in a conversation with God. If a message is helpful, God is the source of the help. If a message is controversial, people must argue with God, not the preacher. If a sermon provokes questions, hearers are motivated to become better acquainted with God, not closer friends of the messenger.

Still important, though, is dialogue between the preacher and those who listen to the preaching. For a sermon to be an act which encourages rather than stifles worship, members of a congregation must have a sense of ownership related to it, an awareness that the preacher is speaking for them as well as to them. Pulpit presentations that do not take seriously people's doubts, inquiries, protests, and problems have little chance of benefiting their listeners in a manner that glorifies God.

Actual dialogue is as important as the dialogical principle. Worshipers need opportunities to talk with their pastors about preaching generally and specific sermons. Crucial insights into the Word of God and needed applications of the Scriptures can come from people who normally sit in church pews as well as from individuals who regularly speak from behind a pulpit.

I have had the privilege of participating in preworship sermon dialogues with Eduard Schweitzer, the noted Swiss preacher. For years, Schweitzer has viewed such dialogues as indispensable items on his pastoral and homiletical agenda. After the biblical text for a sermon has been read to open one of these sessions, all present voice the needs, problems, questions, hopes, and faith which that text brings into focus for them. Later, in worship, when Schweitzer preaches on that text, members of the congregation know they have been a part of the preparation for that sermon, sense that they are taken seriously in the sermon, and realize they have been involved in a conversation with a preacher that has become a dialogue with God.

Preaching Is Biblical

When worship is central, preaching is biblical. Sermons aimed at entertaining or pleasing people, like sermons devoted to airing personal opinions, are totally out of place. In the context of worship, the content of preaching is the gospel.

Preachers rightfully begin where Jesus began—with an announcement of good news, heralding the advent of the kingdom of God. Sermons that fail to rise above the level of newspaper editorials, the platforms of political parties, the mores of cultural traditions, or the harangue of angry moralists have no place in Christian worship. They are not biblical. Similarly, sermons that fail to bring a specific scriptural truth to bear upon the lives of a particular people do not belong.

Christian sermons convey the good news. Sometimes this proclamation may cause discomfort and a recognition of the need for repentance among the hearers. But biblical preaching never locks people into despair and destines them for doom. Christian preaching abounds with assurances of God's grace, the potential for forgiveness, and the eternal reality of hope.

In biblical preaching, the indicative mood is primary—announcing good news. Imperatives—making demands—are a part of the gospel. But they are not and cannot be first. To proclaim the mandates of the gospel prior to or apart from the promises of the gospel is to imply that people have within themselves the capacity to live as Christians. That suggestion neither honors God nor serves the truth. And it hurts people. An illusion is created that an individual can do by human determination and strength what is possible only as a provision by God.

The message of Jesus is the model—"The time is fulfilled and the kingdom of God is at hand; repent, and believe in the gospel" (Mark 1:15). Note that the imperatives, "repent, and believe" follow the indicative, "the kingdom of God is at hand." Obedience to divine demands is possible only because of the divine gift announced by the indicative.

Preaching Is Incarnational

A sermon preached in the context of worship models the incarnation celebrated in worship. Once again the Word is fleshed out. The pulpit is an intersection where the truths of the Bible and the concerns of worshipers collide, ancient texts and contemporary situations meet.

God-honoring preaching is never general. It is as specific as a manger in Bethlehem or a cross on Golgotha. God's love is discussed in relation to clearly identifiable people. Grace is a gift to be extended to a particular person who has sinned. Affirmations of hope challenge the darkest dimensions of a definite, potentially depressing situation. Redemption is a way of life for a congregation, not merely an important doctrine. Christian preaching trades in specifics.

A "timeless sermon" is a serious misnomer, like a "typical congregation." Preaching bears the marks of the temporal—a definite time, place, and people—just as it pulsates with the eternal. The Word becomes flesh historically. Jesus worked at a carpenter's bench in Nazareth in the first century. A preacher addresses people who live in a particular community and work at specific jobs with documentable interests and needs during a definable time period.[46] The timeless gospel becomes timely in every proclamation of it.

The influence of incarnational preaching is both cumulative and immediate. Not every sermon of every preacher can meet the needs of every person in every congregation. However, over an extended period of time, as a preacher and other members of a church worship together, the whole truth of the gospel is revealed to every one. A preacher faithfully shares the good news—sometimes in weakness and sometimes with strength, occasionally plagued by hurt and at times filled with great joy, at moments needing to hear the Word of God every bit as much as any listener and at other moments abounding in certainty. Thus, in the course of a year of preaching, the gospel is declared as deaths are mourned and births are celebrated, as graduations and retirements occur, amid festive moments and periods saturated with problems, when all seems well and when nothing seems right. The Word becomes flesh. In time, the sweep of the gospel is complete. In worship, both the hearers and the speakers of the gospel join in the joyful affirmation "We have beheld his glory" (John 1:14).

Preaching Is Worshipful

Preaching is an act of worship. A sermon is a preacher's gift to God in worship. When worship is taken seriously, preaching is characterized by genuine humility. The preacher focuses on God just as does everyone else. Cognizant of personal sin, a preacher confesses, "I have no right to be here." Overwhelmed by the breadth of God's love, a preacher acknowledges, "The task of preaching is much too great to be fulfilled by one person." Awed by the divine mystery, a preacher admits, "I must try to articulate that which can never be fully described by words."

Such realizations are not excuses for silence and inactivity. True humility enhances, rather than erodes, the authority of the one in the pulpit. A preacher can act because God has acted. A preacher can speak because God has spoken. Any sense of personal sufficiency gives way to a complete dependency on God. The preaching which ensues is marked by a humility appropriate to the worship of Almighty God, preaching which is itself an act of worship.

Aware that a sermon is a gift to God, preachers are challenged to give nothing less than their very best. Who can justify an ill-conceived, ill-prepared, barely understandable gift to God? All sermon preparation should begin, end, and be pervaded by prayer and praise, adoration and devotion to God.[47] Preachers must bring to the pulpit the same qualities of thoroughness, excellence, and integrity that they wish to characterize the other gifts offered by people in worship. An "impromptu approach to the pulpit is an affront to God."[48]

What, then, is the measure of a good sermon? A thoughtful answer to that question demands attentiveness to other questions: Prospectively, "Is this sermon pleasing to God?" Retrospectively, "Was the sermon a worthy instrument for God to use in the ministry of redemption?"

Comments from listeners are poor indicators of the quality of preaching. Søren Kierkegaard observes that the true test of a good sermon is not whether people heard it, enjoyed it, and discussed it over their Sunday meal. Rather, the philosopher points out, the real test may be whether people heard it and found themselves too inspired, too angered, too challenged, or too sick to eat a Sunday meal.[49] From a pastoral point of view, hearing nothing but silence from members of a congregation after a sermon may be more desirable than listening again to traditional comments, "Good sermon" or "I enjoyed the message."

God is the audience in preaching as in all of worship. People overhear the gospel as a preacher carefully relates the story of divine redemption.[50] The meaning of worship is dramatized as the pulpit becomes an altar on which the sermon is offered as a gift to God.

John Knox saw the truth clearly and stated it emphatically: "Either preaching contributes to, provides a medium of, worship, or it is not preaching."[51] "True preaching is very close to praying."[52]

Worship and Mission

The church is mission. To excise mission from the church is to destroy the church. Worship is central in the life of the church. However, every aspect of the church's worship is related to the church's mission. No part of the church's mission legitimately can be divorced from the church's worship.

Worship precedes mission, although it always leads to mission. Perpetual retreat from the world is neither a requirement for nor a product of worship. The essence of worship evokes an involvement in mission among worshipers.

Both worship and mission have their origin in the nature of God as revealed in Jesus Christ. A church worships God because of who God is and what the church is. Similarly, a church is always on mission because of who God is and what the church is. As long as worship is central in a congregation the urgency of mission cannot be forgotten.[53]

Mission couched in worship is always in touch with God. The mission program is not conceived by the church to be supported by the church. Mission is God's work in the world derived from God's nature as understood through Christ. A church which values the worship of God cherishes the opportunity to be a part of the divine action. In fact, a direct relationship exists between what happens in a church's worship and what a church does in missions.[54]

Mission has rightly been tagged "the resonance of liturgy."[55] The dynamism of God's redemptive mission discovered in worship thrusts people into that mission as God's coworkers. One writer declares that the most important moment in worship arrives when worshipers leave the sanctuary. At that time, whether or not worshipers have understood the meaning of the experience in which they have been involved becomes clear.[56] Mission is the natural consequence of worship.

Without a relationship to worship, missions can become a means of self-aggrandizement. A predictable pride in missions is susceptible to error. Almost imperceptibly, people's involvement in missions can become oriented to self-glorification— individually or corporately. In such a situation, mission is far more for the sake of the self than for God.

Nonworship-based mission will not last. No one can for long represent God's love and Christ's presence in the world without regular experiences of corporate worship. "Any ministry without the means of grace in the gathered enactment of the story and the church's memory is impoverished, and, finally, impossible."[57] Missions needs worship. Worship requires missions.[58]

Discoveries made in missions become a part of the content of worship. Concerns related to the world burden the hearts of people who assemble for fellowship with God. Missions activities produce the issues, emotions, and even the language which pervade a congregation's prayers. But missions and worship are reciprocal influences. As people speak with God about pressing needs around them, they discover God leading them to touch those needs personally with love. Don Saliers correctly perceives the pattern—"To pray with the church is to remember the world before God"—and helpfully elaborataes its meaning. There can be "no true serving of others without praying for them: no true praying for them without sharing, literally sharing, their sorrows, griefs, burdens, and joys."[59]

To worship is to declare—as a personal confession and as worldly witness—that God is God. Mission is inherent in that conviction. The praise of God in worship pleases God and witnesses to others about God (Ps. 117:1; Rom. 15:9, 11; Eph. 1:12). In such praise is a desire to involve all of creation in the praise of God, which is the goal of missions.

A recovery of the urgency, intensity, and fidelity appropriate to missions will come in the authentic worship of God. In worship people get in touch with a vision, a motivation, and a power for missions unavailable anywhere else. Missions can begin apart from worship, but missions cannot last without worship.

Worship and Ethics

Worship and ethics are inseparable. Attempts to divide them compromise the Christian nature of both and strike a vicious blow against the wholeness of Christians, individually and corporately.

Unfortunately, the prophetic tirades against inauthentic worship in the Old Testament are sometimes indiscriminately set over against all worship. Persons who espouse responsible ethical action look with suspicion, if not alarm, at statements which emphasize the primacy of worship in a congregation.

Targets of the divinely inspired wrath of the Old Testament prophets were not authentic experiences of the worship of God, but serious abuses of real worship. Amos was disgusted with the festivals of worship which he witnessed in Israel because they had no relationship to even the minimal moral standards of a compassionate life. The rough, plain-spoken shepherd from Tekoa saw persons participate in the most important ceremonies of worship and then ignore the very kinds of people in need for whom God had revealed divine love. The individuals who were lifting their voices to God in the "songs of the temple" were the same as those "who trample upon the needy," "deal deceitfully with false balances," and "buy the poor for silver" (Amos 8:3-6). Little wonder that Amos was angry. And God. But the problem was an absence of true worship, not worship.

Hosea provides an insight into his appreciation for worship by describing the loss of instruments for worship as a punishment for people's sins (Hos. 3:4). This same prophet uses the language of worship—"sacrifice" and "burnt offerings"—to call for demonstrations of "steadfast love" (6:6). —Micah's vision of the "latter days" includes a restoration of true worship (4:1-2), worship in which people find the direction and the power for walking in the ways of God. Note that one of the results of spiritual worship was the establishment of peace (a political-ethical concern). Much like Hosea, using the imagery of worship, Micah calls for justice, loving-kindness, and humility (6:8).

Citing Old Testament prophets to support a deemphasis of worship, even to elevate the importance of ethics, makes the same mistake (sin) which the prophets condemned. Worship and ethics are inseparable. Neither is expendable among the people of God.

Worship devoid of ethical content and challenge degenerates into irresponsible and immoral escapism. Ethics ripped by its roots from worship withers and dies. Each needs the other.

Jesus understood. He positioned Himself in the rabbinic tradition in which people's words and deeds can be both expressions of worship and ethical acts.[60] Jesus demonstrated the primacy of worship by His own behavior. Never, though, was this worship isolated from other people or devoid of ethical values. Jesus taught that people who need to be reconciled to others should restore relationships before going to worship. He told a parable that praised a man who stopped to show concern for a person in need after two other passersby turned away so they could get to the temple. He authoritatively advised a spiritual quality of worship that enhances concern for the moral quality of all of life.

The marriage of worship and ethics blessed by Jesus was celebrated with great faithfulness in the early church. The greater the spiritual meaning of an act of worship, the more valuable it was in ethics-oriented services—whether in the development of an individual's character or a congregation's approach to a social problem. For example, "The early church had a vigorous view of the relationship between liturgical integrity and commitment to the poor."[61]

When worship occupies the center of a church's life, ethics will receive proper attention and courageous expression. Both worship and ethics will be characterized by integrity. So will the church.

Worship Is the Foundation of Ethics

Worshipers bring their whole lives into experiences of worship, offer all that they are and have to God, and then depart to demonstrate the impact of worship on their total existence. Worship is affected by the ethics brought to it by participants. Ethics is an important part of the actual content of worship and an influence on how worship is expressed. Prominent among the consequences of worship is a heightened, better-informed moral consciousness.

Worship is foundational to ethical concerns. How does a person become morally good? Not by developing admirable ideals or embracing correct opinions. Not by thoughtlessly conforming to a respected code of behavior. Not by deciding about which principles have priority and which rules have authority. Maturation in morality is a matter of worship.

God's will is the ultimate criterion for moral convictions and ethical actions in the life of a Christian. God wills that people do in ethics what is done in worship until all of life becomes one continuous act of grateful praise to God. Thus, the first question in ethics is not "What ought I to do?" but "With whom am I in love?"[62] That issue is resolved in worship.

Actually, in the New Testament, worship is a term with a meaning that is as broad as life. New Testament writers had come to understand the "temple" not so much as a building as any place in life where people respond in faith and obedience to the sovereign God as revealed in the risen Christ (see 1 Cor. 6:16).[63] Worship relates to all ethical concerns because worship involves everyone's total existence. Ethics *is* worship lived out in people's lives. "Every detail of private and social life must be ordered in a way that worships God."[64]

Ethics do not (cannot) replace worship. The worship of God is the most important work of the people of God. Ethics become a form of worship. In his classic treatment of Christian ethics, Emil Brunner describes the church's duty "as a worshiping community, to make its distinction from the world plain and clear."[65]

An ethical life begins in the worship of God. Eventually ethics become a form of worship in the world. But, even then, the need for corporate worship is not supplanted. Moral maturity requires regular involvement in the congregational worship of God.

Worship and the Vision for Ethical Action

Cut off from worship, ethical action can become little more than a helter-skelter fidelity to a cultural agenda. Ethical priorities are altered by what is popular or what society thinks is important. No moral concern remains in the public spotlight for long. Special interest groups see to it that an endless variety of issues qualify as "*the* most important ethical challenge of our time." A passion for relevance replaces a commitment to moral substance.

In the worship of God, people confront the commanding vision of ethical action. The constancy of a worship-based focus on Jesus saves congregations and individuals from expending their energies on a rapidly changing social or political agenda. Working for peace, adoring God, advocating economic justice, praising the Lord, feeding the poor, and practicing baptism are actions which belong together. Such togetherness is possible as long as worship exists at the center of life and Jesus is the source of ethical insights. Sustained ethical action among Christians is impossible apart from Christian worship.

Every aspect of worship is fraught with moral significance. None more so, though, than the offering. The offertory in a worship service is a paradigm for ethical behavior in all of life.[66] God expects from persons an offering of every part of their lives. Ethics is a gift worshipfully offered to the continuously gift-giving God.

A call to worship is a summons for people to bring all of their words and actions into the presence of God as means of adoration, causes for reflection, and concerns in need of revision. True praise reveals false idols[67] as it clarifies loyalties and values. Confession creates a vulnerable openness before God through which people can be forgiven for what is unholy in their lives and encouraged regarding what is righteous. Christian proclamation is an announcement of the good news of the advent of God's kingdom with insights into the meaning of citizenship in that realm.

Special acts of worship hold special promise for a true vision of ethical action. Much of the vocabulary and imagery associated with both baptism and the Lord's Supper are integrally related to Christian morality.[68] Baptism is a refutation of individualism and an identification with a community devoted to love and redemption, justice and grace. At the Lord's table, people are reminded of their oneness in need and their chosenness for compassionate service. Reflecting on "the bread of life," persons are challenged to be distributors of bread for all who are hungry physically and spiritually.

Spiritual worship is a profoundly political act. In the worship of God, loyalties are clarified. God has no rivals. Allegiance to a nation, devotion to the workplace, and a passion for personal pursuits are all subsumed under service to God. In the worship of God, freedom is celebrated. Rejoicing in the liberty made possible by Christ, worshipers cannot be content as long as anyone anywhere is in bondage of any kind. Unless, of course, it is a bondage to grace, which, in reality, is freedom.

Social-political structures are threatened by the worship of God. In worship, the ethics of Jesus—often at odds with social entities—becomes the way of life for worshipers. Committed to the worship of God, persons refuse to be a part of anything that cannot be offered to God in worship, and they relentlessly seek to eradicate everything that is a source of displeasure to God.[69] Thus, the politics of prejudice, greed, and war are targets for worship-inspired ethical action.

Worship has protective value for a healthy moral vision. Life cannot be neatly segmented into the sacred and the secular, prayer set over against politics, worship separated from work, and personal evangelism made a competitor of social action. Worship nurtures a godly wholeness in life as well as holiness.

Ethical action is somewhat prone toward the creation of self-centeredness.[70] Worship can keep that tendency in check. Self-centeredness is a sin, the very antithesis of worship. The proper outcome of Christian moral activities is neither a glorification of activists communally or an identification of people as do-gooders individually. Christian ethics cause observers to appreciate good works and give glory to God (Matt. 5:16).

Worship sensitizes persons to the necessity of forgiveness as well as to the importance of righteousness. All people worship God as sinners—sinners forgiven by God or sinners in need of forgiveness from God. Thus, the offer of forgiveness to moral failures is every bit as essential to ethical integrity as an encouragement and applause for ethical victories. In worshipful devotion to God people are exposed to an ethical vision in which it is just as wrong to refuse pardon to people guilty of immorality as it is to reject attempts to live morally.

Worship, Power, and Righteousness

The truest motivation for ethical behavior coincides with the power which makes such behavior possible—gratitude. Gratitude to God. Moral obedience is much more a joyful response to God than a stern-faced act of human determination to do right. Gratitude to God is the basis of ethics. Doxology is its spirit.

Ethical action separated from congregational worship is a cut-flower endeavor which cannot last. God's imperatives related to life in the world are impossibilities for persons who do not know the indicatives of God celebrated in worship. Christian ethics is for people in a dynamic relationship with God that is characterized by constant worship.

Among the saddest, most fatigued, and sometimes obnoxious people in the world are individuals seeking to be good on their own. It is not possible. Such folks become so concerned with straitlaced obedience that they lose sight of Christ-shaped compassion. Legality becomes more important than morality. Institutions take precedence over individuals. The result is good people in the worst sense of the word. Their very concept of virtue is a serious moral flaw.

To ignore worship in the pursuit of ethical goals is to turn away from the very power that makes an ethical life possible. Moral qualities such as "love, joy, peace, patience, kindness, goodness, faithfulness, gentleness, self-control" are not (and never can be) individual accomplishments, but are (always) the "fruit of the Spirit" (Gal. 5:22-23). The God who is worshiped empowers persons to be faithful to the ethical vision discovered in worship. T. W. Manson provides an invaluable insight into the necessity of worship in the ethical life: "The living Christ still has two hands, one to point the way, and the other held out to help us along."[71]

In my own church experience, ethics and worship have often been viewed as competitors. Ethicists have not appreciated worship. Worship rarely has included any reference to ethics.

Congregations tend to incorporate into their worship experiences that which they deem most important in life. Likewise, people make decisions about what is important in life on the basis of what is encountered in worship. Thus, a division of ethics and worship constitutes a serious problem within the church.

In my tradition, issues of personal morality have been embraced in worship. But major social ills have scarcely been mentioned in worship. As a result, church people have sensed affirmation for a double standard of morality—one ethic for the church, the home, and private concerns and another ethic for business, politics, and society. All too often, simultaneously, God has been praised and prejudice perpetuated, the incarnation celebrated and social involvements belittled, prayers of intercession offered but the hungry, imprisoned, and oppressed people of the world ignored.

Only as ethics finds its rightful place in worship can corrections for these faults be realized. In worship alone can public morality and private morality be biblically united. And, God honored—which is the goal of both worship and ethics.

Worship and Administration

What is a section on administration doing in a book on worship? Anyone with experience in local church ministries knows the necessity of administration. In fact, many people have found administrative duties to be the Achilles' heel of meaningful ministry. Administrative concerns always seem to vie for time, attention, and energy that should be channeled more "religiously." Thus, administration becomes a competitor with, if not a distractor from, other ministry concerns. Because administrative matters do not wait without worsening, they win attention. All too often the result is people who are mad, drained, and defeated.

If worship is the central activity in the life of the church and all other concerns are to be seen in relation to it, administration must be involved. But what does worship have to do with choir schedules, budget priorities, logistical arrangements, staff supervision, committee structures, and the like? Everything, really.

Source of Identity

A major frustration in church administration and a source of many of its most persistent problems is a confusion of identity.

People understand the church one way theologically and another way programmatically, institutionally, and financially. Often the two concepts are incompatible. Some people see church administration as a "necessary evil" requiring attention that should go to more "spiritual" concerns. Others dub attentiveness to administrative matters as "being realistic" or "taking care of business."

What is the administrative model to be admired and implemented within the church? The organizational structure put together by a popular multinational corporation? The fiscal program of a prosperous bank? The service-oriented policies of a United Way agency? The supervisory arrangement present in an employee training center?

If a church adopts a business model in its administration, every phase of its corporate life is affected. Business-oriented philosophies, goals, and procedures will shape which church programs are valued, whether or not new ministries are initiated, how offerings are expended (or saved), and expectations related to ministerial responsibilities. The result can be a fiscally sound, organizationally impressive, smooth-running institution which bears only a faint resemblance to a church.

A church that is faithful in worship is a church that will not forget who it is. Of utmost concern in the church is to please God, which means to *be* the church—the people of God—not something or someone else. When concerns for administration are derived from and understood within experiences of worship, the goal of administration becomes the glorification of God through the life of the congregation.

A local fellowship of Christians cannot function as a church if it is not a church. In such a situation, the best administration can do no more than sustain an admirable organization. Identity and ministry as a church are products of a love for God which is faithfully expressed in the worship of God.

Apart from worship, financial campaigns, attendance drives, building programs, and quests for congregational support within a church are devoid of the motivation and power essential to their success. Appeals to duty miss the point—"You ought to be more involved in the church." "The church needs your financial support." People will never do out of duty that which springs naturally from love. Love is the issue in worship.

Who has to urge a lover to spend time in the presence of the beloved? When is it ever necessary to beg someone in love to share a gift with the one loved (or to establish a minimum value for what is to be given)? Who does not want to see every endeavor succeed in the lives of loved ones?

In the worship of God, people learn the value of being together for the corporate adoration of God. That is how a church grows. Yet, in a popular manual on church growth, worship is not even mentioned in a discussion of how and why churches grow in membership.[72] In a prioritized listing of the purposes of a church, the exaltation of God comes after the edification of believers.[73]

Worship nurtures generosity. Gratitude to God finds expression in extravagant giving. Why, then, are so many financial campaigns within churches completely divorced from what happens in worship (except for an occasional "stewardship testimony," a "budget update," or an annual stewardship sermon)?

Worship keeps a church in touch with its true identity. Worship nurtures a relationship with God which is the source of a church's power.

Criteria for Ministry

Worship also sensitizes a church to the appropriate criteria by which to measure its ministry. Administration done without reference to worship can involve a commitment to goals and methods of ministry that hinder, rather than help, people trying to be the church.

The proper vision for a church's ministry is born in worship. As the drama of redemption is reviewed with praise, worshipers see God's favor for people in need. Celebrating the love of God in Christ means confronting Jesus' challenge to serve Him among the lost, the poor, the hungry, and the homeless.

Worship challenges a church's preoccupation with itself, its structures, strength, and survival. One author finds the most God-honoring attitudinal model for the church in the Old Testament story of Abraham's willingness to sacrifice Isaac. "Only he who, at the clear behest of God, is prepared to destroy that which carries the human possibility of the covenant's fulfillment is able to carry forward the covenant."[74]

Discussions of church budgets provide clear insights into the intensity of a church's willingness to follow Jesus' instructions about winning by losing and living by dying. Often the most prevalent questions are: "How will this new program help us?"

"Will this ministry bring us new members?" "Must we not view the line items of our budget as investments upon which we expect significant returns?" Worship-shaped questions are different: "What does God want us to do about this ministry?" "Do we have enough faith in God to take the risk of providing this service?" "Is not faithfulness more important than success?" Worship teaches finance committees and whole congregations to evaluate ministries not in terms of the good received from them but by the good done by them. Church budgets, like all other aspects of the church's life, are to glorify God.

Statistics are of little value in worship. For example, "The number of people in the church is hardly an indicator of its spiritual strength."[75] Through worship, a church is enabled to put numerical figures as they relate to ministries in a proper perspective. "Worship is the vehicle that carries us beyond ourselves and inevitably bids us break the limits of mathematical calculation with an overriding generosity inspired by an overwhelming thankfulness."[76]

What about people—those who serve in a church as employees and volunteers? Does a church measure a person's effectiveness by the same standards embraced by secular organizations? And, what about people in the church who err, fail, or sin? Is the church's commitment to redemption a spiritual concept inapplicable to personnel problems? Or is the church to be a community of forgiveness and encouragement in its supervisory policies as well as in its theological precepts? Worship is the proper context in which these inquiries find their best answers.

Protests are predictable. "We must be realistic." "We have to operate as a good business." Where such aspirations are compatible with the nature of the church, they are acceptable. Otherwise, they are objectionable. In a life of worship, a church learns that its first order of responsibility is not to be a good business, but a good church—a faithful representation of a congregation of God's people.

Administry is the word Tom Oden uses in relation to the administrative concerns of the church. _Administry_ is an old English word that comes from the Latin _administrare_. The meaning is "to manage as a steward." Administration, then, literally means "toward ministry."[77] Church administration shaped within a worshiping congregation involves taking care of the responsibilities which must receive attention in order for the church to be faithful in its God-given ministry.

Conclusion

The worship of God is the most important activity of the people of God. The church has many functions. All are related to worship. Each must be carried out informed by worship. Everything is to be done in the spirit of worship.

John Westerhoff offers a crucial word of encouragement and challenge regarding the centrality of worship in the life of the church. Westerhoff observes, "There remains to the church only one unique and peculiar responsibility; the conduct of public worship." Then he describes the glory and the danger related to worship in the church.

> If the church does nothing other than to keep open a house, symbolic of the homeland of the soul, where in season and out women and men come to reenact the memory and vision of who they are, it will have rendered society and each of us a service of unmeasurable value. So long as the church bids men and women to participate in the liturgies of the Christian faith community it need not question its place, mission or influence in the world. If it loses faith or is careless in its rituals it need not look to its avocations to save it.[78]

Part II
Activity: The Church at Worship

3
An Order of Worship
"Give what is best; This all
my prayer shall be"

Every service of corporate worship has an order, at least in retrospect if not by design. Admittedly, order is more easily discernible in some styles of worship than in others. But all services of worship evidence an arrangement of their constituent parts.

Bible scholars have labored to discover the precise order that prevailed in the worship experiences in the New Testament community of faith. Only a minimal consensus characterizes their findings, however. That is not surprising. Synagogue services influenced Christian congregations with varying degrees of intensity from place to place. Sometimes the worship of an ancient fellowship occurred under the threat of persecution. Thus, activities varied. Services were often abbreviated. Then, too, authors of the New Testament literature reveal a far greater interest in the principles that are to shape Christian worship than in outlines of specific experiences. Early Christian worship was marked by great freedom and festive joy. Not a lot more can be said with certainty about the worship of the primitive Christian community.

Oscar Cullmann's careful study of the early church concludes that the original form of Christian worship included three parts—sermon, prayer, and supper.[1] Obviously, with the passing of time, congregations embraced additional ingredients in their services of worship. Drawing upon 1 Corinthians 12—14; 16:20-24; Colossians 3:16-17, the Pastoral Epistles, and reputable extrabiblical sources, G. J. Cuming reconstructs the order of a worship service common to Christian congregations founded by and/or influenced by Paul. The suggested sequence of Pauline worship is:

Salutation (Grace and peace be with you)
Thanksgiving
Intercession

Bible-reading. Teaching and Admonition.
Psalms (ancient and modern)
Doxology, Kiss of peace
Dismissal (Come, Lord and the Grace)[2]

No doubt, orders of worship varied from congregation to congregation. Also, different orders developed for different kinds of services. Frequently, Christians gathered for a worship service built around baptism early on Sunday morning and later that day regrouped for a service in which the Lord's Supper or biblical exposition was most dominant.

Writing about Christian worship around A.D. 150, Justin Martyr provides the best of the earliest descriptions of the framework for Christian worship. The structure of worship found in Justin's *First Apology* is the foundation upon which later developments in worship have been constructed. The format of worship as reported by Justin is:

Reading of Scripture
Sermon (from the bishop who is seated)
Common Prayer (congregation standing)
Congregational "Amen"
Kiss of Peace
Offertory (not money, but bread and wine)
Consecration Prayer (for the bread and wine)
The Lord's Supper (called Communion)

This service ends with the same kind of abruptness with which it begins. The Lord's Supper is viewed as the climax of corporate worship. No benediction is spoken. Monetary offerings are left with the bishop after the service has concluded.[3]

Clearly, no one generally accepted order of worship exists. There are many. Even if the prevalent New Testament pattern of worship could be identified, a church would be under no obligation to reproduce it exactly.[4] Meaningful worship involves the thought patterns, language, and life-styles of the present in its offerings to God. For example, Christian worship in the house churches of the first century did not include the praise of God by musical instruments. Today, though, orders of worship rightfully provide opportunities for the gifts and leadership of a wide variety of musical instruments in worship.

On the pages which follow, I suggest an order of worship. In no sense should this order be understood as prescriptive, restrictive, or exclusive in relation to alternative orders of worship. My own spiritual pilgrimage has been enriched by diversity in worship experiences. No one order is inherently better than another.

As a leader in worship, I often have planned services that did not follow the sequence of events presented here. Not every service will (or can or should) include all of the elements of worship elaborated on these pages. However, over a period of several weeks, the worship experiences of any congregation can be greatly enhanced if all of these items receive attention.

During one of my early pastorates, I found great joy in leading members of the congregation to study the worship materials printed in our weekly "bulletin." No meaningful order was apparent. Eventually, we reworked these materials to provide a better understanding of each part of the service and the reason for its particular position in the service. Fifteen years later I returned to this church for a "homecoming" celebration. The printed order of service was exactly the same one that had been used during my last service there as pastor. No changes had been made in a decade and a half. Only one aspect of my instruction on worship had been retained—the value of a meaningfully ordered service. What I had said about the importance of flexibility and change in a church's order of worship had not stuck. An order of worship should be a dynamic, not a static, instrument to aid people's praise of God.

Whether or not a congregation's order of worship is printed does not determine the quality of that people's worship. Worshipers need to be aware of where they are in a worship experience and understand the meaning of what is happening. However, a printed document placed in people's hands no more guarantees the fulfillment of those basic needs than the absence of such an instrument makes certain the contrary.

I have known marvelous moments of congregational worship marked by spontaneity and informality. And I have realized the spiritual bankruptcy (at least for me) of well-planned worship events projected in detail by orders printed on slick, multicolored paper. Conversely, I have sensed the lack of seriousness in preparation and the absence of dignity in execution in services which never moved beyond the level of human entertainment to touch God. But I also have experienced the rush of tremendous spiritual joy, adoration, and liberating commitment within a service that was traditional, formal, and liturgical.

At best an order of worship is an aid, a guide, or a nudge for worshipers. Seldom will expressions of worship for everyone present in a service form the same patterns and follow the same sequence at an identical pace. Though words of praise are planned for early in a service, some worshipers may not be able to express genuine praise until near the end of the worship experience. Likewise, some worshipers may not be able to wait until that part of the service planned for prayers to pour out their hearts to God in confessions and intercessions. If an order of worship ever becomes confining, stifling, restricting, or deadening, it defeats the very purpose which it is intended to serve.

The outline of worship which follows is important as a means for identifying and elaborating the contents of a holistic act of corporate worship. This order can be adapted by a church of any numerical size or theological point of view. It requires no particular level of education or type of worship orientation. My concern is neither the development of high church worship nor its opposite extreme. This order invites the involvement of the whole person and the whole congregation—physically, intellectually, emotionally, and spiritually. Within this suggested structure is plenty of room for spontaneity and a hope for surprise. I do not defend the priority of this order against other helpful alternatives. My sole purpose in the work on these pages is the encouragement of worship that is pleasing to God and meaningful to worshipers.

4
Gathering
"Come and worship"

Christian worship is a gathering. Corporate worship happens only as persons unite with each other for the purpose of worship. The very word *congregation* comes from a verb that means "to flock together."[1] The number of people involved is not all that important. Massive congregations of worshipers are thrilling sights. But Jesus promises the gift of the divine presence where even two or three people gather in His name (Matt. 18:20).

When does worship begin? The writer of Hebrews implores Christians not to forsake assembling for worship (Heb. 10:25). An argument can be made that worship begins at the moment people consciously decide to be a part of a worshiping congregation. At this point the words of Hebrews are heeded, God's summons to worship is obeyed, and willful efforts are made to move toward a fellowship of worship.

When worship *should* begin or *can* begin is not always when worship *does* begin. The motives which bring individuals together at a time for worship are as numerous as the people present. Habit is a major prompter. Many people gather for worship as routinely as they go to their places of employment. An elderly lady, weary of loneliness, goes to worship in search of fellowship. A teenager is in worship because she has been told that she cannot have the car during the next week if she does not attend. A young man, who can think of little more than scrambling up the social ladder, skipping as many rungs as possible with every step, has been told that being seen in worship is a "good thing" in his community. An older banker enters a sanctuary, openly declaring to his family, "I just want to feel good again."

Impure motives and complex intentions are not a major problem to God. Rarely do people gather for worship without a mixture of purposes. A desire to honor God has to contend with efforts aimed at self-fulfillment, a mind in search of a different perspective, or a troubled soul desperately seeking to enjoy a moment of peace.

For some folks worship begins during the process of gathering—in the shower when a young woman says to herself, "I'm going to attend a worship service today"; in the car on the way to a church building when a father says to the other family members with him, "Let's begin focusing on what we are going to do in worship today"; walking from a Sunday School classroom into a sanctuary thinking, *I'm looking forward to worship this morning*. For other persons, worship begins after the service is well underway. I have known occasions for worship when I really did not begin to give myself to the purpose of the gathered congregation until joining a recitation of the Lord's Prayer or hearing the offertory music.

God accepts people where they are and, if they are willing, lovingly moves them to where they ought to be. That is a pattern worthy of emulation in worship.

Call to Worship

A call to worship, spoken or sung, is an act of profound theological significance and immense practical worth.

Assuming that all the people present in a worship service are ready to worship is a serious misperception. Minds and bodies, attitudes and interests, may be miles apart. A businesswoman cannot seem to get her mind off a sales presentation scheduled for eight o'clock the next morning. A married couple sits together seething with anger at each other. They fussed all the way to the door of the sanctuary. White-hot wrath does not dissipate quickly. A middle-aged man sits in grief. His mother's funeral was the previous afternoon. Several people are wondering if the service will conclude in time for them to race home and see the opening kickoff of a televised football game. A few people are whispering to each other, inquiring about the absence of some of their friends. Students from one high school are squirming with excitement thinking about their past Friday night's basketball victory over a big rival and wanting to "rub it in" on church members from the losing school. A cluster of adults is buzzing with low-voiced complaints about the temperature of the room. A church leader, who has scanned the printed order of service for the day, comments to a friend, "I don't like the voice of the soloist for today."

A call to worship recognizes the incredible diversity at the beginning of a service, views it as the substance from which a community of worshipers can be formed, and invites everyone present to focus on God. Asking people who have gathered for a service to set aside all of their concerns, anxieties, preoccupations, and cares in order to worship is as completely unnecessary as it is unrealistic. The worship of God does not require a case of temporary amnesia regarding the rest of life. Actually, God desires for all of life to be brought into worship as an offering.

Occasionally, I find special meaning when the sound of a siren on a speeding ambulance, the roar of a jet engine of an airliner flying overhead, or honks of the car horns of impatient motorists filter into a worship center during a service. They are good reminders that worship rightly takes place in this world and seeks no divorce from its concerns. The worship of God is directly related to an accident requiring an ambulance for its victims, to business travel by air, and to volatile internal stress which finds ventilation by a person pounding on a car horn.

A call to worship is as beneficial as it is practical. People can be helped and worship encouraged by a declaration that the time for worship has arrived, by an invitation for participation by every member of the congregation, and/or a question of summons, "Will you now join together in the worship of Almighty God?"

The divine call to worship is the basis of every human call to worship. God acts first. In worship, as in creation and redemption, all of the initiative is with God. A congregation's worship of God is a response to God, to what God has done, and to what God is doing.

Implicit in a call to worship is a major distinctive of Christian worship. Pagan worship is an effort by people in need to evoke a helpful response from their god. Such worship is filled with pleas for the attention of a god accompanied by petitions for the deity's beneficent actions. That is not the nature of Christian worship.

The God revealed in the Bible and in Jesus of Nazareth requires no human attitude or action as a prerequisite for meeting people's needs. God already has acted. The apostle Paul recorded the staggering truth, "God shows his love for us in that while we are yet sinners Christ died for us" (Rom. 5:8). Christian worshipers do not have to beg for God's attention and plead for God's presence. Those are givens. We do not worship God in order to be loved by God. We are loved by God. Our worship of God takes place within that love.

Christian worship is not an initiative taken by people in need seeking to secure the help of the abundantly resourceful God. Divine worship is a human response to God, who previously has acted in history to make possible complete redemption and who presently invites divine-human communion. Worship is not a tactic calculated to win God's grace. Worship occurs because of God's grace. Worshipers gather within God's grace. Worship is a celebration of God's grace.

A *human call to worship* repeats the divine invitation and applies it to a specific congregation. A recognition of the immediate human situation in which worship is to occur can be helpful. Worship is fake if it ignores the conditions in which a congregation gathers and fails to involve each worshiper's total being. Thus, a call to worship may begin with a recognition of an obvious preoccupation among the worshipers, then move to an invitation for all present to focus their attention on God: "This morning we gather with heavy hearts because of the tragedy which has visited our community in recent days." "I'm sure we could spend this entire hour talking about the good things that have happened in our midst this past week." "But now it is time to focus on God, to lay before the divine being our deepest hurts and our greatest joys. Please bring all that you are in this moment into an encounter with God."[2]

Worship is dialogical. A call to worship is an invitation to join a conversation. God has spoken. God's interest in and request for words from worshipers is unmistakable in the Bible: "Ascribe greatness to our God!" (Deut. 32:3); "Sing to the Lord, . . . Tell of his salvation" (2 Chron. 16:23); "Make a joyful noise to God, . . . sing the glory of his name; give to him glorious praise!" (Ps. 66:1-2); "Praise the Lord, . . . Extol him" (117:1); "Ask, and it will be given you" (Matt. 7:7).

A response is in order. Worshipers are invited (and encouraged) to speak to God regarding their adoration of God, their sins against God, their need for God, their requests for God's gifts, and their commitments to God. That is not the end of the dialogue though. The last word belongs to God.

Just as human words are provoked by God's Word, God's word is elicited by human words. A conversation ensues. Communion occurs. A relationship is nurtured. And, if the interac-

tion is really sound, the divine-human dialogue will continue long after the benediction.

Instrumental Prelude

In most services of public worship, an instrumental prelude comes first. Unfortunately (and inaccurately), the prelude is often understood as no more than the surface meaning of the word suggests—a prelude; not an act of worship, but an act prior to worship. Such a perception can cause worshipers to pay little attention to the prelude. A conversational buzz (if not a roar) among worshipers can virtually override the instrumental music.

What is a musical prelude in worship? Is it an ecclesiastical counterpart to an overture in a theater? Or is a prelude in worship more of a minisymphony in which all of the major emotions of worship are represented and the significant movements of worship blended together? Or is a prelude a kind of holy Muzak intended to drown out the noises produced by people gathering for worship?

Neither from a theological nor pragmatical viewpoint is the prelude a "preliminary" to worship. There are no preliminaries in worship. In fact, the prelude does not have to be immovably positioned as the first item on every order of worship. Personally, I like for the prelude to follow the call to worship periodically so as to intensify worshipers' attentiveness to it and appreciation for it.

The prelude is a *transition*. Worship is unlike any other human experience. Corporate worship requires faith-based words and actions unlike any that are common in a workday world. Often worshipers need time to make adjustments, to shift gears, in order to give themselves to an experience of worship.

Gathering for worship, Quakers favor an exercise known as "centering." Time is set aside for people to get their entire beings focused on God. Each worshiper makes an effort to bring together all emotions, thoughts, and needs and to center them on the Divine Being.

The prelude points the way to God. It can be used as a time for centering on God. The prelude encourages all present to bring all of their concerns into a focus on God and to open themselves to a discovery of the divine will.

The prelude is a *connection*. Two or more worlds collide in worship. The world of work, the world of play, the world of family, and the world of need intersect the world of worship. A satisfactory merger of those worlds is crucial to a meaningful experience of worship.

Human concerns do not have to be set aside for divine worship to occur. After all, the humanity of worshipers is a result of the creative activity of the God to be worshiped. True worship incorporates all of the concerns of people and presents them to God in modes of adoration, confession, and intercession. The prelude is a coming together place. Linkage can be established between the kingdoms of this world and the kingdom of God, between the wills of worshipers and the will of God.

The prelude is a *demonstration*. The prelude establishes the essential spirit of worship. It is the first of many offerings to God.

Conversations about whether a prelude is too loud or too quiet, too classical or too popular, miss the point. The prelude is an instrumentalist's offering to God, not to a congregation. By way of the prelude, members of a congregation are encouraged to begin offering their own gifts to God.

Typically, the majesty or the humility conveyed by the prelude depends upon the nature of the service. A special theme or the time of year may also determine whether the musical offering should come from a piano, an organ, or multiple instruments. Stringed instruments bring a helpful solemnity to worship on some occasions. Trumpets are fitting for the fourth Sunday of Advent and Easter morning. Pipe organs and pianos possess a versatility that makes them invaluable musical instruments in all moods of worship.

What the musician or musicians do in the prelude is precisely what all of the other worshipers are to do throughout the service. Worship involves making an offering to God of all that people are and have. The prelude demonstrates that fundamental act.

The prelude is a musical procession into the presence of God. When people gathered for worship hear it, they can take heart. Spirits are lifted. The sound of the prelude is a signal that worship is under way.

Invocation

A prayer is a prayer. Right? Yes and no. Every prayer is an expression to God—an honest attempt at communication with God. But different prayers have different purposes. Public prayer is not just like private prayer. When a prayer is offered as a part of a service of corporate worship, a recognition of its special place in the service and its purpose in relation to the congregation is extremely important.

No prayer is perfunctory in worship. Every prayer, whether its content is carefully written out in advance or developed as spoken, should evidence forethought, an awareness of its public setting and intention. A spoken prayer in public worship is one of the several gifts offered to God by the worshipers. Thus, the nature of the prayer should be consistent with the nature of worship.

An invocation is a unique prayer. Usually, it is brief. God is addressed. All of the worshipers are included in its words.

God's presence in worship does not have to be requested. Worship is initiated by God. The presence of God precedes the gathering of worshipers. An opportunity to encounter God in worship is the reason people are assembled. An invocation acknowledges God's presence with a spirit of gratitude.

Certain requests are appropriate in an invocation. Though God's presence in worship is a given, requests are in order for God's guidance in worship, acceptance of a specific service, and approval of the worship of the people present. Such requests in prayer steer clear of a self-centered motivation for worship that is concerned only with receiving a blessing. They demonstrate a singular interest in worshiping God through offerings that are pleasing to God.

The invocation can establish the spirit in which a service of worship should proceed. This public prayer at the beginning of worship reflects the nature and purpose of worship generally and the intended direction of the various elements of worship which will follow its "Amen."

Greetings

"Old Mrs. Brown!" That is what everybody called the woman. I do not know the rest of her name. Mrs. Brown lived midway up a long hill nearly two miles from where our church met. People rarely visited Mrs. Brown because her house was dirty and filled with offensive odors. No one in Mrs. Brown's family encouraged her involvement in the church. She was the only member of that household who cared for the church.

Mrs. Brown had no means of transportation. She walked wherever she went. The church was one of her regular destinations.

In fact, Mrs. Brown was present almost every time the church doors opened. She walked to and from worship, two miles each way, regardless of the time of day or the nature of the weather. When she was absent from a service, invariably someone said, "I wonder where old Mrs. Brown is."

Whether or not Mrs. Brown benefited from what happened in worship, I do not know. Her educational level was low. Her comprehension was minimal. Nevertheless, Mrs. Brown faithfully attended worship—walking up and down that long hill in all kinds of conditions. Mrs. Brown did not have much to offer the church. Her gift to God was her presence in worship, a gift which she offered with generosity and sometimes with sacrifice. Of course, that gift was enough. Mrs. Brown needed the affirmation of a welcome to worship, the encouragement of greetings shared among the worshippers, and the assurance that her presence was pleasing to God.

No person's presence in worship should ever be taken for granted. Only each individual alone can know the cost of attendance in any one service. All present in worship, though, need to sense the importance of their efforts to participate. A person's presence in worship is a precious gift of worship.

Being present before God means being present with all who have gathered to worship God. Worshipers benefit from acknowledging each other as well as responding to God. In reality, the former can be an integral part of the latter.

Greetings in worship should evidence the uniqueness of the gathering. Worship is not just another social "get-together." Every person's presence in worship deserves more than a routine, "We're happy to have you here today." God is in the midst of the people. Greetings take place in the name of Christ. Each person's presence is affirmed for the glory of God.

The early church developed specific forms of greetings. Often just prior to a celebration of the Lord's Supper, worshipers exchanged "the kiss of peace," sometimes called the "holy kiss" (cf. Rom. 16:16; 1 Cor. 16:20; 1 Pet. 5:14). Not only did that kiss constitute a greeting, it established the kind of communion appropriate for worship. "It is not easy to be indifferent or hostile towards a brother or sister with whom one has exchanged a personal token of love."[3]

Though an actual kiss is no longer exchanged between most worshipers, some form of passing "the peace" remains an important act of greeting. Various ways exist for an exchange of peace.

In some congregations worshipers shake hands with each other. At times specific words of greeting are voiced among those present, "Peace to you." However this greeting is done, it is a planned act of worship that is to be carried out with sincerity and spontaneity. When properly done, this means of greeting allows all present to see each other as representatives of God's grace to each other.

Another ancient form of mutual acknowledgment among worshipers was a specific spoken greeting:

> The Lord be with you
> *And also with you.*
> (or *"And with your spirit."*)[4]

Based upon the text of Ruth 2:4, these words offered assurance to each worshiper: "Here you are welcome"; "Here you will find sustenance"; "Here, under the shadow of God's wings, you are protected."[5]

During a time of greetings, emphasis can be placed on the importance of presence in worship. However, this observation is not to be confused with an enlistment or an attendance campaign. The point to be made is the importance of a person's presence in worship as a gift of worship.

God calls for people's presence in worship.—In recent years, the importance of a person's physical presence in worship has been eroded by the popularity of "watching worship" by means of the electronic church. Listening to a worship service on the radio or viewing a corporate worship experience on television can be very beneficial to people who are completely unable to be present in a worshiping congregation. However, not even faithful attentiveness to broadcasted worship services can replace personal participation in a worshiping congregation if that is at all possible.

Spiritual dynamics are present in a worshiping fellowship that cannot be duplicated in any other setting. Walking in the woods alone or watching a sunrise with a loved one can be a spiritual experience. But no such act qualifies as a meaningful alternative to worshiping God as a part of a congregation of worshipers.

Worshipers need each other's presence.—The unity of a worshiping community is a source of spiritual encouragement for each individual within it. No one is alone. Every person is aware that a common purpose pervades all who are present.

"Being there" in worship carries an importance which is difficult to overestimate. Unless people are present, "there," corporate worship cannot take place. Anyone who can give no more than personal presence in a service of worship benefits from a reminder that presence is no small gift. An individual's presence in worship honors God and also makes a positive contribution to the experience of other worshipers.

According to an often-told story, Dwight L. Moody once met with resistance when talking with a man about his need for membership and involvement in a church. Moody walked over to the fireplace by which the two men were seated, lifted a flaming coal with a pair of tongs, and set the coal aside by itself. The famous evangelist returned to his seat and remained there in silence watching with his friend as the separated coal ceased flaming and finally died. The man who earlier had protested the worth of Christian fellowship said, "I see your point."

A church fellowship has no counterparts. Its nature is much more that of an organism than that of an institution, organization, or club. The uniqueness of the faith community is dramatized in worship. The importance of the personal presence of all worshipers is evident. Each individual is special and significant. Persons are neither interchangeable nor dispensable. No one individual can make up for the absence of another individual. Biblically understood, the whole fellowship suffers even more from the absence of one of its members than does the individual who is absent. Worshipers (all) need each other (every one).

Faith in Christ requires a person's presence in worship.— Followers of Christ are not people who have arrived, persons who have mastered life completely, individuals who have achieved perfection. Every Christian congregation is a fellowship of failures, strugglers, seekers, outcasts, and sinners. The life of faith is a life of worship. Every person of faith needs regularly to join with other persons of faith in expressing praises, confessing sins, receiving forgiveness, studying the Scriptures, nurturing love, growing in grace, and thereby adoring God in worship.

Any act (gift) of worship as important as presence merits attention, affirmation, and encouragement as a part of worship.

5
Praising
"All Glory, Laud, and Honor"

A mother told me the story. One Wednesday afternoon, she called her young son to come inside and get ready for choir practice. The little fellow was playing with his friends. Immediately, though, he stopped what he was doing and ran toward his house. As he was hurrying away, one of his playmates shouted, "Where are you going?"

The boy's response was, "I'm going to praise the Lord!" Then, in almost the same breath, though an obvious second thought, the child yelled back over his shoulder, "Haven't you ever praised the Lord? It's fun!"

That childhood declaration captures the nature of the praise which belongs in worship. To praise God is to adore God, honor God, give thanks to God, glorify God, and exalt God's name. Most of the time this kind of praise is enjoyable, if not outright fun. Appropriate to the exultant praise of God are confetti, balloons, crepe-paper streamers, colorful banners, candles, whistles, horns, and bells. Worthy sounds of praise include bugle blasts, choral "alleluias," and a wide range of words and phrases lifted high by human voices.

All worship is filled with praise. Praise is nonnegotiable for Christians. Every experience of the public worship of God involves all persons present in the praise of God. Devoid of praise, worship is compromised.

What is praise? Most worshipers know its sound better than its meaning. By definition, praise is "the grateful acknowledgment of reality."[1] But that seems stiff and rational. To a certain extent, praise is mercurial and inexplicable. Praise is adoration. Praise involves exaltation. Praise moves in and out of thanksgiving. Praise bows before the mystery of God, glorifies the revelatory nature of God, magnifies the majesty of God, lauds the love of God, and rejoices in the presence of God.

Words of Praise

In the worship experiences of my childhood and youth, congregational involvement in praise was restricted to the singing of hymns, songs, choruses, and "The Doxology." Occasionally, a member of the congregation was requested to offer a public prayer. But apart from singing, most members of the congregation had no opportunities to use their voices in worship. Worshipers did nothing else together. All of the speaking was done from behind the pulpit.

An act of worship as crucial as praise deserves (demands) congregational participation. Scripture writers acknowledge this truth through multiple requests for people to praise God. The psalmist calls upon all of the earth to "Make a joyful noise to God,... give to him glorious praise" (66:2) Paul suggests that the extension of God's grace to all people is to increase declarations of divine praise (2 Cor. 4:15).

Congregational expressions of praise are integral to worship. Adoration is basic. Ralph Martin calls the adoration of God "the most appropriate and salutary response" of the human spirit to the God encountered in worship. "Adoration confesses that there is more in God than our finite minds and limited capacities can absorb."[2]

Thanksgiving is essential. Thanksgiving is in order because of both who God is and what God does. People rightly praise the holiness of God. Gratitude is expressed for God's self-revelation in Jesus Christ. As the story of salvation is pondered, thanksgiving abounds. Realizing that the gift of redemption is available to all people—to every individual—prompts an explosion of ecstatic joy that defies expression.

Spontaneous Words of Praise

Spontaneity has been important in worship historically. Frequently, the phrase "Thanks be to God" has resounded through worshiping congregations. This expression of praise can be prompted by silent meditation, a reading of the Scriptures, an announcement of the assurance of God's pardon for confessed sins, an insight from the preacher, a prayer of gratitude, or the declaration of God's invitation to salvation.

In recent years, I have come to a new appreciation for the

word *hallelujah*. Roots of the term run deep into the worship traditions of Judaism. Derived from *hallelui,* the imperative mode of *hillel,* which means "to praise," and *Jah,* an abbreviation of Yahweh, which means God, "hallelujah" is "praise be to God."[3] Few terms carry the heights of ecstasy, the depths of devotion, and the breadth of love contained in "hallelujah." Historians indicate that the early Christians often repeated and sang together some form of this word for twenty or thirty minutes at a time. Still today, the word *hallelujah* has a lively presence in Christian congregations around the world.

When worshiping with people who speak a different language, I find the term "hallelujah" to be a major source of union. The meaning of the word is readily understood by everybody. To say the word is to communicate joyous praise. To hear the word is to find inspiration for celebration. Expressing "hallelujahs" binds worshipers to God and to each other.

Litany of Praise

Not all fellowships are comfortable with spontaneous expressions of praise in worship. Even in services in which vocal participation on the part of all present is encouraged, some people are reticent to speak aloud. For these reasons alone, a litany of praise is a valuable ingredient in public worship. There are other supportive factors as well.

Unfortunately, in Free Church worship, *litany* is often viewed as a bad word. Fearing even a hint of rigidity and suspicious of a prescribed act of worship, people shy away from any use of a litany. Such fears and suspicions are ill-founded. A litany is virtually identical with the widely accepted practice of "responsive readings." The difference is that a responsive reading is usually for the edification of members of the congregation and a litany is addressed to God. A litany of praise is among the most ancient forms of worship known.[4]

By means of a litany of praise, every member of a congregation can be involved in the praise of God. No one is left out. If God-glorifying statements such as "Thanks be to God" or "Hallelujah" are not likely to be spoken spontaneously in a worship service, then these important words of worship can be lifted to God by the voices of all present unified in a litany.

Hymns of Praise

Though I write from within the Free Church tradition maintaining profound appreciation for it, I am tempted to argue for one fixed item in every order of service—a hymn of praise. Worship involves much more than praise. But worship cannot involve less. Praise is essential. Affirming that "the raison d'etre of the church's life is to show forth the praise of God who has called the redeemed to himself,"[5] I find it inconceivable that the worship of God can take place without a musical presentation of praise to God.

A hymn of praise early in every worship service is both theologically and pragmatically sound. God merits praise. As soon as people enter God's presence, praise is in order. Practically, praise lifts the gaze of worshipers from themselves and focuses their vision on God. Praise has the power to silence criticisms and to facilitate redemptive relations.

While singing a hymn of praise to God, worshipers join a cosmic choir intent on heralding the greatness and goodness of God. Individual sentiments are sounded as worshipers sing, "Praise to the Lord, the Almighty, the King of creation! O my soul praise Him."[6] A union with all of creation occurs, though, as a congregation sings, "All creatures of our God and King,... Thou burning sun,... Thou silver moon!... Ye clouds,... Thou rising morn, ... Ye lights of evening,... O praise Him."[7]

Visiting a magnificent cathedral on one of the small islands across the bay from Venice, Italy, I learned an important lesson. The beauty and grandeur of the building were overwhelming. I knew, though, that not enough people resided on this island to fill this cathedral, even if every one of them attended a service of worship in it. On my way out of the structure, I asked a resident of the island about its size, "Why was it built so large? Obviously, on this island, you do not need a place of worship with this much space in it." The man's answer rebuffed me even as it instructed me. "We built it for the glory of God!"

They built it for the glory of God! That is the spirit appropriate to a hymn of praise. No holding back. No repressing emotions. No guarding against what others think. Full throat. Full organ with all of the stops open. Pianist plays fortissimo. Add strings and horns as desired. Praise is without moderation. "Praise, praise the Father, praise the Son, And praise the Spirit, Three in One! O praise Him, O praise Him! Alleluia! Alleluia! Alleluia!"[8]

6
Listening
"Speak to My Heart"

Worship is a dialogue. In a dialogue, more than one person speaks. For a conversation to occur, listening is as important as speaking. Listening is essential to worship.

Unloading is a part of worship. Worshipers rightly lift from their hearts and set before God concerns and anxieties, sins in need of forgiveness, intercessions on behalf of others, pleas for divine guidance, reasons for giving thanks. However, at some point, telling has to give way to listening. As much effort must be exerted to hear God speak as has been devoted to being heard by God. Worshipers cannot be forgiven, counseled, directed, encouraged, comforted, and inspired by their own words. God's word is needed. The divine word must be heard. God's word is always available in worship. But worshipers have to listen in order to hear it.

Silence

"We need more silence in our worship services." A laymember of the congregation was speaking. Each week all the ministers of the church responsible for worship leadership met with a cross section of people from the congregation to talk about worship. We asked for honest feedback. This comment about silence caught most everyone by surprise. Over a period of several weeks, one or more worship services had included moments of silence. Obviously, though, the length of the silence was not enough for this businessman.

I was eager to hear the man's reasoning. "How much silence do you want?" I asked. After a pause, someone in the group said, "At least three minutes." At that point, the group fell silent. Finally, one of the ministers spoke, "Do you have any idea how long three minutes is in public worship?" Further discussion revealed a consensus opinion in that group of laypersons. Worship services need more silence.

As worship planners, we decided that a three-minute period of silence in worship would be our goal. We agreed, however, that for this amount of silence to be meaningful, we would have to prepare for it. Because our Sunday morning worship services were broadcast by radio, we had to make arrangements to fill those three minutes with something beneficial for those who listened.

During the month that followed that worship planning session, longer and longer expanses of silence were incorporated into our worship experiences. Finally, one Sunday morning, three minutes were set aside for silence. Admittedly, for the first thirty seconds or so, there was a lot of coughing, foot shuffling, and squirming. Then the congregation seemed to settle into a unique peace. Silence prevailed. But it was not the silence of sleep. It was the silence of waking up, of coming alive.

Writing on worship from the perspective of people in the pews, Craig Douglas Erickson observes, "To reach spiritual maturity, one must apprehend the silence of God. In worship it is the silence that is the stepping-stone to maturity."[1] Taking seriously such comments, certain passages within the Bible take on new meaning. Habakkuk was told, "The Lord is in his holy temple; let all the earth keep silence before him" (Hab. 2:20). Elijah heard the voice of God not amid dramatic turbulence but in stark silence (1 Kings 19:12). I think that often in worship people are more intent on reproducing the wind and fire and the earthquake than on preparing to hear the "still small voice."

Some folks actually fear silence. Every moment of the day, even those devoted to study or sleep, has to be filled with sound. Noise seems to provide security. Such a passion for sound makes virtually impossible quiet moments of personal introspection which can produce redemptive, even if discomforting, honesty.

In worship, silence is far more than an absence of sound. Silence constitutes a vital part of the divine-human dialogue. In silence, worshipers can experience interchanges with God that will not be known where silence does not prevail.

Silence is appropriate at several different points in corporate worship. Exactly where a period of silence is scheduled in a particular service depends on its purpose in that experience. As a general rule, times of silence are more beneficial to worshipers if they are preceded by an explanation for the silence or suggestions for its best use. Silence for the sake of silence makes no contribution to worship. Worshipers merely use the time to develop a grocery list, to think of calls which need to be made, or to turn off their thought processes completely. Beneficial silence in worship is purposeful silence. There are numerous options.

Centering

The term is borrowed from the Society of Friends. With considerable discipline Quakers, intent on the worship of God, sit in silence seeking to focus on God. The purpose of centering is not for worshipers to look inward in search of themselves but to seek a vision of God.

In the time of Jesus, rabbis often requested persons to experience an hour of silence as a prelude to worship in a synagogue. Such a practice (whatever the length of time involved) has a mighty potential. Many people who gather for worship have not experienced any substantive silence for days. Quiet moments in which nerves can relax, breathing can slow down, and the clutter of irrelevant thoughts can dissolve can be immensely beneficial in making possible an encounter with God. In silence, the entirety of life can center on God.

Hearing

Silence is an aid to worshipers immediately preceding or following readings of God's Word. The truths of the Bible deserve more than passing attention. Both preparation for listening to the Word of God and reflection on the meaning of the Word are important. If moments for these purposes do not occur in corporate worship, in the lives of many people they will not occur at all.

A time of silence for hearing is also of value at the conclusion of worship. Some congregations stand or sit in silence just after the benediction and prior to the musical postlude. Before departing from a sanctuary, worshipers listen for God's voice reinforcing the truths just encountered, calling for commitment, and perhaps directing them to care for some specific need.

Meditating

Meditation can serve as a significant act of worship. Truthfully, though, unless persons have extensive preparation for it or possess a unique discipline regarding it, meditation needs direction, prompters, and/or instruction. Specific suggestions from worship leaders enrich periods of meditation.

All worshipers can be requested to meditate on a specific hymn text or a particular passage from the Bible. A work of art, such as a traditional depiction of Jesus as the Good Shepherd or a more contemporary presentation of Jesus with outstretched arms overlooking the buildings of the United Nations, is a good prompter for meaningful meditation. Occasionally, worshipers can be aided in their efforts to relate to God by meditating on one part of the place of worship—the significance of a centered pulpit, the reason for a baptistry, the implications of a Communion table. Thereby worshipers can confront both the gift and the demands of the gospel, the blessings and responsibilities of salvation in their lives. The result well may be a worship-enhancing confession of need, request for help, renewed commitment, or declaration of praise.

Confessing

Confessing is hard work, especially confessing sins. God demands more honesty than many people are comfortable practicing. Frequently, providing silence in worship is a means of encouraging confession.

Here again, aids to worship are appropriate. A statement of confession to be read in silence can be printed in the order of worship. No worshiper is under any obligation to use the published words personally. Often, though, such a statement helps worshipers get their own words flowing. In silence, some confessions to God will be made that otherwise will be ignored or repressed. Likewise, God's redemptive response to confession may be better known in silence than amid sounds.

Praying

Not all people have an opportunity to voice an audible prayer in every service of worship. Yet no experience of worship should be concluded until all present have had time to pray. Intense prayer is difficult while others are speaking or singing. Silence is welcome.

Many ancient orders of worship include provisions for praying in corporate silence. Each worshiper is unique. Thus, praying silently, individual worshipers can offer to God praises, intercessions, thanks, and requests in their own ways. Whether or not the exact words are actually spoken, meaningful moments of silent prayer lead to the exclamation with which John Chrysostom concluded wordless prayers in the fourth century: "And grant unto us with one heart and one mouth to glorify and magnify thy glorious and majestic Name."[2]

In addition to periods of silence in worship services generally, at certain times of the year and in specific kinds of worship experiences, expansive stretches of silence are in order. In a worship service on the Saturday evening prior to Easter, little needs to be said. Little *can* be said. Corporate silence allows people to participate in the cosmic silence of which the eleven disciples in Jerusalem were a part immediately prior to Jesus' resurrection. Many congregations favor a completely silent observance of the Lord's Supper as a way of worship while New Year's Eve becomes New Year's Day.

Silence is helpful in worship. Silence may be an inevitable result of worship.

Scripture Readings

A visit to the Santa Groce church in Florence, Italy, introduced me to the phrase and the concept of "the people's Bible." Frescoes of scenes from biblical narratives originally covered all of the interior walls. At the time the church building was constructed, most of the people were poor and illiterate. The frescoes were intended to inform worshipers of the content of the Scriptures. Because of the paintings, the building in which worship takes place is itself "the people's Bible."

What a wonderful image of the desired relationship between a congregation of worshipers and the revelation of God in the Scriptures. In churches generally, and in the worship services of churches particularly, the Bible should be prominent. The eyes, ears, minds, and hearts of worshipers are to be confronted by the Bible in Christian worship.

What has happened? A rather secular-minded friend talked with me about his recent visits in the worship services of several different Protestant congregations. His complaint focused on a lack of Scripture, "In most services, I heard only two or three verses of Scripture read just before the sermon," he said. "That's not enough. When I go to church, I want to hear the Bible!"

A sad irony exists. Many congregations in the Free Church

tradition use the Bible in corporate worship far less than their sister fellowships in other denominations. Often the Bible is not as prominent in the worship experiences of people who proudly identify themselves as "people of the Book" as in the services of Christians with more officially prescribed patterns of worship.

Why?

The Bible contains the worship materials of our predecessors in the faith. When we read the Bible aloud in worship, we participate in the very God-directed process out of which the Scriptures came and in which they have been preserved. No wonder writers of the Scriptures urged the reading of the Scriptures in worship. The author of 2 Timothy 4:13, in words that carry divine authority, declares, "Attend to the public reading of scripture." That was the tradition in which Jesus stood as He read from the scroll of Isaiah during His visit to a synagogue worship service in Nazareth (Luke 4:16-17).

God can work through public readings of the Bible. More is involved than refreshed memories. The message of the Bible is able to affect in the present the very kind of experiences from the past that it reports. Hearing the Scriptures read can result in convictions, conversions, and transformed actions. As the author of 2 Timothy 3:16 says, "All scripture is inspired by God and profitable for teaching, for reproof, for correction, and for training in righteousness."

I have found great value periodically in using an act of worship which is standard in the Church of Scotland. At the beginning of a period of public worship, someone brings a large Bible into the sanctuary, proceeds down an aisle with the book in hand, then places the open Bible on the pulpit. The imagery is potent. Every aspect of the worship service which follows exists under the authority of the Word of God. What transpires in corporate worship is not the result of the whims of human opinions or the ideas of an individual's imagination but the product of obedience to the divine will discovered in the Scriptures. People's thoughts are subservient to God's Word.

Debates exist about how much of the Bible should be read in a service of worship. No pat answer to that question exists. Personally, I am inclined to the opinion of the more the better. After all, what God has to say to worshipers through the Bible is far more important than what worshipers have to say about the Bible, about God, or to each other. One prominent Protestant writer concludes that the historic practice of reading three biblical lessons each Sunday—an Old Testament passage, an Epistle selection, and a Gospel reading—is not too much.[3]

Every leader of worship does well to do a six-month review of the Scriptures that have been read in the public worship services of a church and ask, "How much of the Bible have the people in worship had an opportunity to hear over the past half year?" A documentable tendency exists for congregations and their worship leaders to develop a rather restricted canon of Scripture. Understandably, people turn to their favorite biblical texts again and again. But the whole of the Bible is worthy of attention.

In the late 1960s and early 1970s a group of scholars from many different denominations worked together to develop a three-year cycle of suggested Scripture readings for worship. The product of their labor is commonly referred to as a "lectionary." Congregations which follow the Bible readings suggested by this lectionary do not find themselves limiting Scripture readings to their personal preference and are exposed to the narratives and teachings of the whole Bible.

Resistance to the lectionary among Free Church worshipers is understandable and predictable. A lectionary certainly does not have to be used for worship planners to incorporate the whole expanse of the Scriptures in the services of a church. A lectionary is optional. But that is not the case with readings from the Word of God in the worship experiences of a church. "People of the Book" ought to be at the forefront of those suggesting and practicing an extensive use of the Scriptures in Christian worship.

In addition to the value inherent in the textual truths read, Bible readings constitute an important act of witness. "The constant reading of the scriptures in worship bears testimony to the fact that Christianity considers itself a historical religion centred [sic] upon the revelation of God in Jesus Christ."[4]

How?

The Bible can be presented in worship regularly without its truths becoming perfunctory. God's Word in the Bible is as fresh for people today as it was for those in previous generations. That freshness should be apparent every time biblical passages are read.

The significance of paying attention to the reading of the

Bible in public worship can be emphasized by a brief period of preparation for listening. A choir or the entire congregation singing one verse of a hymn such as "Break Thou the Bread of Life" or "Holy Bible, Book Divine" can be helpful. Always beneficial as well is a short prayer requesting illumination and understanding in relation to the Scriptures to be read.

Scriptures can be sung as well as read. In any given service, if one presentation from the Bible is read, another portion of the Scriptures can be presented musically. Many of the psalms and other Old Testament texts have been set to music that can be sung by a choir or a soloist. Several New Testament passages are available in this form also.

Members of worshiping congregations have a right to participate in public readings of the Bible. Where the same translation of the Scriptures is available throughout a worship center or when a passage of the Bible is distributed in printed form, worshipers can read the Scriptures in unison. Personally, I find such readings deeply moving—the people of God reading the Word of God as with one voice. Responsive readings of the Bible in which all members of a congregation have a part are popular in many churches.

The Bible belongs to all of the people in worship. That fundamental truth can be dramatized helpfully as a variety of persons are enlisted to do Scripture readings. Over the course of a year, I like for representatives from all segments of the congregation to serve in this capacity. Often I plan to begin corporate worship on Easter morning with a woman from the congregation reading the staggering words which God entrusted to the women at the empty tomb. Many times an elderly gentleman can read the final testimony of the apostle Paul with great feeling. I well recall the powerful impact of Luke's birth narratives read by a young child as the first act of worship on a Christmas morning.

Readings from the Bible do not have to be confined to the pulpit (unless members of the congregation cannot hear adequately otherwise). A helpful reminder that the Bible is a book for all people is registered when individuals stand before their respective seats in the worship center and read a verse of Scripture. Some pastors prefer to step away periodically from the pulpit and stand on the floor level with the congregation when reading from the Gospels. Their physical movement reiterates the truth that God's grace has descended into the lives of all in need.

As a child, I wondered why people always stood to pray but remained seated for the reading of the Bible. Of course, the posture of prayer should demonstrate honor and respect for God. However, hearing God's Word seemed to merit every bit as much attention as worshipers conveying their words to God. More recently, I have learned that at least since the fourth century many congregations have stood whenever a portion of a Gospel has been read. I understand.

Amen

During a preaching mission in Eastern Europe prior to recent reforms, I found many people begging for Bibles. One woman in particular stands out in my mind. As my wife and I departed from an evening worship service in Timisoara, Romania, this woman, with whom we had talked earlier, ran alongside our bus window yelling, "Don't forget. Please ask someone to send me a Bible."

While worshiping with Christians on mainland China, I listened to people reflect on the trials they faced during the oppressive revolution fomented by Chairman Mao. In Nanjing an older man described a nightly ritual. At midnight, a small group of Christians gathered at an appointed spot, dug up the copy of the Bible which they had buried there (the only Bible in the community that had not been confiscated by the Red Guard), and read together from God's Word.

Perhaps persons who take Scripture readings for granted could be helped by the testimonies of these Romanian and Chinese Christians. In worship, reading the Bible is much more than "taking a text" on which to speak. Reading the Bible aloud in corporate worship is breaking the "bread of life."

In locations where the Scriptures are not readily available to all people, Bible readings in worship are often followed by spontaneous expressions of congregational praise: "Thanks be to God." "This is the Word of God." "Amen." Not a bad idea everywhere.

7
Praying
"Our prayer attend"

Worship without prayer is as inconceivable as a meal without food. In each instance, the two go together. All who sit at a table at mealtime are expected to eat. Similarly, everyone who gathers for corporate worship is to be involved in prayer. Prayers are essential components in public worship. When true to its proper nature, worship itself is a form of prayer.

Public prayer differs from private prayer. Both are important. However, a failure to distinguish between the two can hinder corporate worship rather than contribute to it. Worship is a communal act. So is every prayer offered in public worship.

In public prayer, the proper personal pronoun is "we," not "I." Praying in the first person singular is a vital part of Christian living, but such prayer belongs exclusively in private. Alone before God, people can honestly voice their individual prayers in pathos and happiness: "I have sinned." "I praise you God." "I pray especially for these concerns." When worshiping with other persons, however, individuality is to give way to community. Public prayer is a prayer of all the people of God even if spoken aloud by only one of them.

In corporate worship prayers are always offered *from* the congregation and *for* the congregation, but never *to* the congregation. Prayer—public or private—is addressed to God. Always. If God is not the intended audience of a prayer, what is spoken fails to qualify as prayer regardless of the speaker's aspirations for it.

Corporate worship is not a compilation of individual actions. From intention to completion, it is communal. Any person who offers an audible prayer in worship speaks to God from amid the fellowship and on its behalf declares to God what others want to say and silently join in saying. As one worshiper prays aloud, other worshipers ought to be able to sense identification with the person and experience the sensation of participation in the verbal offering being made to God.

How best to address God in a public prayer is a question with no single resolution. Two factors interact to create a tension out of which this kind of prayer is offered—intimacy and reverence. In no sense is the person praying a stranger to God. God is known as Creator, Redeemer, and Perfect Love. The language of intimate love is natural as the person speaks to God. However, the individual speaking the prayer also acknowledges God as transcendent and perfect holiness, the Wholly Other. Respect and reverence are prerequisites to prayer which affect every word spoken in prayer.

Debate continues on whether public prayers should address God as "Thee" or "You." Supporters of the former suggest that the language of the sixteenth century conveys a reverence for God which cannot be captured in more modern terminology. They have a point. "Thee" carries a dignity that is elusive to "You." However, far too often the dignity conveyed by the use of this pronoun for God is compromised by a subsequent confusion in language which develops as the one praying seeks to be consistent in the terminology of the prayer. Words become cumbersome—*Thou knowest; Thou shouldest; Wouldest Thou bless?* With noticeable uncertainty, the person praying seeks to decide when to say "Thee" and when to say "Thou" or "Thy."

Of course, employing "You" as a pronoun for God in public prayer is not without problems also. What is gained in terms of communicating intimacy can be lost if the prayer seems casual or irreverently colloquial. God is the Holy Redeemer not "the man upstairs" or "our buddy in heaven."

Pronouns are not the issue, really. Most important are the attitude of the person praying and the spirit in which the prayer is offered. Consistency is helpful. An individual should choose between "Thou-language" and "You-language" and stay with that choice through an entire prayer, not randomly mixing the two. But the use of neither set of pronouns can suffice for the offering of words in a manner that breathes reverence and compassion, intimacy and dignity, devotion and a will for action.

A Call to Prayer

Prayers pervade worship. However, special periods of prayer within worship merit attention and preparation. A call to prayer, spoken or sung, is helpful.

The Bible is the best resource for words which summon people to prayer. Quoting Jesus' statements about prayer can quickly and succinctly establish the importance of this act of worship: "Ask, and it will be given you; seek and you will find" (Matt. 7:7); "Whatever you ask in my name, I will do it, that the Father may be glorified in the Son" (John 14:13). Paul's prayer-related admonitions are worthy of repetition: "In everything by prayer and supplication with thanksgiving let your requests be made known to God" (Phil. 4:6); "Continue steadfastly in prayer" (Col. 4:2); "I urge that supplications, prayers, intercessions, and thanksgivings be made for all" (1 Tim. 2:1). A line from Hebrews offers assurance, "Let us then with confidence draw near to the throne of grace" (Heb. 4:16).

The Old Testament also contains excellent calls to prayer. A summons to prayer and a promise regarding prayer are combined in 2 Chronicles 7:14-16. Many of the psalms can be helpful, especially by use of paraphrases in which singular words are made inclusively plural: "O Lord, open [our] lips, and [our] mouth[s] shall show forth thy praise" (Ps. 51:15); "Cast your burden[s] on the Lord" (55:22); "Let us kneel before the Lord, our Maker!" (95:6).

Calling attention to a time of prayer and to the nature of prayer increases the likelihood that temptations to use prayer for nonprayerful purposes will be rejected. Far too often public prayers have been turned into soapboxes. Understanding what prayer is *not* is as essential as seeking to comprehend what prayer is.

Public prayers are not:—Preaching or teaching.—A sermon or a lesson may be offered as a prayer. However, a prayer is neither a sermon nor a lesson. A prayer addresses the God being worshiped, not other worshipers. God is not in need of human instruction. *An announcement.*—Sometimes a prayer is turned into a bulletin board. "God please bring us all back to the evening worship service scheduled for 7:30 in the chapel and help us to remember that a nursery will be provided and a social hour will follow it." I cringe when I hear such a mockery of prayer. I cannot imagine how God is affected. *An address to the congregation.*—One Sunday morning during the offertory prayer, I heard a deacon abuse prayer ruthlessly. He began praying with a proper word of thanksgiving to God, then launched into a harangue aimed at the congregation. "Our attendance is down. We're not being faithful. We're not visiting prospects." By the end of his monologue, this well-meaning man had dropped the name of God from his address altogether. It was just as well. There was no prayer. *A wish list.*—Occasionally, I actually hear the word *wish* within a supposedly prayerful petition. "We *wish* our church could grow stronger." "We *wish* you would take care of the needy." Implicit is a suggestion that prayer is some form of magic. Such an idea has no place in worship. *Private prayer.*— What is helpful in private prayer can be harmful in public prayer. To pray aloud in worship is to move beyond the self and to embrace all of the worshipers in what is said to God.

Congregational Prayer

Some of my most vivid memories of childhood worship experiences involve recollections of congregational prayers. Our church building was small enough that a person located any place in it could pray aloud and everyone else present clearly hear what was being said. I heard a few individuals pray often enough that I could almost speak their prayers with them. They said the same words in the same sequence every time they prayed. However, there were others who prayed with freshness and intensity each time they were asked to lead a prayer. I benefited from hearing the prayers of these individuals.

An interesting phenomenon in the prayer life of our congregation struck me as humorous as well as serious. Sometimes a worship leader called on someone to pray who, for whatever reason, did not want to lead in a prayer at that time. The man (it was never a woman) responded, "I pass to brother so and so" and named the individual who was then expected to pray. On one occasion, "I heard three "passes." In retrospect, I like both the honesty and the participatory nature of such prayers.

A major drawback in large worship centers is an inability for people throughout the congregation to be called on to lead and to participate in the various prayers of a service. In such situations, different individuals can be invited to the platform to pray. Also, by distributing a printed prayer, all present can speak to God in unison. Congregational prayers offered to God in unison are as ancient as the worship of the New Testament community of faith (Acts 4:24). Providing a time for silent prayers is also important in such settings. Every worshiping congregation needs to experience its identity as a praying congregation.

Each spoken prayer in worship has a distinct purpose. The offertory prayer and the prayer of invocation are offered for different reasons. Their contents should not be the same. A prayer of dedication is unlike a prayer of thanksgiving. Prayer gifts to God can be enriched considerably if the distinctive nature of each prayer is taken seriously. That does not happen accidentally, though. Forethought is required. Worship leaders perform a helpful ministry to the congregation by helping all who pray aloud in worship to understand the function of their specific offerings.

A variety of prayers is important in worship. *Adoration* is basic, yet often problematic. If people's orientation to prayer is primarily one of petition, adoration can prove difficult. In prayers intended to praise God, requests are not present. Adoration requires discipline, but it is the discipline of love. In this kind of prayer, people in love with God pour out to God the reasons for their affection. Incidentally, if a prayer of adoration is considered too difficult, the whole experience of worship is in jeopardy.

Prayers of *confession* reflect the needs of the worshipers and obedience to requests from God. Worship is the context in which sins are to be set before God in honesty and repentance declared. The person who leads a prayer of confession should be sensitive to the demand for specificity without violating the principles of confidentiality and good judgment. True penitence for some sins demands a private confession which does not provoke public conversations.

A prayer of *thanksgiving* can follow a declaration of forgiveness, the proclamation of the gospel, or a reflection on God's blessings. The more specifics are verbalized in this prayer, the more the entire congregation can be involved in it. Thanking God for all good gifts is in order. But thanking God for supportive friends, a glorious sunset, the cry of a newborn baby, and fresh strawberries is even better. This prayer ascends to the peak of its potential when it can honestly include problems and pains among its reasons for gratitude.

A prayer of *petition* is most common among worshipers. Every person has needs to be offered to God in the form of requests for help. Before God, most people's hands are open—if not to extend gifts to God, certainly to receive gifts from God. The person leading this public prayer can provide insight into the comprehensiveness of God's care as requests for divine assistance focus on matters such as a troubled relationship, the removal of fear, and preparation for a final exam.

Prayers of *intercession* guarantee that worship is not viewed as an escape or a retreat. The cares of the world are embraced in these words to God. Interestingly, in sincere intercession, something happens to the one praying. Voicing a need to God becomes an occasion for accepting the responsibility, with God's help, to attempt to meet the need described. As God's assistance in the world is requested, a service-oriented partnership with God is accepted.

A prayer of *dedication* articulates all that is happening in worship. Confessions become commitments. Words take off in the direction of deeds. Abilities are made resources for ministries. What is placed in a collection plate is offered as a symbol of the gift of all of life.

Other forms of prayer are also beneficial in worship. The types just identified, however, are of fundamental importance. All of these prayers can be positioned at various time throughout a service. For example, a prayer of thanksgiving may precede the collection of tithes, a prayer of adoration can serve as an invocation, and a prayer of dedication may end a sermon and be followed by an invitation. However, the location of a particular prayer does not have to remain the same in every experience of worship.

No prayer is more beautiful or more appropriate in corporate worship than the one provided by the One who taught us to pray. The Lord's Prayer encapsulates the concerns of the gospel and provides a means by which all worshipers can speak to God together. A public recital of the Model Prayer from Jesus can be very meaningful. One of my favorite means of concluding a service of worship is to invite the entire congregation to stand and to serve as a mass choir singing Malotte's "The Lord's Prayer."

Pastoral Prayer

In recent years, the pastoral prayer has come under attack, and the value of its presence in worship questioned. One writer labels the pastoral prayer as "one of the major problems in Protestant worship."[1] Another author describes this prayer as "a bowl of wet, soggy noodles dumped on a helpless congregation."[2]

I object. The only problem with the pastoral prayer under attack is that it has been poorly done. When properly offered, a pastoral prayer can communicate with God and perform a priestly ministry among the worshipers.

Pastoral prayers require sensitive preparation. Ministers who have not pastored their people will find this prayer almost impossible. Identification with the hurts and joys, anxieties and hopes, failures and successes, which pervade the congregation is the major source of strength in this prayer.

Amen

Historically, the "amen" at the end of a prayer was spoken by all members of a congregation. Thereby, everyone joined in the prayerful offering made by an individual in their midst. Many times, in fact, "amens" from a congregation were sounded throughout a prayer. In this way, the petitions of one person were supported by all of the people declaring to God, "so be it," "let it be." If verbal "amens" are not deemed acceptable in a particular congregation, each worshiper is at liberty to offer an "amen" to God silently.

Planned or Spontaneous?

In relation to all prayers in public worship, questions are frequently raised regarding their preparation, substance, and freedom. Should prayers be planned or spontaneous? Is it all right to write out a prayer in advance of speaking it aloud? Why does prayer need any order or classification at all?

Congregational worship is an experience comprehensive enough to include planned prayers and spontaneous prayers, prayers formed instantaneously and prayers carefully prepared in advance. A pastoral prayer definitely needs preparation—at least general forethought if not specific planning. To spend multiple hours getting reading to speak to people for God, then to give no thought at all as to how to speak to God on behalf of people seems incongruous (if not insensitive and unwise). Prayers from members of the congregation are best offered in the manner which is most comfortable for the people praying. Personally, I prefer not to call on a person to pray in public without some advance notice. This gives individuals an opportunity to gather appropriate thoughts and to consider how they best can be voiced to help the congregation and to honor God. Free prayers can be premeditated.

Public worship imposes certain concerns on prayer that are absent if one is speaking to God in private. Writing about prayers in corporate worship, Isaac Watts, the noted hymnwriter, warns against "an entire dependence on sudden emotions and suggestions of thought."[3] Likewise, the popular and often-quoted preacher, Matthew Henry, declares, "It is requisite... that we offer not any thing to the Glorious Majesty of Heaven and Earth, which is confus'd, impertinent, and indigested."[4]

8
Confessing
"We share our mutual woes"

Every Christian's life moves back and forth along a continuum that includes high spiritual aspirations and dismal personal failures, a commitment to righteousness and an awareness of sinfulness, a resolve toward ethical obedience and a realization of moral error. Thus, the rhythm of Christian worship includes both repentance and renewal.[1] Confession is essential to both.

Within the worship practices of the Free Churches, not every service includes a specific time devoted to confession. Even so, the element of confession has to be integrated into other aspects of worship if a worship experience is to be holistic. "The Confession of Sins is…a necessary element in a full act of worship."[2]

From the *Didache*, a manual on church order dating from the late first century or early second century, comes direct instructions for Christians: "On the Lord's day, come together, break bread, and give thanks, having first confessed your transgressions, that your sacrifices may be pure."[3]

Where confessions occur in a particular service varies. Most worship planners prefer for confessions to be made early in worship, often immediately following ascriptions of adoration and praise to God. That location is consistent with the classic pattern of worship based on the experience of the prophet Isaiah (Isa. 6:1-6). However, confessions are also appropriate after Scripture readings and prayers. Sometimes a period of confession is in order as a response to a sermon. The one invariable regarding the positioning of confessions relates to the Lord's Supper. If a worship service contains a celebration of the Lord's Supper, confession must precede this communal act.

Since true confession before God always (eventually if not immediately) forms the content of a prayer, some congregations incorporate confessions into their other prayers. Nothing is wrong with that. However, confession merits a place of special attention in orders of worship, occasionally if not regularly.

Confession of Sin

Confessing sins is the hardest work of worship. In this act, worshipers have to confront the dark sides of their natures with stark honesty and ponder the consequences of their unforgiven sins realistically. Nobody likes to do that. But all need the experience.

The Bible provides both the precedent for this act of worship and the correct perspective from which to view it. A confession of sins was an integral component in the worship practices described in both Testaments: "When a man is guilty . . . he shall confess the sin he has committed" (Lev. 5:5); "When a man or a woman commits any of the sins . . . by breaking faith with the Lord, . . . he shall confess his sin" (Num. 5:6-7); "I will confess my transgressions to the Lord; then thou didst forgive the guilt of my sin" (Ps. 32:5); "Confess your sins" (Jas. 5:16); "If we confess our sins, he is faithful and just, and will forgive our sins" (1 John 1:9).

Most people need assistance in making confessions. Culture conditions us to disguise our weaknesses, cover our faults, reject guilt, and remain silent about our sins. Worship demands a dramatic turn around from that—confession at all costs. Not surprisingly, help is needed.

Confessions of sins can be done congregationally and chorally. A statement of confession read in unison by the entire congregation is valuable. So, too, are musical arrangements of confessions which allow all members of a worshiping fellowship to identify with the words being sung by a few. But, at some point, personal confession is a necessity—each individual one on One with God, supported by the realization that all of the other worshipers present are similarly engaged. None of these acts of confession is mutually exclusive of the others. In fact, each can be encouraged and strengthened by the others.

In corporate worship, personal confessions of sins are best done in silence. Printed directions or suggestions placed in the hands of each worshiper can help: "Confess your acts of disobedience to God. Confess your sins which have hurt other people. Confess your impure thoughts and immoral attitudes. Confess your part in the sins of your society. Confess the sins you imagine to be secret." Of course, all of these instructions can be spoken rather than written.

Also beneficial to personal confession are periodic reminders (printed, sung, or spoken) of the confessions of others: "Woe is me! For I am lost; for I am a man of unclean lips, and I dwell in the midst of a people of unclean lips" (Isa. 6:5); "Have mercy on me, O God, . . . For I know my transgressions and my sin is ever before me. Against thee, thee only, have I sinned, and done that which is evil in thy sight" (Ps. 51:1, 3-4).

Request for Forgiveness

Confessions of sins flow naturally into requests for divine forgiveness. Actually, the two movements constitute one act. They are separated here for the purpose of emphasis.

Confessing sins is never an end in itself. A realization of sinfulness precipitates a recognition of the need for forgiveness. Hopelessness has no place in Christian worship. What is needed from God is provided by God. God invites and encourages the request for forgiveness that is essential to sinners. God seeks sinners every bit as much as sinners seek God.

How we phrase our request for forgiveness is not especially significant. Every worshiper is at liberty to seek God's forgiveness through words and thoughts that are honest and meaningful to the person. Though congregational petitions may take shape in traditional terms, personal pleas for forgiveness are bound by no norms. Here again the language of the Bible can help: "Blot out my transgressions. Wash me thoroughly from my iniquity, and cleanse me from my sin! Purge me, . . . Hide thy face from my sins, . . . Create in me a clean heart, O God, and put a new and right spirit within me. Cast me not away from thy presence, . . . Restore to me the joy of thy salvation" (Ps. 51:1-2, 7, 9-12); "God be merciful to me a sinner!" (Luke 18:13). When an individual worshiper has trouble finding the right words to seek God's forgiveness, these words from prior worshipers can be used. Equally as powerful, though, are honest cries from worshipers, whether traditional or not: "God, help!" "I've blown it God and I need You"; "I'm sunk. Please pick me up, God"; "Help me to be able to start all over, to have a new beginning, O Lord."

Requests for divine forgiveness are invariably marked by obvious sincerity and spoken (even if silently) with intensity. These petitions, however, are to be offered with confidence—not because of who the worshipers are or what they have done, but because of who God is, what God promises, and how God responds to pleas for forgiveness.

Assurance of Pardon

Christianity never locks people into their sins. Neither does Christian worship. Even the call for an honest confession of sins rests on the divine promise of redemption.

The truth of God's promise of forgiveness is far too important to be left unspoken. After enduring the trauma of detailing their sins before God, worshipers need assurance that God hears them with love, treats their wrongs with grace, and delights in granting forgiveness. For conscientious persons, that assurance cannot be heard too often.

A congregation of worshipers must take great care not to deal with people's sins in a manner of harshness, rejection, and condemnation, all of which are inconsistent with God's loving bent toward redemption. The severity of sin is beyond description. Jesus was crucified because of our sins. Even so, in relation to sinners, God desires pardon rather than punishment, reconciliation rather than revenge, salvation rather than condemnation. ("For God sent the Son into the world, not to condemn the world, but that the world might be saved through him," John 3:17.)

Judgment is not a prerogative of the church. Judgment belongs to God alone, the only capable judge. A congregation's failure to convey the good news of God's pardon to penitent sinners and to cooperate with God in the redemption of their lives is as wrong as the sins that have been confessed.

The language of the Bible deserves repetition at this point in worship. "If we confess our sins, he [God] is faithful and just, and will forgive our sins and cleanse us from all unrighteousness" (1 John 1:9).

Continuing in worship beyond the confession of sins is impossible if the sins are not forgivable. If an assurance of God's pardon cannot be claimed, worship ends, and it concludes in killing despair, not life-giving devotion. But pardon is possible. Divine forgiveness is available.

After an experience of confession in worship, even the worst of sinners has a sense of God-given cleanliness. The full resources of God's strength can be claimed in future struggles with temptations. Those realizations create a surge of joy and thanksgiving in need of expression. The assurance of God's pardon is meaningfully followed by a prayer of thanksgiving or an anthem of celebration or, more preferably, some form of congregational praise.

Confession of Faith

Buoyed by the freedom experienced in a confession of sins and the subsequent joy which is realized as penitence meets pardon, worshipers are ready to confess their faith. Such a confession is as important as it is appropriate.

In the New Testament, strong emphasis is placed on a confession of faith in Jesus. "If you confess with your lips that Jesus is Lord and believe in your heart that God raised him from the dead, you will be saved" (Rom. 10:9). The source of that statement is personal, but its proper context is social. In 1 Timothy 6:13, the writer indicates that a confession of Christ is to be made in the presence of many witnesses. First Timothy 3:16 may embrace the actual content of such a confession that was offered in worship as a hymn. Jesus describes the importance of people's confessions: "Every one who acknowledges me before men, I also will acknowledge before my Father" (Matt. 10:32).

The anticreedal posture of Free Church congregations often creates suspicion even at the mention of a confession of faith. However, meaningful, noncreedal, public declarations of faith are possible. A singing of the Gloria Patri is such a statement. Praise is offered confessionally to the majestic, eternal, Triune God. Succinct but powerful is the ancient confession, "Jesus Christ is Lord." Every congregation can speak these words in union with enthusiasm.

Important also in public worship are personal stories of faith, often called "testimonies." No statement of faith is more moving than one which comes from a person who speaks of the value of faith in good times and bad. If the place of worship is small enough and its accoustics are good enough for people to be heard from any location in the congregation, spontaneous words of this nature can be invited. If people cannot be heard, from time to time, various members of the congregation can be invited to the pulpit to share insights from their spiritual pilgrimages.

Confessions of faith honor God. They also encourage worshipers seeking to be faithful.

9
Proclaiming
"We Have a Gospel to Proclaim"

Worship *is* proclamation—all of it, at least implicitly. Proclamation is a part of worship—a major part of it explicitly.

In worship and *through* worship, the great truths of the Bible are proclaimed by words and actions: "In the beginning God" (Gen. 1:1). "Holy, holy, holy is the Lord of hosts" (Isa. 6:3). "Thou, O Lord, art a God merciful and gracious, slow to anger and abounding in steadfast love and faithfulness" "With what shall I come before the Lord?...He has showed you,...justice, ...love kindness" (Mic. 6:6, 8). "All have sinned" (Rom. 3:23). "God is love" (1 John 4:16). "For God so loved the world that he gave his only Son, that whoever believes in him should not perish but have eternal life" (John 3:16). "If you confess with your lips that Jesus is Lord and believe in your heart that God raised him from the dead, you will be saved" (Rom. 10:9). "The Spirit helps us in our weakness" (8:26). "If God is for us, who is against us?...[nothing] in all creation will be able to separate us from the love of God in Christ Jesus our Lord" (Rom. 8:31, 39).

In worship and *through* worship, the story of redemption is told and retold, and a strange thing happens. At first worshipers hear the bad news about human sin and the good news of God's grace singularly, intimately, as if the whole of salvation history has taken place for each of them individually. Then comes an awareness of the larger community and a vision of the inclusiveness of God's gracious action. Suddenly, there is an urge to shout the good news to others, a compulsion toward a cosmic exclamation. What worship proclaims to worshipers, worshipers desire to proclaim to the world.

Often we only associate proclamation in worship with the delivery of a sermon. Certainly preaching is a major component in worship, but proclamation in worship is larger than any one medium. Numerous media serve the cause of proclaiming the gospel.

The Sermon

Sermons dominate worship in many Protestant congregations. Free Churches, particularly, tend to equate worship and preaching. In some churches, the sole measure of a worship service consists of the effectiveness of the sermon and the nature of people's visible response to the preaching.

Motivated by a desire to emphasize the importance of all acts of worship, I am tempted to respond to an overemphasis on preaching by understating the significance of a sermon. But one error is not corrected by another error. Preaching is endowed with tremendous value as an act of worship.

Historically, preaching is older than Christianity. However, since the inception of Christianity, the two have never been separated. Students of Christian origins find no time when sermons were absent from corporate worship. "There is nothing in early Christianity more basic to its life than oral proclamation of what is called God's word."[1] The apostle Paul writes, "Faith comes from what is heard, and what is heard comes by the preaching of Christ" (Rom. 10:17). James White interprets the sermon as an act of worship theologically, "In worship, God gives of God's selfhood to us through human speech, and we, through God's power, give ourselves to God through our speech."[2] Thor Hall concludes that no other "medium of ministry is capable of facilitating such a full and representative encounter with the gospel as the ministry of preaching, rightly understood."[3]

A sermon is an act of worship. A sermon is a preacher's offering to God, which God immediately uses in the work of divine redemption. These realities influence both the spirit in which preaching takes place and the shape of the sermons offered to God and overheard by the worshipers.

Spirit

The spirit of preaching is the spirit of worship. A sermon has no place in a service of Christian worship unless it is a medium of the Word of God that brings worshipers into a closer relationship with Christ for the glory of God.

Christian preaching is biblical.—The Bible is more than the background and the literary basis for preaching. The Bible is the content of a Christian sermon. The gospel is more than the foundation and inspiration for preaching. The gospel is the content of preaching. Luther saw the truth long ago, "The preaching of the Word of God *is* the Word of God."[4]

A Christian sermon is a word event. Preachers and listeners join each other in a faith-reflective engagement with the Word of God. The sermon is not to be confused with a preacher's comments about the Bible, personal counsel based on the Bible, or individual interpretation of the Bible. Accurately understood, every sermon is an "execution" of a biblical passage. The sermon proclaims what the Bible proclaims.[5]

When preaching degenerates into sharing opinions or offering advice, it loses its potential as a medium for God's Word and forfeits its right to be included in worship. "The preaching of the Gospel is concerned with news, not views; it is the proclamation of Good News, not the tendering of good advice."[6] A sermon devoted only to telling people what to do fails to celebrate God's grace "and thereby undercuts the *sine qua non* for bold Christian action. In forfeiting the gospel story it detaches people from their legitimate birthright as participants in that ongoing story."[7]

Citing or reading a passage of Scripture as the text for a sermon is no guarantee of biblical preaching. More than once a preacher has used a biblical text as a prelude to arguing for the acceptance of a personal point of view and supporting that argument with a series of emotions-pricking anecdotes. A sermon does not have to be textual to be biblical. But to qualify as a gift to God appropriate in Christian worship, a sermon has to be biblical.

Christian preaching is confessional.—The classic definition of preaching comes from Phillips Brooks—"Preaching is the bringing of truth through personality."[8] The words of a human being, a distinct personality, are media for God's Word. The personal dimension of preaching can be ignored only at the risk of great peril.

"Sermons are exercises in faith."[9] A preacher is obligated to be honest in all proclamations from the pulpit. At times honesty may require a preacher to declare, "I need to hear the truth of this sermon as much as I need to proclaim it." Or "The implementation of this biblical teaching in my actions has fallen short of the strength of my verbal affirmations of its authority and validity."

Preachers are no different from other worshipers struggling with temptations, needing forgiveness, and longing for grace.

Attempts to hide this reality when delivering a sermon bring to preaching a falseness, a superficiality, which has no place in a life of faith or an experience of worship. The apostle Paul readily acknowledges that the truth of the gospel resides in "earthen vessels" (2 Cor. 4:7). The confessional nature of this man's proclamation is worthy of study and emulation: "I have been a fool!" (12:11). "What has happened to me has really served to advance the gospel" (Phil. 1:12). "I know how to be abased, and I know how to abound" (4:12). "Not that I have already obtained this or am already perfect; but I press on" (3:12).

In his *Journal*, Emerson writes of hearing a preacher who tempted him to resolve that he would not go to church again. The preacher gave no indication of how truth and life relate. In another *Journal* entry, recorded just after a worship experience in Concord, Emerson explodes, "Cease, O thou unauthorized talker to prate of consolation and resignation and spiritual joys in neat and balanced sentences, for I know these men who sit below."[10] The great writer was angered by the chasm between truth and life created by a sermon that bore no evidence of an awareness of the multiple, dreadful needs of the people in the worshiping congregation.

A sermon that fails to touch persons where they live lies about the gospel. The good news is that God's grace can be experienced in the worst and the best of human situations and at all points in between. Being told of what happened to Jacob at the Jabbok River, to Peter by the campfire in Jerusalem, or to Paul in Rome is of little benefit to worshipers unless they are assured that what happened then can happen again. God can be encountered today where people struggle, hurt, rejoice, and pray.

Christian preaching is convictional.—"Woe to me if I do not preach the gospel!" Paul writes to the Corinthians (1 Cor. 9:16). His words pulsate with the urgency which should pervade preaching. Jeremiah pictures the intensity of the impulse as he writes of the Word of God, "Then is in my heart as it were a burning fire shut up in my bones" (Jer. 20:9).

Phoniness in the pulpit can be spotted from the furtherest pew. No preacher ought ever to proclaim publicly what is not believed personally. If a person enters a pulpit neither possessing nor possessed by Christian convictions, silence is preferable to speech.

What is believed? If preaching really is a means by which

people are led to salvation, how can anyone preach devoid of passion? In a sermon, a preacher speaks of the only comfort which can calm grieving people, the only peace which can still rampant anxieties, the only forgiveness which can break the grip of a grinding guilt, the only hope in a context of despair. Does the preacher believe that? If so, urgency is irrepressible. When a preacher conveys a message which can mean life for dying people, which is the meaning of preaching the gospel, that preacher cannot speak without conviction and convicting.

Within a Christian sermon, nothing is inconsequential. Dealing with divinely given truth can never be a casual, take-it-or-leave-it affair. Pressing for a decision is appropriate. A listener's response to the content of a Christian sermon has consequences that stretch into eternity.

Shape

What is the shape of a sermon that conveys the Word of God and serves the purpose of worship? Multiple answers to this question are acceptable. Each has value. Deciding which preaching format to use in a specific service of worship depends on the aim of the particular sermon as discovered in dialogue with God.

Expository preaching is presently enjoying great popularity. In the best expository sermons, the central idea of a biblical text is expounded. Often the outline of a sermon is determined by the arrangement of the text being treated.

Every sermon form is characterized by dangers as well as values. The greatest potential danger in expository preaching is the tendency never to move outside a biblical text. A preacher can facilitate a remarkable understanding of a scriptural passage within its original context. However, if no attention is devoted to that passage's significance for the present, the incarnational principle of preaching is violated. It is not enough for people to know what God expected of the Christians at home in first-century Corinth. Worshipers need to know what, according to the Bible, God expects of them where ever they live today.

A classic form of expository preaching, sometimes called "old expository preaching," avoids the danger of distance, a lack of engagement, irrelevance. Three major sections make up each sermon. First comes a careful study of the biblical situation. Exegesis aids an understanding of what the text meant in its original setting. Second, attention is devoted to the enduring truth of the text, the message for all times. Understandably, this part of the sermon is usually rather general in nature. However, in the third section of the sermon, the focus turns to the meaning of the text for people in the present. Specific applications of the biblical passage are elaborated.

Evangelistic preaching is also highly acclaimed. In a sense, all preaching is evangelistic. New Testament evangelism is the work of seeking to bring all of life under the lordship of Jesus Christ. No sermon can stand outside the scope of that concern and be worthy of time and attention in worship. Commonly though, the term "evangelistic preaching" is used more narrowly, defining a sermon aimed at leading people to an initial declaration of faith in Christ. In that sense, it is a distinctive form of preaching.

Evangelistic preaching relies heavily on persuasion. A positive decision from at least some of the listeners is desired—their acceptance of Jesus as Savior. However, responsible persuasion requires an adequate foundation. Problems arise when pleas for people to accept Christ are repeated fervently without much explanation of what all is involved in that acceptance.

James Cox notes the significant fact that in the evangelistic sermons of the Book of Acts, calls to repentance and faith always followed narratives detailing the mighty acts of God in history.[11] That sequence is important. Recital theology belongs at the forefront of evangelistic preaching. Before people are invited to meet God in Christ, they need to know the identity of this God and be given some insight into divine activity within history. Any normal person desires the promise of happiness and a sense of security. But not all people feel the same about those gifts when they understand that to accept the joy of salvation is to be met with the demand to advocate justice and the responsibility to practice righteousness. The God of redemption is committed to all of that. And so are the people of God. Evangelists must be clear, from the beginning, about the nature of salvation.

The fervor of evangelistic preaching is never to be stifled. However, enthusiasm in sermon delivery is always to be subservient to the nature of authentic religious experience. God desires the kind of unconditional commitment from people which can only be made where there is intellectual, emotional, and volitional freedom. A passionate preacher neither honors God nor aids people in need of redemption by seeking to do individually through the power of oral delivery what can only be done by the Spirit of God. True faith is social as well as personal, characterized by understanding as well as feeling. People accept Christ and come to redemptive faith by responding to what God has done, not by yielding to the persuasive rhetoric of a powerful preacher. Any confusion between these two is dangerous beyond description.

To understand the gospel is to preach evangelistically and enthusiastically. In such preaching there is no question about who does the saving and how.

Doctrinal preaching typically has few fans. That unfortunate fact is based upon negative stereotypes born of a serious misunderstanding. Frequently, doctrinal preaching is caricatured as abstract, heavy, irrelevant, dry, and boring. How wrong!

Christians cannot grow, individually or corporately, apart from doctrinal preaching. What people believe about the nature of God, the person of Jesus, the presence of the Holy Spirit, the viability of hope, the priority of grace, and the scope of redemption makes a difference in every phase of life. A group of people will fail to function as a church if they do not know what it means to be a church. Faithful ministry depends upon beliefs that have integrity.

Probing questions demand doctrinal answers: Why does a good God allow so much evil in the world? When people die, is it always God's will? Why does God seem to have a bent toward violence in the Old Testament and insist on peace in the New Testament? How can a church proclaim redemption, then not act redemptively toward people in need? What is the relationship between faith and works? Is salvation solely a matter of belief or is behavior important?

Doctrinal preaching properly done is powerful. James Stewart describes it aptly:

> Here is no academic speculation or cold, insipid moralizing; here is no dull collection of views and impressions, schemes and theories; here is a Gospel, able to bind up the broken-hearted, proclaim deliverance to the captives, and bid a distracted world stand still and see the glory of the coming Lord.[12]

Ethical preaching makes specific the demand which accompanies the gift of salvation. Helmut Thielicke's massive treatises on theological ethics grew out of a pastoral concern for preaching. Thielicke's intent in his monumental work coincides with the aim of ethics-oriented sermons—to spell out the nature of people's faith in relation to themselves, their neighbors, their world, and its structures in the midst of where they live in secularity.[13]

Ethical preaching is not easy. It is almost always controversial. Ethical sermons require extensive preparation and careful evaluation.

Preachers do well to examine regularly their personal motivations in the preparation and delivery of ethical sermons. If they discover a desire to endorse a partisan political platform, to attack an individual or a group of individuals or to air individual convictions rooted in cultural mores rather than biblical morality, they best cease and desist. Similar action should be taken if one's dominant mood in ethical preaching is anger, hostility, resentment, jealousy, or envy.

The best ethical sermons are rooted in love and saturated with grace, just as other types of sermons are. Preaching can be prophetic, compassionate, and redemptive all at the same time. Addressing moral concerns and attacking social ills provide no justification for stern-faced, hard-hearted, finger-pointing tirades heavy on condemnation and silent on redemption. Denunciatory preaching needs the correction of the gospel of Christ in which demands rest on indicatives, and responsibilities are viewed as opportunities to experience the joy of obedient service.

Of extreme importance in an ethical sermon is a presentation of alternatives for positive action. Christian preaching does not leave its listeners with frustration and despair. For example, a sermon on the problem of hunger must do more than create guilt. After raising worshipers' consciousness about hunger, specific suggestions should be made as to how people can translate Christian concern for the hungry into helpful actions. If a sermon calls attention to an ethical problem without offering solutions, a preacher does best not to deliver it until helpful recommendations consistent with the gospel can be included.

Devotional preaching plays a significant role in worship on special occasions. Devotional preaching is not to be confused with giving a brief devotional talk or leading a short period of meditation. A devotional sermon is as strong in potential, purpose, and practice as any of the other sermonic forms. Devotional preaching nurtures the Godward vision that is basic to worship.

Sometimes in worship, human words seem extraneous if not inappropriate (or absurd). On these occasions the best sermon is one which retells a biblical narrative. How many worship services on Easter have been robbed of explosive joy by pulpiteers who felt obliged to amass impressive arguments in an attempt to prove the resurrection of Jesus? Who can explain or prove that mystery by rational debate? Easter morning is not a time for theological apologetics and scientific arguments but for confessions of faith embodied in the shout, "He is risen!" A similar principle applies to public worship on Christmas Day. The incarnation does not need a homiletical explanation (as if that were possible). No Christmas sermon can improve on the infancy narratives from the Gospels. A wise preacher just retells the holy story and identifies with worshipers caught up in wonder and a celebration of God's glory.

Other sermonic forms are available to preachers. Most homileticians list numerous additional possibilities: topical preaching, narrative preaching, confessional preaching, autobiographical preaching, dialogue preaching, monologue preaching, apologetic preaching, pastoral preaching, and life situational preaching. Several of these sermon classifications overlap. However, enough alternatives are available that any preacher serious about a sermon to meet a specific objective in worship can find a homiletical form that will help and, with hard work, can produce a sermon that is a worthy gift to God.

The form or the subject of a sermon may determine the location of the act of preaching in a particular service of worship. Sermons do not always have to be delivered at the same point in worship. In every instance, the question to be answered is where in a service the sermon best serves the purpose of worship and benefits the worshipers. Many times when worship includes the baptism of a new Christian, the sermon is scheduled early in the service. That way the meaning of baptism can be explored from the pulpit prior to the act of witness from the baptistry. A sermon can take place near the conclusion of worship if it is a fitting consequence of or response to the praise, confession, and Scripture readings which have occurred earlier.

I recall a worship service which included baptism, the Lord's Supper, and a sermon. In that experience I did the sermon in four parts—the first from the baptistry, the second from behind the pulpit, the third at the Communion table, and the fourth standing on the floor level with the congregation. Such seg-

mcntcd prcaching can bc valuablc to worshipcrs as it is offered to God, especially in a service where worship develops around several different foci.

Preaching a sermon is not the only form of proclamation of importance in worship. Other media serve well. But preaching is unique in its ability to challenge, to encourage, and to guide people regarding their faith. Preaching not only conveys the gospel, it participates in the gospel. H. H. Farmer summarizes its significance, "Preaching is that divine, saving activity in history, which began two thousand years ago in the advent of Christ and His personal relationships with men and women, and has continued throughout the ages in the sphere of redeemed personal relationships."[14]

"Visible Words"

Some people might object to considering baptism and the Lord's Supper from the perspective of Christian proclamation. The importance of both baptism and the Lord's Supper involves much more than proclamation, but proclamation does occur.

Most likely, any singular classification of baptism or the Lord's Supper will be challenged. Each is a worshipful act of identification, of confession, of communion, of offering, and of celebration. Yet each is more than any one of these and more than all of them together.

Baptism and the Lord's Supper set forth the gospel. Each is an enacted parable. However, both events have meaning within themselves and point to meaning beyond themselves. A phrase from Augustine best captures the nature of these two crucial acts of worship—*verba visibilia,* "visible words."[15] Baptism and the Lord's Supper are dramatic actions which proclaim the gospel, whether or not they are accompanied by spoken words.

Baptism

Not much was said about baptism in the congregation in which I spent nearly the first two decades of my life. Its importance was downplayed. After all, "immersion is just a symbol." Despite what was said or not said about baptism, great pressure was exerted on everybody to "get baptized." Often the topic of baptism generated heated discussion in meetings with "sister churches." Occasionally, a Baptist association "withdrew fellowship" from a congregation with a questionable baptismal policy. Baptism was considered "not very important," but it sure did seem important.

I presumed the official view was the correct one. In our church, baptisms were always scheduled for Sunday evening services. I assumed that if baptism really was very important, it would have been made a part of Sunday morning worship.

Historically, baptism is older than Christianity. However, the act always has been an integral part of Christian experience. Followers of Christ are to be baptized people—baptized not because Jesus was baptized but because Jesus declared that His followers should be baptized.

The New Testament is rich with imagery that provides insights into how early Christians understood the act. Baptism is described as a union with Christ in His death and resurrection (Rom. 6:3; Col. 2:12), a rebirth (John 3:5), incorporation into the church (1 Cor. 12:13; Gal. 3:28), and reception of the Holy Spirit (Acts 2:38; 22:16). Baptismal images include a burial (Rom. 6:1-11), a bride's prewedding bath (Eph. 5:26-27), putting on new clothes (Gal. 3:27), and being washed or cleansed (1 Cor. 6:11; Heb. 10:22).[16]

None of the New Testament writers suggests that baptism is a "mere symbol." Of course, water is a symbol. So is burial in water.[17] However, participation in a symbolic act involves identification with the reality that the act symbolizes.

The act of baptism is filled with meaning, though it points to a prior act with even greater meaning. Baptism does not create a redemptive union with Christ. That union occurs prior to baptism by means of God's grace being received with a total commitment in faith. Baptism is an act by which people physically identify themselves with Christ, a postconversion dramatization of conversion.

Baptism deserves a prominent place in Christian worship. Theologically, it can never be a casual or promiscuous act.[18] In relation to worship, baptism is neither a preliminary to be taken care of so worship can proceed nor a postscript available for those who want to remain after worship to see it. Baptism is an act of worship.

Prominently identified as a rite of initiation or a mode of entrance into a Christian congregation, baptism is also a distinctive act of proclamation. The proclamation is embraced in and conveyed by the action involved. Worship leaders do well to maximize the declarative power of baptism.

What does baptism proclaim? What is the content of the message delivered from the baptistry? Answering these questions means considering baptism from two different perspectives—that of the church and that of the church plus the person being baptized.

By means of baptism, the church makes several gospel-oriented statements. Baptism proclaims *what God has done in Christ.* The death, burial, and resurrection pattern of baptism by immersion projects the crucial acts in Christ's ministry of redemption. James White writes, "A baptism is always an act of evangelism, proclaiming the good news of God's love."[19]

God's love is the reason any person can enter a baptistry. No one is baptized because of merit or self-worth. The identity of every child of God is a product of God's grace. God accepts people who are unacceptable and sets their lives on a course dominated by compassion.

In baptism, *a church says something about the nature of its fellowship.* The people of God form *a community of obedience.* A church is made up of people who have obeyed Christ's directive about baptism regardless of the cost and inconvenience involved and the charges of foolishness to be endured. No one has to be excluded. The church is *an open community.* All of its members are sinners who have met Christ and been baptized. Superiority and inferiority are irrelevant concepts in this fellowship. God's grace is the only reason the community can exist, and God's grace is for everybody.

One frequent writer on worship makes an interesting proposal related to the church's nature as revealed in baptism. Every fellowship of believers is contingent upon the love and gracious acceptance of God dramatized in baptism. Thus, Michael Marshall suggests that the baptistry should be located at the entrance to a church's sanctuary. Marshall writes, "We should physically, literally, and architecturally enter the church through the baptistry."[20] I do not know the logistical ramifications involved in implementing such a plan. But the instructional value of the arrangement makes good sense theologically.

Through baptism a church identifies itself also as *a supportive community.* Gathering to witness the baptism of a new believer reinforces the truth that members of the fellowship of faith are never on their own. Christians are bonded to each other as well as to Christ. Every person of faith has the support of a family.

Baptism communicates more truth than that which comes from the church. In the baptistry, the person being baptized becomes a witness, a herald. Numerous messages are declared as the person is dipped into the water.

God owns me. Succinctly stated, that is the basic confession of baptism. In the patristic period, church leaders used oil to trace the sign of the cross on the forehead of a newly baptized person. The intent was to identify the person as God's possession much like slaves were branded to indicate their owners and soldiers were tattooed with the mark of their emperor.[21] Actually baptism itself sufficiently proclaims God's ownership of a person.

When I am baptizing a new Christian, I ask why the person has come to the baptistry. "What confession brings you to this water?" By way of response, the least that can be said is "Jesus Christ is Lord!" But no more needs to be said. By submitting to baptism, a person proclaims allegiance to the God revealed in Christ.

Overfamiliarity can deaden people's sensitivity to even the most significant acts of worship. Some folks view baptism like they would school graduations, club initiations, and piano recitals. Conversely, I well recall occasions on which I have baptized persons who knew that the declaration of this act would result in condemnation and rejection from their families and former friends. A proclamation-event with such serious consequences ought never to be viewed with a familiarity that reduces it to a matter of routine.

In the apostle Paul's writings on baptism, he seems unable to decide if it is an act of death or resurrection, a heralded renunciation or a declared affirmation. No wonder. Both are involved.

Baptism conveys a person's *renunciation of a former way of life, of Satan, and of existence apart from God.* By the second century, this baptismal message had been formally incorporated into baptismal services. While standing in water, a person being baptized declared, "I renounce thee, Satan, and all thy service and all thy works." In some places, this statement was followed by the new Christian symbolically spitting in Satan's face. The renunciation was spoken while facing west, the place of darkness. Afterwards, the person turned toward the light of the east to profess Jesus as Lord.[22] The significance of these actions was enhanced by the fact that many baptisms in the early church took place at daybreak.

Complementing the renunciation and death communicated by baptism was the baptismal proclamation of *affirmation* and *resurrection*. Early in the life of the church, baptism became the major ingredient in worship-based celebrations of Easter. New Christians were required to undergo a year of training in discipleship prior to baptism. Then, as Christ's resurrection was celebrated, new Christians were buried in and raised from baptismal waters. The message was as unmistakable as it was powerful, *"A new life—life in Christ—has been accepted."* Often, as people walked out of the waters of baptism, they were given new clothes to wear, a further symbol of their new life, of "putting on Christ."

A person's submission to baptism is also a nonverbal proclamation of *loyalty and unity in relation to a community of believers.* "I want to become a part of this fellowship of faith. I am identifying myself with these disciples of Christ." Those words capture the unarticulated testimony of the act.

Does such a treatment of baptism in worship make too much of the event? Hardly. At best it is an aid to continuing baptism without making too little of it.

The Lord's Supper

Periodically, I like for an entire worship experience to center on the Lord's Supper. To emphasize this meal's capacity for proclaiming the gospel, I sometimes replace the pulpit, which is front and center in the sanctuary, with the Communion table. This obvious change calls attention to often overlooked biblical-theological truths about the Lord's Supper.

Reflecting on the impact of a congregation's celebration of the Lord's Supper, the apostle Paul chooses the term *katangellein,* meaning "proclamation," to describe the meal. It is the word most commonly used to denote the preaching of the *kerygma.* After an examination of 1 Corinthians 2:1; 9:14, Romans 1:8; and Philippians 1:17 and following, one student of the New Testament writes, "The apostle clearly saw no great distinction between the *kerygma* as preached in his public evangelizing mission and the same gospel as presented to believers at the Lord's table."[23] The Lord's Supper is a proclamation event.

Through the years, Christians repeatedly have been impressed with the preaching power of worshipers eating together the bread and drinking together the cup of the Lord's Supper. John Wesley judged this corporate meal to be a church's greatest means of evangelism and call to Christian conversion. The Lord's Supper is the gospel in action. By means of this meal, all of a person's senses are involved in the worship of God. In many denominations, the Lord's Supper is considered the central act of worship.

Early Christians shared the Lord's Supper every time they gathered for worship. For many years, a separation of the ministry of the word and the ministry of the table was inconceivable. Eventually, though, in some places these two acts of worship occurred independently of each other. Now, in the Free Churches especially, preaching is assigned the position of central importance in worship. The Lord's Supper is relegated to occasional observances.

New Testament images—Insights into the nature of this special meal can be derived from the basic images used by New Testament writers making reference to it. The Lord's Supper is an occasion of *thanksgiving* (Acts 2:46). Many contemporary Christians speak of this meal as the Eucharist—a term which comes from the Greek word which means to give thanks (*eucharisteo*). *Communion* is another New Testament metaphor for the Supper (1 Cor. 10:16-17). This term is also used as a title for the meal, perhaps the most popular name for it. In his Corinthian correspondence, Paul refers to sharing the Lord's Supper as partaking in *koinonia,* a term rendered as "communion" by translators of the *King James Version* of the Bible and as "fellowship" by most other translations of the Scriptures. A third biblical metaphor for the meal is *commemoration* (1 Cor. 11:24). Celebrating the Lord's Supper means remembering Christ's work. In this instance, though, memory is much more than passive reflection. "This is a meal of 'remembrance,' not in the historical sense of the word, but in the sense of *anamnesis,* waking up, opening the eyes; in the sense of 'remember who you are.'"[24]

At least two other images of the Lord's Supper can be found in the New Testament. Among Free Churches, however, neither of these metaphors is as popular as the first three. These two terms are often connected with a sacramental view of the Lord's Supper—an unacceptable interpretation of the event to some groups. But the issues involved reach far beyond denominational lines. Controversy swirls around references to the Lord's Supper as a *sacrifice* (Heb. 13:15) and as the *presence of Christ* (Mark 14:22, 24).

Certainly the meal is related to sacrifice. Historically, the sacrifice of Jesus is recalled. Presently, a sacrifice of praise is offered. In no sense, though, is what happens around the Lord's table a repetition of what happened on the cross of Christ.[25] And, as for the issue of presence, the words of Jesus can be repeated—"This is my body.... This... is my blood"—without the Catholic doctrine of transubstantiation being accepted.

Christian proclamation—Patterned after the meal which Jesus shared with His disciples in the upper room, biblical descriptions of the Lord's Supper (like 1 Cor. 11:23-25) embrace four fundamental actions. Each one has potential as a vehicle for Christian proclamation.

First, Jesus "took." The earliest celebrations of the Lord's Supper began with worshipers offering to God the elements—the bread and the wine—needed for the meal. Encapsulated in this act is the essence of worship itself—returning to God what has come from God.

The Lord's Supper proclaims the *reality of God's ownership* of everything and the *necessity of a Christian's stewardship.* Also communicated is the *spiritual potential of ordinary matter.* In the hands of Jesus, the first-century staples of bread and wine took on a religious significance that endures into the present. An event from earlier in His ministry foreshadowed the action of Jesus in the upper room. When a little boy placed his five loaves of bread and two fish in the hands of Jesus, an entire multitude was fed. From around the Lord's table the message goes forth that gifts entrusted to Jesus can become effective ingredients in His ministry of love throughout the world.

Second, Jesus gave thanks. The meaning is simple, similar to Christians' practice of saying a "blessing" before a regular meal. God is recognized as the source of all that is good.

The Lord's Supper proclaims the *necessity of gratitude* among the people of God. Thanksgiving is in order for what is on the Lord's table. More important, though, gratitude is the fitting response for people who participate in the Lord's Supper. No one is worthy of the experience. Forget merit. Every worshiper's participation in Communion is a result of God's grace. Little more can be said than, "Thanks be to God."

Third, Jesus "broke." In the upper room Jesus tore apart a loaf of bread and poured out the wine to be consumed. He did not risk the disciples interpreting His actions on their own. Jesus spoke of His body being broken and His blood being spilled in the ultimate act of redemption. More than the crucifixion was involved. Jesus poured out the entirety of His life in a ministry aimed at providing salvation for sinners.

The heart of the Supper's proclamation is contained in the third of Jesus' actions. The Lord's Supper declares *God's love.* A discernment of the inclusive nature of this love is almost overwhelming. God extends love to sinners who crucified the Son.

Such love had been apparent from the beginning of Jesus' ministry. Frequently, Jesus ate with sinners. In fact, this was a matter of major controversy. The inclusive nature of Jesus' love was a significant factor in His death. No one accused Jesus of bad theology. But numerous people resented the time He spent eating with sinners.

The Lord's Supper proclaims *the cross.* No message could be any clearer than this one—a broken body and spilled blood. And why? For the sake of sinners, even those who did the killing. Thus, the Lord's Supper proclaims *salvation.* In one writer's words, "The very center of salvation is shown forth"[26] in this meal. All people can be beneficiaries of Jesus' redemptive actions.

Worship and the meaning of the Lord's Supper in worship are greatly enhanced when, in observances of the Lord's Supper, bread is actually broken and wine or juice is poured. These visible actions impact worshipers in a manner impossible to achieve by verbal descriptions. If a worship leader desires to speak, comments are in order regarding the unity of the church as symbolized by the loaf but also regarding the necessity of brokenness in the ministry of redemption. "Just as truly as food must be destroyed before it can be of use to us, so He had to be destroyed before He could savingly serve us. We must be broken ere we deeply bless."[27]

The Lord's Supper proclaims *communion.* As Christ is received in faith, people experience the benefits of His passion. Life "in Christ" is life in constant fellowship with God. Other people are involved also. All who share in the divine life of Christ, share life with each other. Among Christians, life together is sustained by the repetitious acts of giving and receiving. Implicit, if not explicit, in this fellowship is the proclamation of *how all of life ought to be and can be through Christ.*

Fourth, Jesus gave. In the upper room the disciples munched on bread and drank wine. They were sustained by what Jesus provided. Under the shadow of the cross with a certainty of Jesus' death, the disciples learned of the gift of life.

The Lord's Supper proclaims that *Christ gives Himself for us,* and thus that *salvation is a gift.* All that worshipers do in the Lord's Supper is a response to what God has done. The initiative is with God—in salvation, in the Supper, and in worship. Any person who cannot gratefully receive what is not deserved, what cannot be earned, and what no one dares expect, cannot know Christian redemption. Salvation is available as a gift or not at all.

A basic principle throughout the Bible is that people are blessed in order to be a blessing. Responsibility accompanies the reception of a gift. Receivers become givers. The Lord's table is no different. The Lord's Supper proclaims that *as Christ gives Himself to us, we are to give ourselves to one another.* In the early church, this declared truth was reinforced immediately. After a service, worshipers took the bread and wine left over from the Supper and distributed them to poor and hungry people in the community.

After everything has been said and written about the meaning of the Lord's Supper and the truths it proclaims, still more remains. No one will ever get at all of it. The Lord's Supper is a mystery and the proclamation of *mystery.* "Something happens at the Lord's table that doesn't happen anywhere else in the church's worship."[28] However, that "something" defies definition. Why was it in the breaking of bread and sharing the cup that the Emmaus travelers recognized Jesus though they had traveled with Him for hours without any recognition? I do not know. But I am confident that a similar occurrence is possible today as people break the bread and drink the cup of the Lord's Supper in worship.

This significant act of Christian proclamation merits sensitive preparation. Variations in the methods of its observance can enhance its meaning. Careful thought is in order regarding the nature of the elements to be used and the manner of their distribution and reception. Good decisions about concerns such as these strengthen the meal's potential to be used by God for the proclamation of the gospel.

Other Media

Even the strictest Puritans would have been pleased with the worship centers and worship services which I knew as a young person. A priority was placed on plainness. The aim was achieved with perfection. Generally, walls were bare except for two small boards—one on each side of the pulpit area—used to post attendance figures and other statistics related to Sunday School and Training Union. In my home church, the only art in the room where we gathered for worship was a pastel painting of the Jordan River which had been done on the concrete blocks that formed the back wall of the baptistry. I liked it. As a child, sometimes I thought I could see a ripple in the painted blue water.

Then proclamation meant preaching only. For that matter, worship meant preaching. Other media for proclamation were never considered. Our choir did not do *anthems, oratorios,* and *cantatas.* Those very words were thought to sound a bit "high church." Besides, our fellowship did not include any musicians skilled enough to direct such presentations.

Then a pastor arrived who introduced the congregation to skits. This same man later brought to our church an evangelist who used a flannel board and a black light to tell the gospel story. People listened as if for the first time. At least, I know I did.

Years passed before I became fully aware of the proclamation potential of nontraditional media in worship. Flannelboard presentations and chalk talks had made the point. I began to understand God's love for all creation and desire to use all of creation in the ministry of redemption. Studying the meaning of the incarnation was revolutionary. If God can offer salvation to the world through human flesh, God can speak the gospel through a variety of media.

An antiaesthetic bias in worship is understandable. All attention is to be focused on God. Then there is the latent danger of object worship, an idolatry of art. Here again, though, abuses and misuses do not justify no use. In worship today, there is more danger of an idolatry of self and a sanctification of tradition than of an unhealthy appreciation for art forms. In fact, the utilization of different media in declaring the gospel can aid deliverance from a preoccupation with selfish thoughts and interests.[29]

Music is a tremendous medium for proclamation. At times I have been confronted best by the claims of the gospel through a choir's singing of an anthem, a children's chorus combining music and movement, a choir and a symphony orchestra together interpreting the biblical Christmas narratives, or an a cappella solo of "Amazing Grace." Worship-sensitive church musicians can serve as unrivaled proclaimers of the gospel.

Visual art is another avenue for sharing the message of God's love and redemption. Just about the time my worship-related thoughts were changing significantly, Broadman Press published a book on worship written by a respected Baptist author. In that volume, Gaines Dobbins addresses the issue of art in worship writing, "A church that neglects art in worship is missing a divinely given opportunity."[30]

Drama can also convey and create God-honoring convictions about the gospel. Oil paintings from the great masters can heighten worshipers' understanding of the plight, pathos, and joy of Jesus.

Once, in a Sunday morning worship service, I did a dialogue sermon with a sculptor. As I spoke from the pulpit about the prophet Isaiah, he slapped together moistened clay and molded it into a bust of King Uzziah. Out of our interchanges, verbal and nonverbal, worshipers gained new insights into what happened when Isaiah visited the temple at the time of Uzziah's death.

What is appropriate and what is not? Helpful guidance comes from a book on worship: "The sole criterion for all liturgical art is that it must be transparent to the mystery of God in Christ."[31] To be beneficial in worship, art, like all other ingredients in a service, must serve the purpose of worship and not seek to take worship captive in order to serve itself. Paul Hoon details the criteria for art's effectiveness as a medium of the gospel:

> If art will subordinate its vision of Reality as Beauty to the Christian vision of God as the Holy; if art will address man not with pleasure but with judgment and mercy that beget salvation; if art will let its love of the vitalities of existence be chastened with the paschal Life of the Gospel.[32]

Offended by an excessive and manipulative use of emotions in worship services, for a time I overreacted. I failed to acknowledge the normal role of emotions in spirituality. My propensity to trust the rational alone has been challenged by people like Michael Marshall, who writes, "Logic is only one of many motivations in worship, and it is probably the least powerful."[33]

Worship is an experience that involves the total person. That includes emotions. Art forms in worship bring the gospel appeal to people's emotions in a superlative manner.

Robert Webber, with whom I share a similar pilgrimage in worship, describes an experience of worship during a visit to a church in Moscow. A proliferation of art served as an unforgettable proclamation of the gospel. Webber's reflections on that occasion articulate the hope that a variety of art forms can be incorporated into worship:

> In a rare moment of spiritual release, the aesthetic side of my person was set free to worship God. Color, sound, light, texture, and smell lifted me up to the praise of God, and I felt as though I was joining all creation in the praise of his blessed and holy name.[34]

10
Singing
"We'll join the everlasting song"

Acquaintances of Paul Tillich tell of the great theologian's encounter with a distressed student who came to him confessing troublesome doubts. The student asked for Tillich's help in resolving numerous nagging questions. In his sensitive response to this young fellow, Tillich played a recording of "Credo" from Bach's *B Minor Mass*. Though an astute thinker, Tillich realized that the only satisfactory answer to the student's quest would be found in art not science, not in sharper reasoning but in singing. "I give my love, my loyalty, my heart."

Music can take us where the intellect alone cannot go. The intellect can find in music an integrity of expression unavailable in reasonable, verbal declaration. Music has the capacity to convey praise and joy, concern and sorrow, in a manner that defies a captivation in words. Thus, music, heralded by one writer as "God's second greatest gift to humanity,"[1] is of inestimable importance in corporate worship.

Music is a medium through which every act of worship can find meaningful expression. God can be praised by music. Convictions of faith can be sounded through music and thereby strengthened. The pathos of true penitence can be communicated musically. Assurances of divine forgiveness can be announced musically. Music is a major medium for the proclamation of the gospel. By means of music, an invitation can be extended and a decision of faith celebrated.

Throughout this volume I have used a variety of phrases from different musical texts to identify the various divisions of my discussion of worship. My purpose is to suggest that music does not belong in any one part of a worship experience alone. Music has a proper presence in every expression of worship.

Toward what end? What is the purpose of music in worship? Before responding to those inquiries, though, perhaps another question deserves attention. Can worship occur without music? That answer is easy—yes. Not only *can* worship take place devoid of music, musicless worship *does* occur regularly. (Numerous forms of corporate worship through silence have already been discussed.) Music is not essential to worship. That realization is beneficial in forming an accurate response to the first question.

Music is an aid to worship, an enhancement of worship. Music assists worshipers in fulfilling their corporate task. The purpose of music in worship, then, in the same as the purpose of every other act of worship—to honor, please, and glorify God. Baptist church musician Hugh McElrath warns that if music cannot assume this secondary role in relation to worship, its presence in the church cannot be justified.[2]

The value of music in the worship of God is evident in the Bible. Old Testament worship abounded with joyful music. King David appointed singers to assure the presence in worship of people who could "raise sounds of joy" (2 Chron. 15:16*b*). The psalmist prized musical expressions in worship and encouraged both choral and instrumental contributions: "O sing to the Lord a new song!...Make a joyful noise to the Lord,...break forth into joyous song!...Sing praises to the Lord" (Ps. 98:1, 4-5). Old Testament writers favored a redundancy of praise in worship. They summoned the involvement of every musical instrument available—the human voice, harps, lyres, cymbals, trumpets, timbrel, strings, and pipes, to cite a few. A premium was placed on loudness—"loud clashing cymbals!" (Ps. 150:5); "singers...should play loudly on musical instruments" (1 Chron. 15:16*a*).

Not as much has been written about the use of music in New Testament worship. However, the importance of music in the primitive community of faith is irrefutable.[3] A glimpse into the early church's musical offerings to God is provided by Ephesians 5:19 and Colossians 3:16. More important than New Testament descriptions of musical activities in primitive Christian worship, though, is the significant presence of musical literature in the content of the New Testament. Much of what the early church sang in worship has been preserved in the Scriptures.

No consensus exists on the precise number of hymns in the New Testament. Scholars agree, though, that their influence is considerable. Our best theological insights into the nature of Christ are contained in the early hymnody of the church. Classic examples of this musical literature are John 1:1-18; Philippians 2:6-11; Colossians 1:15-20; and 1 Timothy 3:16.

In Christian worship, the positive potential of music rests on both theological and practical foundations. The specific values of music in worship become more apparent as an order of worship is developed and various possibilities for musical contributions within that order are studied.

Congregational Singing

Music can unite a worshiping congregation like no other activity. A real community of worship is formed as one voice joins another in obedience to the biblical admonition to worship God with singing. Diversity is utilized to create harmony. Participating in worship through congregational singing allows every person present to please God and encourage other worshipers.

In meaningful worship, people experience an emotional release. Congregational singing is the perfect vehicle to carry unleashed feelings into the presence of God as gifts of worship. Singing to God is as natural as crying because of a sad story or laughing at a joke. God invites musical expressions that represent a wide range of emotions. Songs to God may be conveyed in high-pitched happiness or interspersed with sorrowful sobs.

Congregational singing is to be a purposeful act in worship, never merely a time filler or a matter of routine. By means of corporately voiced songs, a call to worship can be sounded, praise can be declared, faith can be confessed, a text from the Bible can be heralded, repentance can be invited, a prayer can be offered, and sacrifice can be encouraged. Over an extended period of time, the worship of a church is strengthened if congregational singing is utilized in service to all of these purposes.

Instrumental Offerings

Some groups early in the Free Church tradition banned the use of musical instruments in worship. Reasons varied. Some argued from the precedent of an absence of musical instruments in the earliest forms of New Testament worship. Their historical knowledge was accurate, but their reasoning was faulty.

Primitive Christian worship took place in family dwellings and other locations where musical instruments were unavailable. Strict fidelity to this pattern of worship would require an abandonment of church buildings as well as prohibition against musical instruments. Other people assumed that instruments of music belonged to "worldly" buildings and activities. The pipe organ especially was viewed as an instrument that belonged in a "music hall."

In the church of my childhood, a piano was the only musical instrument permitted in worship. Eventually, that changed. The transition involved the addition of a second piano. Piano duets were considered indicators of great strides forward in our church's musical progress. Finally, a few other musical instruments were allowed in worship.

Granted, a musical instrument can dominate a worship experience. An insensitive instrumentalist can function more as a tyrant hindering worship than as a minister aiding worship. Like most pastors, I have witnessed members of a congregation angered by instrumental excesses in worship. However, misuses and abuses in instrumental music do not provide an adequate rationale for the absence of instrumental music in worship.

Skilled instrumental musicians can make substantial contributions to worship. Indeed, the mood befitting each act of worship can be established by the leadership of musical instruments. Not only can the proper use of musical instruments encourage greater musical participation on the part of all worshipers, sometimes a run on a piano keyboard, the somber resonance of a burst from a pipe organ, or the victorious blast of a trumpet can convey to God sentiments that many worshipers can find no way to express on their own.

Musical instruments serve a purpose in worship that is very different from their presence in a concert. When people gather to enjoy a music recital, instrumentalists are expected to call attention to their musical expertise and to the importance, beauty, and versatility of the instruments which they play. When people assemble for worship, though, all of the attention belongs to God. A musical instrument has a place in worship only as long as it contributes to that focus on God.

A Ministering Choir

A choir is a worship prompter integrally related to the entire congregation. Choir members enable other worshipers to make a better musical offering to God.

Choirs come from congregations. To forget this truth is to risk an elitist mentality among choir members and to open the door for a congregational resentment against what is perceived as a musical clique. This point is far too important to go unnoticed.

At times I like for a choir to be assembled after worship has begun. A processional of choir members during the opening hymn can serve this purpose. Also of value occasionally is having members of the choir seated in the congregation as worship begins, then moving together to the choir loft at a specified time in the service. Such action dramatizes the bond which exists between members of the choir and other members of the congregation.

Sometimes, having members of the choir move away from their normal location in the sanctuary and to stand amid the congregation is helpful for a specific act of worship. For example, I am fond of an entire congregation singing Handel's magnificent "Hallelujah Chorus." Because of the difficulty of this piece for untrained musicians, congregational participation is aided by members of the choir positioning themselves throughout the congregation. The result may not be musically flawless, but what a joyous expression of praise! All worshipers in the service become a part of a choir offering its music to God.

At times a choir may sing to or for a congregation of worshipers, but God remains the ultimate audience. However, a presentation from a choir can qualify as Christian proclamation every bit as much as a sermon. Intended as a gift to God, such a musical declaration is directed to members of the worshiping body. Also, a worship service can be enhanced by including a piece of music that most of the worshipers cannot sing. In that situation, the choir sings for the congregation. Members of the choir present a musical gift to God on behalf of all who are present. When a choir fulfills this function in worship, a congregation benefits from being able to read the words which are being sung.

Selecting Music

What kind of music is appropriate in Christian worship? No one answer to that question satisfies all of the people interested in it. For any person to suggest the acceptability of one musical form to the exclusion of all others is an act of great audacity (if not outright insensitivity). Variety in church music benefits a congregation even as it serves the basic purpose of worship.

Contemporary musicians are blessed by multiple options from which to choose in fashioning the musical expressions for a worshiping congregation. *Hymns* are basic. Though the definition of a hymn has expanded across the years, a hymn is a form of prayer which is sung to God as an act of praise and devotion. B. L. Manning accurately states a dominant conviction among people in Free Churches, "Hymns are for us dissenters what the liturgy is for the Anglican. They are the framework, the setting, the conventional, the traditional part of divine service as we use it.... We mark times and seasons, celebrate festivals, and expound doctrines by hymns."[4]

Psalms are just what their name implies. Today numerous sections of the Old Testament psalms are available in easily singable musical forms. Congregational worship can be enriched as contemporary voices unite in the praises, laments, and thanksgivings of their worshiping predecessors in Israel.

Canticles are the biblical texts of songs and prayers found outside the psalms. For a straightfoward declaration of a scriptural text by means of music, the canticles are superb. Among the most popular of the canticles are "The Song of Zechariah" (the *Benedictus* in Luke 1:68-79), the "Song of Simeon" (the *Nunc Dimmitti's* in Luke 2:29-32), and the "Song of Mary" (the *Magnificat* in Luke 1:46-55).[5]

In many churches *gospel songs* are popular. These musical pieces are more given to individualism, recitations of personal experiences, and exhortations toward listeners than any of the other musical forms mentioned. A vigorous debate continues regarding the appropriateness of gospel songs in corporate worship.[6]

The God whom we meet in worship is the God of grace. Fortunately, God accepts less than perfect musical offerings just as less than perfect persons. Worshipers are obligated to give to

God the best of which they are capable in all offerings, music included. When a congregation meets this one criterion, people who judge those worshipers negatively are in danger of severe judgment.

But what is good? Or best? Answer to those inquiries are matters of taste and appreciation. And both taste and appreciation are determined by cultivation and growth or the lack thereof. A church's views on the music appropriate for worship should be dynamic, not static.

Much of the disruptive controversy about church music in local congregations stems from personal preferences—individual likes and dislikes related to music. I know the issue well, both personally and institutionally. As a college student, when I stepped into the religious world that existed beyond my local church, I first resisted worship music that was different from any I had known in the past. Having experienced a rather steady diet of music from a paperback edition of the "Stamps-Baxter Quartet Book," I looked with chagrin on pieces of music that had been standard fare in the hymnals of my denomination. But I struggled. And changed. Eventually, I grew.

I still enjoy getting together with friends around a piano in someone's house and singing a hand-clapping, foot-patting selection like "I'll Fly Away." However, I now know the difference between music appropriate for private enjoyment and music suitable for public worship. Usually, when involved in an uninhibited rendition of something like "Swing Low, Sweet Chariot," I am much more aware of individual pleasure, of feeling good and having fun, than of an effort aimed at worshiping God.

For persons to insist that the music of worship be restricted to their individual favorites reveals an attitude which is inconsistent with the very nature of corporate worship. Some musical forms which do not serve the purpose of a worshiping congregation can be valuable in private devotion. But to impose one's privately appreciated music upon the public as a matter of personal preference is wrong. Participation in corporate worship requires an overriding interest in how a large number of people can worship God most fully.

Worship strengthens a person's spiritual muscles (as discussed earlier). And worship becomes better and better as worshipers become stronger and stronger. To grow comfortable with one type of music alone and to be intolerant of new musical expressions (texts or tunes) in worship is to impede the kind of growth which inheres in worship and contributes to better worship.

Music is an art form with mass appeal. In many communities, the worship music of local churches is the best live music available. Some people attend worship to hear the music. Though that motive for participating in worship is less than satisfactory, it need not be denigrated. With patience and prayers, motives can be improved. The major danger in such a situation is the temptation for musicians to begin performing for the congregation. Then music becomes an end in itself. Winifred Douglas addresses that issue directly, "No valid church music was ever made merely to be listened to as a sensuous pleasure."[7]

Most everyone who writes about church music suggests criteria by which music appropriate to worship can be selected. Prevalent on most lists are questions such as: Is it biblical? Does it appeal to the whole person—intellect, will, and emotions? Is it true to experience? Does it nurture a sensitivity to God? Is it worshipful? Does it unify the congregation? However, perhaps the best guiding principle for evaluating music to be used in worship comes from a man who has been called "the supreme religious composer."

For Johann Sebastian Bach, music, theology, and worship were all intertwined. On many of his musical compositions, some of which were not prepared specifically for the church, Bach wrote the letters "I.N.J." for the Latin words "In the Name of Jesus." According to Bach, all music is "for the glory of God and the instruction of my neighbors." That's it! Certainly Bach described the spirit which should be prompted by and pervasive in the music which is made a part of authentic worship.

11
Offering
"We Give Thee but Thine Own"

The offering is the pinnacle act in worship. Likewise, all of worship is an offering. The self-emptying of Jesus is the model. Unless a person offers the total self to God, true worship does not occur. Actions devoid of self-giving do not qualify as the worship of God regardless of the ecclesiastical nature of the site where they happen, the spiritual flair with which they are performed, or the holiness of the language which accompanies them.

At the center of a psalm often called a "Psalm of Worship" (Ps. 96) is a reference to the act which occupies a central place in worship—"bring an offering, and come into his [God's] courts!" (v. 8) Likewise in the New Testament, the apostle Paul describes the essence of "spiritual worship" in terms of making an offering—"present your bodies as a living sacrifice, holy and acceptable to God" (Rom. 12:1). An offering, a costly gift, is a prerequisite to praise-worthy worship, the fundamental act of God-honoring worship.

So central in the Christian life is the concept of offering that during the first three centuries after Jesus' ministry, a Christian was called an "offerer." A person who had been excommunicated from the church was labeled "forbidden to offer."[1] Making an offering to God was viewed as an act of great privilege, which declared the nature of a person's faith and constituted "the heartbeat of divine worship."[2] The terminology by which Christians are known has changed. But the centrality of offerings in Christian experience remains.

The offertory time in public worship deserves careful attention. What happens in this period is indicative of the nature of the whole worship experience. To enter this phase of a worship service perfunctorily and to interpret it as a spiritualized method by which an institutional church seeks to meet its annual budget misses the point entirely. At issue in the offertory is what will be given to God. People's level of participation in the offering (not the size of their gifts) is a revelation of the true character of their spiritual commitment.

Offerings from the congregation are appropriate at any point in a worship experience. Theologically, however, the offertory is best positioned near the conclusion of worship. Within the dialogical nature of worship, an offering of the worshipers' gifts is understood as a reaction to all that God has given. In reality, the gratitude which generates true Christian generosity is not likely to be experienced until after worshipers have realized forgiveness for their sins and have been confronted by the drama of redemption. Offertory gifts from worshipers constitute a response to the multiple, inestimably valuable gifts of God—especially "his inexpressible gift!" (2 Cor. 9:15).

Dedication

The offering is much too significant an act of worship to exist without an introduction and a statement of dedication (declared among the worshipers or addressed to God in prayer). As worshipers are requested to offer their gifts to God, a reminder of the nature of sacrifice can be beneficial.

Money is not sacred. Talents are not holy. Each becomes an item of spiritual significance only as it is dedicated to God. That transformation is captured in the image inherent in the word *sacrifice*. The term comes from the Latin *sacer,* meaning "sacred," and *facere,* the verb for "to make." Thus, to offer a sacrifice is to give that which has been made sacred.[3] Offered as gifts to God, material matters, personal abilities, and expenditures of time become vital spiritual realities.

Before the offerings from a congregation are actually collected, worshipers can be helped by a reiteration of the responsive nature of what is being done. Calling attention to words like these penned by J. E. Fison can sensitize people to the true nature of giving: "God on the cross gave all, and God on the cross took all. God on the cross offered all, and God on the cross received all."[4] Following a statement of this nature, a worship leader may ask, "How, then, can we give less than everything to God?"

Human gifts are dedicated to the glory of God, Creator of all good and perfect gifts. No question about that dedication is tolerable in worship.

Musical Offering

In most worship services, some form of music accompanies the passing of offering plates. Financial gifts are offered to God in a context of music. Unfortunately, a tendency exists to interpret the instrumental or choral offertory as background music or a nice cover-up for extraneous noise generated by the congregation. The importance of the musical offertory is far more theological than functional.

During the offertory, musicians model the intent of this act of worship for everyone present. They give to God the fruit of their labor. Personal talents are offered to God in a spirit of commitment which is strengthened through worship. Other members of the congregation are thereby encouraged to offer to God the products of their abilities and labors as well as the skills themselves. At this moment in worship, as in no other, sensitive persons see the indissoluble relationship which exists between work, prayer, and worship.

Opinions differ as to what type of music is best in this part of a worship service. Instrumental offerings are probably most prevalent. However, worship leaders like Don Hustad see a problem here. During an instrumental presentation, the minds of worshipers are likely either to wander distractingly or to focus on the musical skills of the instrumentalist. This moment in worship is far too crucial to risk such a negative potential. Hustad prefers a sacrifice of words—by means of a solo, a selection from the choir, or a congregational hymn.[5] If Hustad's perception is correct, a congregational hymn would seem to be the safest choice.

In planning worship, I see the musical offertory as an opportunity to involve a variety of people in worship leadership who otherwise will never assume that role. When individuals dedicate their different talents to God by providing offertory music, they perform an exemplary act of worship. They model the essential meaning of the offertory. Young persons, especially, should be encouraged to share their musical abilities before God in this part of the service. In so doing, they please God and encourage others to do the same.

Personal Offering

Will Campbell writes of Grandma Bettye: "She wore the flannel bathrobe to church the very first Sunday after Christmas. Because it was the prettiest thing she had ever seen, and the Lord deserved the best."[6] That is the attitude behind an offering appropriate to the Lord God. Worshipers give their best.

Sadly, sometimes worshipers' motivations for participating in the offering get caught up in a harmful legalism. They ask: How much must I give to be fair to God? Should I tithe the net or the gross of my paycheck? Is a gift of 10 percent of my extra income really necessary? Such inquiries imply ownership. Worshipers see themselves as deciding what part of their possessions to offer God, a highly presumptuous thought. Viewed from the perspective of the Bible, stewardship is at stake in the offertory, not ownership. Participating in the offertory in worship is a form of people giving an account of their handling of God's possessions. Every gift returns to God that which already belongs to God. The giving, though, is important as an act of love, faith, and commitment.

Any haggling over minimum and maximum percentages in giving compromises the basic spirit of the act. A worshiper seeking to determine "How much of what I have is mine and how much of it belongs to God?" needs correction and instruction. Meeting a legalistic requirement in making an offering falls far short of participating in real worship. The truest response to the revelation of God in Christ is a desire to give everything to God.

To understand what is at stake in an offering, as well as in the entire worship experience of which it is a part, necessitates a look at the crucifixion of Christ. Christ's obedient death on the cross is the ultimate act of worship, the epitome of worshipful giving. "He gave himself completely that the father might be glorified."[7] All of life is involved in this kind of giving—mind and heart, intention and action, will and work. Such an offering extends to God a gift that can be used in the redemption of all creation.

Originally, the offering was not a time in worship for passing collection plates throughout the congregation. In its earliest forms the offering consisted of worshipers bringing to the altar the fruits of their labors. Often monetary currency was scarce.

The altar was piled high with meats, vegetables, and other goods—all offered with gratitude and intended for the glory of God. During the offering, worshipers brought forward also the bread and the wine to be used in the celebration of the Lord's Supper that followed.

Here again is a merger of the sacred and the secular, work and prayer, in worship. Making an offering is a liturgical act with ethical significance. Today, as worship moves to the offertory moment, worshipers should ask, "Are the fruits (products) of my labor appropriate to place on an altar as gifts to God?"

The apostle Paul elaborates the horizontal implications of a worshipful offering. More than once this itinerant man on a mission refers to the collection taken in worship by the term *koinonia,* meaning fellowship (2 Cor. 9:13; Rom. 15:26). Paul understood that monetary gifts dedicated to God form the substance of valuable ministries to people in need. Throughout his travels, Paul encouraged contributions to provide assistance for the needy Christians in Jerusalem. Material gifts take on spiritual significance as a means of building up the *koinonia.* Paul succinctly states his theology for such giving in 2 Corinthians 8:9. "You know the grace of our Lord Jesus Christ, that though he was rich, yet for your sake he became poor, so that by his poverty you might become rich." J. G. Davies explores the depths of the meaning in these words from Paul. "Our response in gratitude to his self-impoverishment must be self-giving, for giving to others is giving to Christ who gave himself for us."[8]

The essence of an offertory gift is captured in a prayer from the *Book of Common Prayer.* Worshipers do well to remember these, or similar, words as the offertory time in worship arrives.

> Here we offer and present unto thee, O Lord, ourselves, our souls and bodies, to be a reasonable, holy, and living sacrifice unto thee . . . and although we be unworthy, through our manifold sins, to offer unto thee any sacrifice, yet we beseech thee to accept this our bounden duty and service: not weighing our merits, but pardoning our offenses.

Invitations

A critical, perhaps climactic, moment in worship arrives when worshipers are invited to make an offering to God that involves far more than material goods. This invitation is true to the basic rhythm of worship. The good news of God's Word has been declared. Worshipers have been confronted by a divine love—incomprehensible to human understanding but incarnate in Jesus who came and is coming. A response is in order—a response that cannot be satisfied unless a person's soul is involved. Praise, prayer, and stewardship move to the brink of their fullest expressions as worshipers contemplate giving the entirety of their lives to God.

Integral to the gospel of Christ is an open-ended invitation for all people to know Christ as Savior and Lord. Presentations of the drama of redemption are incomplete until everyone who witnesses them is invited to become a participant in it. Worship leaders are right in summoning all people within the sound of their voices to become beneficiaries of God's grace, recipients of salvation through Christ.

The invitation to Christian discipleship has been entrusted to the church by God. Nowhere in the life of a church is this invitation more fittingly extended and its acceptance encouraged than in divine worship.

Also in order during this period of worship are invitations for Christians to renew their basic commitments to God. In some instances, worshipers are asked to make public a visible indication of this private internal action. Often an important dimension of spiritual rededication is a formal identification with the worshiping congregation. For that reason, many worship leaders invite people to join the membership of their churches even as they urge others to unite with Christ.

For many years, I heard no other invitations offered in worship. Then I made a discovery. The offertory generally and the spoken invitation to discipleship specifically present a wonderful opportunity for inviting numerous expressions of ministry. What happens in worship has to take some form in the world. By means of detailed instructions, worshipers can be challenged by alternative ways to flesh out their faith in much needed acts of mercy. This part of the invitation well may be designated as "A Calling Out of Gifts."

This special form of invitation should be present in a service only as needs for ministry dictate. The substance of the invitation will vary considerably from time to time: "A teacher is needed for the seventh-grade girls' Sunday School class. The local hospice organization is seeking three new volunteers. Our downtown boys' club is looking for someone to lead recreational activities on Tuesday nights. A group of older women in our church has asked for someone to meet with them once a month and lead a Bible study. If you can respond affirmatively to any of these needs, I invite you to let me know so these needs for ministry can be matched with ready ministers."

In worship, the offertory begins with a recognition of the self-emptying Christ who reveals the God who gives everything. The offering does not end, though, even if a particular service concludes, until worshipers have given everything to God. When that happens, the worship which fills a sanctuary leads naturally to a way of life in the world which can best be described as worshipful.

12
Departing
"God Be with You"

Departing from worship is an act of spiritual significance akin to that of gathering for worship. When an experience of corporate worship has been fulfilling, there is an irresistible almost inevitable temptation to resist departure. In much the same manner that Peter wanted to remain amid the awesome glory and mystery of the "transfiguration" experience, many worshipers want to remain in the strength and security of a worshiping congregation rather than to reenter daily routines. At the end of public worship nothing less is at stake than the nature of faith and the authenticity of the experience of worship. Is faith an otherworldly preoccupation? Is worship a means of escape? Or are both faith and worship gifts from God which make possible a life of meaning, joy, and service in this world?

Parting Words

For some people, the conclusion of worship is a frightful moment. A recently widowed woman has to return to an empty house. Cancer cells remain in the bone marrow of a middle-aged man. A college student faces a major test on Monday morning and knows that his car probably will not start after the worship service. The family is still quarreling. How easy to view a worship center as a place of seclusion and protection, a good place in which to remain.

Worship should conclude, not merely stop. Sensitive comments at the end of a service can be as important as the welcome which is extended when worship begins. If persons have responded publicly to the invitation, sharing their commitments can be beneficial to everybody. New Christians bear evidence that God remains active in the world, calling people into salvation through Christ. Individuals expressing a desire to become members of a church reinforce worshipers' awareness of the importance and power of a fellowship of God's people. To conclude worship by celebrating such decisions is an inspiration.

Giving specific directions for the departing worshipers is also valuable. "So now we go, not to fragment the church and to be separated from each other but to exist as the dispersed people of God, a united church active in the world." "Go in God's Name, not to be alone, but to be with those who need you." "Go from this place, not to forget what has happened here but to remember, and in remembering to find strength for service."

Worshipers can be encouraged by hearing (or repeating) a reaffirmation of their identity. "As you go, do not forget 'you are a chosen race, a royal priesthood, a holy nation, God's own people'" (1 Pet. 2:9). Paul's question to the Romans can birth a conviction to sustain departing worshipers—"If God is for us, who is against us?" (Rom. 8:31) A pastoral statement of assurance can increase worshipers' confidence that they live in the world, as in the sanctuary, by God's love and grace—"Grace to you and peace from God our Father and the Lord Jesus Christ" (Eph. 1:2).

Blessing or Benediction

Biblical worship always concluded with a blessing (though not always with a benediction as presently understood). In the Old Testament, the blessing was voiced by the priests and was intended to convey to individuals the truth that the power of the worshiping assembly would go with each of them personally. In the New Testament, Christ was celebrated as the blessing. Worshipers were dismissed in His name and with assurances of His grace. Worship in the early church invariably ended with a blessing.[1]

William Willimon makes the important point that a blessing at the end of worship grows out of a responsible theology of providence and bears witness to the total significance of the Christian religion.[2] God is the author of this blessing. A worship leader only reminds people of its reality. The peace of God can be experienced anywhere in the world as well as in the worship center. God remains close to members of the community of faith whether they are gathered or scattered. The blessing is not a magical formula—it is a biblical fact. God is for us. God is with us.[3]

The spoken benediction need not be a plea for God's accompaniment as worshipers depart. God has already promised the divine presence. This prayer embraces that assurance and gives thanks for it. When people realize that they are as much in the presence of God when they step through the exit from the sanctuary as when they assemble within it, reentry into the world takes on new meaning.

A traditional benediction can take the form of a biblical blessing. Two passages of Scripture serve that purpose beautifully. From Numbers 6:24-26, "The Lord bless you and keep you: The Lord make his face to shine upon you, and be gracious to you: The Lord lift up his countenance upon you, and give you peace." And from Jude 24-25, "Now to him who is able to keep you from falling and to present you without blemish before the presence of his glory with rejoicing, to the only God, our Savior through Jesus Christ our Lord, be glory, majesty, dominion, and authority, before all time and now and for ever. Amen."

Musical Postlude

Unfortunately, a postlude in worship is often considered "traveling music," intended to cover the noisy shuffling of people leaving the sanctuary. For that reason, I often ask worshipers to remain in their seats until the postlude is concluded.

The postlude is a *reflection*. In a sense, the postlude is an excellent summation of a worship service. Obviously, for this function of the postlude to be realized, planning must be done. However, when properly anticipated, the postlude provides a time for reflecting on the primary theme or themes of the worship experience.

If the focus of worship has been on the majesty of God and the glory of praise, the postlude can offer a superb final statement of inspiration and exaltation toward those ends. If a service has been more meditative in mood and devotional in substance, the postlude can reflect that spirit as well.

At the conclusion of worship, people need a time to reflect on what has been said and done—to review the reasons for praise, to recall prayerful petitions, to remember the Word of God read and proclaimed, to recount the commitments made and the offerings given.

Also, the postlude is a *transition*. Just as the prelude serves to usher people from the world into worship, the postlude serves to usher people from worship into the world. However, it is never a mere pushing out. Within the postlude is encouragement to apply what has been discovered in worship to all that will be experienced in the world.

What Martin Marty writes of an "amen" relates as well to a postlude. It is "not so much the end of anything as an escalator, a traffic control movement, an agent to move people to a new stage."[4] The postlude precedes that moment when people exit a service in a sanctuary for service in the world. The postlude blinks the signal indicating that the time has come for words to become deeds, for faith spoken to become faith in action, for ministry to move beyond contemplation to implementation.

During the postlude, people pick up on the themes of a service and apply them to their tasks in society. How do I praise God on my job? Where do I find those in need of my mission? In what way can I proclaim my faith? How can our family represent the church to someone this week?

In a real sense, the postlude is *another benediction*. The final sounds of instrumental music form a benediction on behalf of the entire experience of worship. From a piano, an organ, or other instruments come the musical strains which mean "so be it" and "yes."

Not only is an "amen" sounded in response to the various themes of the preceding service, an "amen" sounds as an affirmation of worship itself. Thus, the postlude becomes an invitation to yet another prelude, the gift of another offering. Worship is affirmed and celebrated. More worship is encouraged and invited. People are helped in their spiritual pilgrimages. And God is glorified.

Part III
Responsibility: The Church for Worship

13
Affirming Variety While Assuring Unity in Worship
"Now to His temple draw near"

In a personal letter to a friend, Hugh and Anne Bromehead described an experience of congregational worship among the General Baptists who met in Amsterdam under the leadership of John Smyth in 1609.

> We begin with a prayer, often read some one or two chapters of the Bible; give the sense thereof and confer upon the same; that done, we lay aside our books and offer a solemn prayer... the first speaker he propoundeth some text out of the scripture and prophesieth out of the same by the space of one hour or three quarters of an hour. After him standeth up a second speaker and prophesieth out of the said text the like time and space, sometimes more, sometimes less. After him, the third, the fourth, and fifth etc., as the time will give leave. Then the first speaker concludeth with prayer as he began with prayer, with an exhortation to contribution to the poor, which collection being made is also concluded with prayer. This morning exercise begins at eight of the clock and continueth unto twelve of the clock. The like course of exercise is observed in the afternoon from two of the clock unto five or six of the clock.[1]

Though set in a fictional context, Will Campbell's description of a worship service in the Church of the Almighty in Jesus' Name Amen carries a ring of truth. The author's words bring to mind actual experiences which are common in some congregations. The pastor is speaking:

> ... We don't have a printed bulletin that's sent to the printer on Tuesday for next Sunday's service. You know what I'm talking about!... They'll have all this fancy stuff. Processional, Call to Worship, Invocation. Or whatever they call it when the preacher gets up and reads something out of a book. Congregational

Hymn. Offertory. First lesson. Second Lesson. Responsive Read-ing. All that. Sermon. Recessional. Prayers of Intercession. All that...Now brother, we don't write it down in advance because we don't know what the Spirit has in mind for us to do until He leads us to do it. We don't have printed on a piece of paper Processional, Call to Worship, Hymn, Sermon, Lift Up Serpents! We lift up serpents when the Spirit of the living God tells us to lift up serpents! Not when some elder or bishop or pope tells us to. You know what I'm a-talking about out there![2]

In his very fine treatise on worship, Paul Hoon verbally sketches a worship service similar to many I have known per-sonally. Details vary at points, but, in general, the service is a very familiar one.

The congregation engages in a buzz of conversational small talk while the organist competes for attention....The choir...enters on the opening hymn in hesitation-waltz step. The minister ...conspicuously takes up a position as master of ceremonies, and fetches out of his hip pocket a hand edition of the New Testament from which he will presently read a few verses as springboard for his climactic "message," preparing himself from time to time with a draught from a prominent glass of water. The opening invocation becomes a sermon with everyone's eyes closed, and the "responsive reading" which follows, with the congregation sitting, concludes with the solo, "The Holy City." Two hymns follow.... The service then proceeds with the offer-ing, prefaced with an urging to present "folded money that will make Jesus smile," and the collection plates are retained at the rear of the auditorium while the ushers count the money as the minister's "morning prayer" wanders....Next follows a long and pretentious anthem....After the sermon and recessional, the benediction...is pronounced from the rear of the church and immediately after an "Amen"...organ chimes sound "God Be with You Till We Meet Again." The service ends with a mounting cre-scendo of conversation competing with fortissimo organ postlude.[3]

A vision of the author of Revelation provides an inspired description of worship offered by a cosmic congregation. Hav-ing listened to the singing of a new song before the throne of God, John writes:

Then I looked, and I heard around the throne and the living creatures and the elders the voice of many angels, numbering myriads of myriads and thousands of thousands, saying with a loud voice, "Worthy is the Lamb who was slain, to receive power and wealth and wisdom and might and honor and glory and blessing!" And I heard every creature in heaven and on earth and under the earth and in the sea, and all therein, saying, "To him who sits upon the throne and to the Lamb be blessing and honor and glory and might for ever and ever!" And the four creatures said, "Amen!" and the elders fell down and worshiped (Rev. 5:11-14).

Four experiences of worship. Each is distinctively, if not radically, different from the other three. Can such widely diverse activities possibly be envisioned as only variations of one primary activity and thus understood in relation to a unity of purpose? How different can expressions of worship be and each continue to be considered worship? What, if any, are the minimal requirements of worship, the essential characteristics of worship?

Human beings differ from each other dramatically. Little wonder, then, that human expressions of worship vary considerably—formal, informal, orderly, chaotic, rational, emotional. Congregations differ in their understandings of meaningful worship. Thus, great variety exists in worship practices.

No one individual can tell another precisely how to worship honestly. However, certain general guidelines for worship can prove helpful in maintaining its integrity.

All Worship Should Conform to Biblical Teachings About Worship

Christian worship is obligated to take the Bible seriously. Preparation for worship involves a study of the Bible as a divinely inspired medium of divine revelation.

Historically, worship practices have been shaped by two major approaches to the biblical literature. Some Christians assume that the pattern of worship in the New Testament is to be replicated in every age. The fact that New Testament descriptions of worship are sketchy and varied is not considered a problem. If a worship practice is present in the primitive community of faith, so the reasoning goes, that act of worship merits repetition today. Activities on which the New Testament is silent best be left out of contemporary worship.

Other Christians treat New Testament descriptions of worship very differently. Again attention is devoted to the worship practices of the early Christians. However, those first forms of worship are considered illustrative more than prescriptive or restrictive. In worship, these Christians do what was done by their predecessors in the faith, but more. Matters on which the Scriptures are silent are assumed acceptable. Unless an action is specifically forbidden in the Bible, it is considered an appropriate expression of worship.[4]

Positively, each of these approaches takes the Bible seriously. That mentality is to be applauded and emulated. The Word of God does make a difference in the total life experience—work and worship—of the people of God. Negatively, though, to treat the Bible as a detailed description of worship—the form and sequence of which all Christians are to follow—is to err. Well-intended efforts never to do less or more than was done in the worship of the early church, according to New Testament descriptions of it, and never to vary the pattern misunderstand the nature of the Scriptures. The Bible is a worship book abounding in materials from worship and for worship, but the Bible is "not a book on how to worship."[5]

New Testament writers address the spirit and the content of worship rather than establish normative forms of worship. In fact, variety not rigidity characterizes the worship practices of the early church. Efforts to reproduce faithfully a worship service developed by first-century Christians in Corinth or in Ephesus may or may not be of value. Available today are means of glorifying God and honoring Christ that were unavailable then (instruments of music for example). Worship then was conditioned by influences that are no longer factors in worship planning (limited times for meeting and the unavailability of worship centers outside family dwellings). However, the general insights into the nature of worship which emerge from the biblical narrative on worship are of extreme importance. They deserve more than acknowledgement. Biblical observations about worship can serve as helpful guidelines for understanding and planning worship and as beneficial criteria for evaluating worship.

A Spirit of Response

Christian worship is a response to God. Human actions follow divine actions. God always has the initiative in creation, redemption, and worship.

How people view God shapes the manner in which people worship God. Unfortunately, numerous faulty understandings of

God persist. Some people see God as a rather remote entity whose attention has to be attracted and whose love must be wooed. Worship, then, is the initiative of people intent on earning God's favor—saying good words and doing good deeds to win God's approval. Others view God as a deity basically disgusted with people, distrustful of human actions, and prone to anger. For these folks, worship is a personal initiative aimed at showing God that people can do right, appeasing God's wrath, and courting God's favor. For some people, God is a heavenly bookkeeper devoted only to fairness and justice. For them, worship is an attempt, at their initiative, to strike a bargain with God—"I have come to worship, so don't let anything bad happen to me." Or "So much has been going wrong in my life that I have come to worship in order to plead with God to stop the punishment and give me peace." Some people perceive God as a divinity who wants to do good for people but must be pampered, begged, and flattered before doing so. Developed with such an understanding, worship is an endeavor to constantly bombard God with pleasantries and niceties so as to move God toward appreciation for the worship offered and demonstrations of divine care toward the worshipers.

Worship as an act of human initiative is not Christian worship. The nature of Christian worship is that of a response—a response to God and to certain givens from God. God has demonstrated a love for people that does not have to be requested and cannot be earned. God loves us. God offered the gift of Christ that all people might be able to experience salvation. No one has to beg for that gift or plead for the presence of Christ. God has transcended human concerns of fairness and justice with an eternal commitment to grace. Our acceptance of God is not conditioned on how we worship or on whatever else we do and say but upon God's grace. God is the source of worship as well as the object of worship.

Worship is a gift from God to be returned to God as a gift. Never is worship a contractual negotiation or a quasi-legal form of religious plea bargaining. Christian worship is a response to the God who has been, is, and will be active on behalf of redemption with love.

The Importance of Order

Biblical worship is ordered worship. At times, Old Testament worship was too ordered. Form killed spirit. Rituals took the place of authentic celebrations. However, ordered acts of worship were reformed and revitalized, not abandoned. New Testament worship also was characterized by order. Not one order, but order.

Order is important in worship pragmatically as well as theologically for worship leaders and members of a congregation. Apart from some objective order of worship, a service can be subjected to and distorted by the random whims and moods of a worship leader. More broadly, a tendency toward individualism among worshipers is always strong. Order can check that tendency, which fragments a congregation if left unchecked, and can contribute to a unifying bond among worshipers.

God, the God who is worshiped, desires order. Creation re veals this divine preference as does redemption. Out of nothing ness God brings into existence an ordered creation. Chaos is a result of sin. In Christ, God takes on an ordered life so as to make salvation possible. Persons who give their lives to Christ experience a radically new order, an order different from any they have known before—a new creation.

Actually, a plea for order in worship may be a bit misleading. Every service or worship has an order—good or bad, helpful or harmful, explicit or implicit. Even among avowed nonritualistic congregations, rituals emerge. Informality is elevated to a formal status. So-called spontaneous acts of worship regularly occur in the same sequence accompanied by boasts (identical in wording and almost legalistic in spirit) of complete liberty. Order is inevitable. The issue, however, is order which is beneficial, an order in worship which aids worship. That requires effort. That is the kind of order in worship which God wills.

But what about freedom? The Spirit of God is the author of liberty. How, then, can the worship of God be other than free?

Freedom and order are antithetical only in extreme situations in which each has been abused. Sadly, that happens. Order can become rigid formalism. Freedom can be turned into formless chaos. Neither of these extremes has a rightful place in Christian worship. However, in worship even as in the world, order and freedom can complement each other and actually reinforce each other. A society under law provides an order which makes freedom possible. Freedom apart from a foundation of law and order quickly deteriorates into a captivity to anarchy. In worship a proper order provides worshipers the means by which and through which to express their faith freely. Devoid of a meaningful order, worship disintegrates into a series of unrelated individual impulses that make little sense. Spontaneity becomes enslaving rather than enriching.

By definition, Christian worship is ordered. Paul writes of the divine will for worship, "All things should be done decently and in order" (1 Cor. 14:40). By definition, Christian worship is free. The same apostle writes, "Do not quench the Spirit" (1 Thess. 5:19). Worship takes place within a tension created by these two definitions—between order (that can become formalism) and freedom (that can become formless chaos).

In worship an appreciation for freedom causes a gratitude for order because order keeps free expressions responsible. Worship requires freedom. Order is the foundation of freedom. Free expression is a fundamental in meaningful worship. But this freedom is not to be confused with disruptive antinomianism. Under God, the truest work of freedom gives order to life and to worship.

Even Free Churches acknowledge the authority of certain forms. Among Baptists, for example, people who prize freedom, authoritative worship forms can be found. At the very heart of Baptist convictions is an insistence on one form, and one form only, of baptism—the immersion of a believer.

From a Baptist writer comes the interesting suggestion that order should characterize what is done in worship as freedom should characterize what is said.[6] Stephen Winward finds this principle in the New Testament and the earliest postbiblical accounts of Christian worship. In relation to the Lord's Supper, for instance, freedom in worship does not justify an alteration of what happened in the upper room. The form of the Lord's Supper is set. Yet within that form worshipers find plenty of freedom for contemporary expressions. From time to time, words and emotions vary considerably in Communion, but the form of the Supper remains the same.

Both order and freedom serve worshipers and work best when people are not conscious of either. Caught up in the adoration of God and determined to make a worthy offering to God, worshipers are grateful for a meaningful order that guides them toward the realization of their purpose and for a liberty which encourages their honest expressions and allows their spirits to soar. But if asked about the nature of that order and the specific provisions of freedom present, worshipers would, no doubt, be bewildered. Neither order nor freedom has been the object of their focus. Their sights have been, and are, set on God.

The Necessity of Understanding

Worship readily acknowledges mystery and bows before it. However, what is said and done in worship should not mystify worshipers. Shared understanding is an essential ingredient in the type of worship commended by the New Testament. Word forms suggest a fundamental truth. Only when *common* understanding exists can there be *communion* and thus *community*. A community of worshipers requires communion with God that is marked by a common understanding of the words, actions, and symbols involved.

Shared meanings for every aspect of a service are prerequisites to corporate worship. The alternative is individuals sitting together in a place of worship but engaging in private devotions in isolation from one another. That alternative does not qualify as corporate worship. The worship of a community of faith is a unified expression, not a composite of individual expressions. Such oneness in voice and action is possible only when worshipers share a common understanding of the experience and its constituent parts.

Histories of worship document the emergence of new forms of worship in every century. The essential nature of God has not changed, but the nature of certain expressions of God has been reshaped. Only when worship is dynamic, when changes that enhance meaning occur, can a broad-based understanding of worship be assured and the integrity of worship maintained. Continuing worship with words, phrases, actions, gestures, and symbols that have lost their meaning is an exercise in futility.

Discretion is important. Obviously, some aspects of worship cannot change (and the activity around them still be considered worship). God is both transcendent and immanent. Jesus is Savior and Lord. The Holy Spirit counsels, comforts, and encourages. A sacrifice of praise is basic. Confession is mandatory. Commitment is essential. These are givens. Where an understanding of these worship-related truths is absent, change will not help. Innovation is out of order. Instruction, reorientation, and direction are needed. The basic content of Christian worship cannot be altered without the nature of worship itself being destroyed.

The manner in which God is addressed, Christ is exalted, and the Spirit celebrated can change, however. Words of confession in one generation may not adequately convey the penitence of people in another generation. If persons do not find meaning in speaking to God by means of words from a sixteenth-century English vocabulary, new forms of communication are in order. "Hast" can become "has" and "wast" can become "was" without destroying the sanctity of worship or offending the holiness of God. Commitment in worship is not negotiable. However, an individual may as readily (and acceptably) blurt out to God, "Here's my life!" as more formally state, "Thou knowest O God my interest in living as Thy servant."

In the entire history of worship, few reforms approach the magnitude of those instituted by the Roman Catholic Church in the years since the Second Vatican Council. At the heart of the monumental changes in that fellowship has been a relentless drive toward common understanding—worshipers understanding the Bible and understanding worship. In service to that objective, Latin was dropped as the official language of worship and priests began to read, to preach, and to pray in the language of the people to whom they minister.

What an example! A lack of understanding of the words and actions of worship is a problem anywhere, whether or not a foreign language is spoken. Such a situation demands reform. We must make every effort to be certain that people understand and correctly interpret the meaning of worship. Only then can worship be authentic because only then can worshipers be united in their offerings.

An insistence on shared understanding in worship is concerned with more than relevance and irrelevance, familiarity and strangeness. At stake is the question of what best communicates the gospel to people and expresses the worship of these people to God. In answering that basic inquiry, the primary source to be consulted is theology, not psychology or aesthetics. People must understand the components of worship in order to participate meaningfully in worship. And that understanding must have theological integrity to assure expressions of worship with which God is pleased.

The Centrality of Praise

Praise dominates biblical worship. Both Testaments resound with exclamations of praise and requests of praise. Worship without praise is unthinkable.

"But how?" "How can we offer praise to God? Look at our world. People are starving. Drugs are destroying whole communities and ruining (if not killing) individuals. Violence creates a permanent fear. In our own congregations people are grieving over lost relatives, worrying about a lack of finances, and struggling with other incredible difficulties. Praise seems out of place. Praise seems possible only if we shut our eyes and play like everything is all right. How can we praise God when things are such a mess?" Excellent question.

Praise is a response to God which grows out of the *content* of faith rather than the *context* of faith. Praise is a product of understanding the nature of God, not looking around in the world. Praise is born of a vision of God's sovereignty rather than a study of human difficulties. But praise is not a form of denial or an expression of escapist blindness.

Praise fills the Psalms. So does reality. The twenty-second Psalm is an example of realistic praise.

An outcry comes first. With words drenched in pathos, words that Jesus used to express His agony while on the cross, the writer shouts to the heavens, "My God, my God, why hast thou forsaken me? Why art thou so far from helping me, from the words of my groaning?" (v. 1) What congregation does not contain people who readily identify with these questions and the sentiment behind them? A woman with a spouse in an intensive care unit of a local hospital, a family whose daughter is confined to a drug rehabilitation center, and a recent graduate who has been fired from his first job all know a sense of solitude and struggle with thoughts of forsakenness. That is how the psalm begins. But that is not how the psalm ends.

Before he is finished speaking to God, the psalmist declares, "In the midst of the congregation I will praise thee" (v. 22) and observes, "Those who seek him shall praise the Lord!" (v. 26). What has happened? Are these last words misplaced? Has the psalmist lost his mind? No. The psalm is of one piece. Not even life-threatening difficulties can silence praise for God. God is praised because God merits praise regardless of the situation out of which the praise is offered.

One evening in Pineville, Kentucky, I had the great joy of listening to a dramatic recitation of the biblical text of Job while watching the faces, painted like stained-glass windows, of the people speaking. That night in the hills of Eastern Kentucky I learned something important about praise. After rhythmically detailing the demise of Job and the horrors with which he had to contend, the chorus came to the confession of the sufferer. The pace of the actors' words slowed noticeably. No smiles were apparent. Every syllable of every word was spoken with great effort. "The Lord gave, and the Lord has taken away; bl... bless... (The term seemed to stick in the throats of the readers. They seemed unsure that they could voice the word *blessed*. But they did.)... bless sed be the name of the Lord." The praise did not come easily, but it did come.

Words of praise do not always flow from one's lips like a gushing stream. They may falter and trickle toward expression. Sometimes to speak the word *blessed* before God requires every ounce of willpower and effort a person has. That is all right. God accepts praise offered amid great stress with no smiles even as blessings born of peace and spoken amid convulsive laughter.

Praise is not an irresponsible disregard for problems. Praise arises amid problems (e.g., 1 Pet. 4:11; Rev. 19:7). The basis of praise is the nature of God as revealed in the good news of the gospel. An absence of praise indicates the lack of a vision of God. Worship requires both. Worship envisions God and expresses praise.

All Worship Should Exhibit a Dignity in Expression that Complements the Holiness of God

What happens in worship? What really takes place every time people worship God? We dare to approach God Almighty. We speak to the One whose words set the world in motion and made possible our redemption. Think of that! We stand before the Sovereign of the universe, the Righteous Judge of human nature, the Lover of all nations, the Savior of all people. Conscious of the magnitude of an act of worship, we must not stumble into the divine presence thoughtlessly, casually glide through activities which, when done correctly, give God pleasure, or address God as if speaking to a newspaper salesperson or to a colleague seated across a desk from us.

Have we lost a healthy sense of fear and trembling in the presence of the Holy God? Who do we think we are, ambling into the presence of God and casually accepting responsibility for divinely ordained ministry? Where are the carefully framed words and studiously dramatized acts which convey the eternal importance of the One in whose name we gather? Does God not deserve better from us than anyone else—or everything else? Does God not merit our best?

Every word and act in worship constitutes a witness about God as well as an offering to God. The manner in which God is worshiped is a message about how God is perceived, how God's holiness is to be reverenced and approached. Of concern in worship, then, is not only giving to God what is best, what God deserves, what is consistent with God's nature, but giving to God that which most accurately reveals the nature of God to others.

People will have difficulty understanding that God's Being requires reverence if they know worship services that are not reverent. Similarly, if people participate in worship services that reflect no careful preparation and serious execution they will not grasp that God is interested in their lives. When prayers are offered perfunctorily, hymns are sung routinely, sermons are preached "off the cuff," and both confessions of sin and faith are regularly ignored, the message conveyed is that God doesn't care, that God is not concerned with the integrity of worship. How dishonorable to God! What a disservice to people interested in a right relationship with God!

When prophets denounced cultic actions in the Old Testament, they were challenging the discrepancy that had developed between the nature of divine worship and the nature of God. The character of God was not accurately disclosed in people's worship of God. Mindless routines in worship indicated the existence of a god who can be satisfied with form without substance. An absence of ethical actions in the lives of the worshipers suggested a god interested only in belief and unconcerned with behavior. A passion for religious rituals wed to a disinterest in social justice implied a divinity concerned exclusively with the spiritual nature of people.

God would not have it. The one true God! God's Word was voiced through God's prophets. "Come to Bethel [a place of worship], and transgress" (Amos 4:4)! "My people are destroyed for lack of knowledge.... You have forgotten the law of your God" (Hos. 4:6). "They shall not pour out libations of wine to the Lord; and they shall not please him with their sacrifices" (9:4). "Rend your hearts and not your garments" (Joel 2:13). "Woe to those ... who sing idle songs" (Amos 6:4-5).

The applications of this principle change with times and places, but the principle remains the same. Acceptable worship in God's sight is worship that truthfully reveals the nature of God in people's sight.

Occasionally, a misguided concern for understanding, relevance, and witness is the culprit behind defective worship. Current questions about music styles appropriate for worship demonstrate the issue. In recent years, "Christian music" has appeared. Musical forms of a secular origin are appropriated as media for sacred truths. Thus, Christian musicians produce works which are acceptable to radio stations that play only popular music and are suitable for inclusion in rock concerts. Their rationale is to give a secular witness for Christ. Through their music, these performers voice a testimony about Jesus in settings where religious rhetoric is usually mocked. The motivation and intention are admirable. But is this music appropriate in corporate worship?

Materials that are suitable for a broadcast over the public air waves and materials that are appropriate as corporate expressions of the worship of God within a church may be different. In some instances, music which conveys a much-needed Christian witness in a secular setting can hinder and disrupt rather than help and contribute to the kind of congregational worship which complements the nature of God.

The same principle applies to sermons, readings, and all other ingredients in public worship. We ought to examine every potential act of worship—What does this lead people to believe about God? Is the holy nature of God reverenced or offended by this word or act? How secular can the medium of a religious message become without the medium diluting the message? Can a religious word, song, or act become so caught up in a nonreligious form that its religious dimension is completely obscured? Even spiritually motivated efforts to be relevant to society, yet which are sure to be an affront to the dignity of God, have no place in worship.

The apostle Paul seems amazingly tolerant of the presence of spiritual excesses in people's lives. However, Paul expressly forbids demonstrations of such excesses in public worship. A disorganized, difficult-to-understand, haphazard service of worship does not complement the nature of God and accurately communicate the divine will for order, truth, and community.

What is appropriate in private worship is not identical with what belongs in corporate worship. In privacy, little attention may be given to the words and gestures of worship. Honest expression is the goal. However, public worship is different. In corporate worship, individual preferences and idiosyncracies have to be subjected to communal needs. The likes and dislikes of a person become subservient to the communication of fundamental truths about the nature of Almighty God within the community of worshipers.

Michael Marshall provides an excellent principle by which we can make decisions about appropriate acts of worship: "Informal, then, but never trivial; supernatural, but never unnatural; tailored for the immediate but never trapped in the relevant and the banal."[7] Whom we worship is far more important than how we worship.[8] But how we worship must clearly depict the nature of the God whom we worship.

All Worship Should Embrace a Variety of Forms Sufficient to Provide for the Diversity of Human Needs

Failure to provide for variety in worship represents a blatant disregard for human diversity. To stifle variety in worship is to display a sad insensitivity to the multiple dynamics of worship which is to rob some people of the possibility of meaningful worship.

Few, if any, worshiping congregations can claim a true homogeneity among their members. Most fellowships of worshipers consist of people who are vastly different from each other. Emotional needs are diverse. Some people come to worship needing to laugh and to celebrate while others arrive on the verge of an outburst of sobbing and a display of tears. Almost always worship includes persons needing comfort and others hoping for a stirring challenge. Also, the levels of spiritual maturity among worshipers vary significantly. One person wants no more than to be fed by the preacher and inspired by the choir. Another is adamant about involvement in every part of the service. Some individuals seek a corporate service filled with ringing declarations of judgment, hoping that a sense of guilt will be a proper penance for whatever caused the guilt. Others long to hear assurances of God's love, forgiveness, and acceptance.

Worshipers have different personalities. A take-charge person sings loudly and makes an offering with a flair. A more reserved individual desires to participate in worship quietly and unobtrusively. Members of one family can hardly wait for a bombastic blast of praise from the organ. Seated on the same pew with them, though, is a fellow who thinks such an instrumental sound is distasteful and totally out of place.

Though no one service can be expected to provide adequately for the needs of everyone, a composite of services—worship experiences that take place over the course of a month—should include numerous details planned to meet a variety of needs. Personal tastes and abilities, even as various levels of spiritual maturity, are important factors. However, the first two principles cannot be set aside. Worship should always be biblical and fundamentally consistent with God's nature.

New Testament worship was characterized by much greater variety than can be found in the experiences of most churches today. A basic structure of worship persisted, but within that structure great variety developed.

Given the diversity in every gathering for worship, a service of worship should seldom be constructed entirely around one theme. Of course, by its very nature, worship is multifaceted, embracing many themes, moods, words, and actions. In all likelihood, every congregation contains at least one person in need of every facet of worship. For one person worship becomes most full during the hymn of praise, while for another the confession of sins is an avenue into the presence of God. Hurting people find help during a prayer of intercession, while folks buoyant with joy find release in a litany of thanksgiving. Pilgrims in need of instruction can be fed by the sermon. Persons ready to declare their faith can respond to the invitation. Individuals who crave quiet communion cherish moments of silence as a time to make their offerings.

Christian worship is an experience big enough to include all kinds of people with all kinds of needs. Limits do exist, however. Variety in worship is appropriate as a means of involving as many people as possible in the praise of God. Variety as a product of human selfishness is an entirely different matter.

Immature perceptions of God's nature and inadequate understandings of divine worship must not be allowed to dictate worship practices. Any activity which seeks to reduce God to human categories and to restrict the worship of God to self-defined conditions for feeling good is not worship. How people feel about the worship of God and judge the nature of God are not nearly so important as how God feels about people's worship and how God judges everybody.

Worship does not have to meet the demands of spiritual immaturity. Neither is it to placate the selfish desires of people who seek God as an equal or seek to have God perform for their pleasure. A major responsibility of any worship leader is to compassionately nudge people toward a proper adoration of God and a suitable confession before God while stringently guarding against all attempts to confine God to the models of certain mental images, to restrict God's Spirit to the possibilities of only one set of emotions, or to treat God as the boy next door or a doting Jewish mother.

Conclusion

Frankly, all of my suggestions about worship are offered with a degree of hesitancy and a large dose of humility. I do not presume to know the mind of God so well that I can determine what gives God pleasure. At the same time, I cannot tell people what is and what is not meaningful worship for them. At best, all I can do is point to certain guiding principles about worship that are available to everyone in the Scriptures.

The Bible leaves no doubt about the conclusion of worship that is indicative of the best experience of worship. It is not: "What a terrific sermon"; "The music today was outstanding"; "I am so pleased with the attendance this morning"; or "I thought the altar flowers were unusually pretty." Most desirable is the comment, "I have been in the presence of God."

When people experience God's presence, worship does not conclude when the benediction is spoken. Rather, people move from the sanctuary into the world with a strong sense of the presence of God, and thus live every day so that all of their words and actions have about them the character of worship—each is a form of devotion of God.

14
Providing Meaningful Worship
"That we fail not man nor Thee!"

An experience as a visiting preacher in a nearby church led me to recognize the reality of irrelevance in many experiences of corporate worship. I arrived at the church office early so as to make an acquaintance with someone and to look over the order of worship planned for the morning service. The chairman of the deacons greeted me and escorted me to a hall just outside an entrance to the sanctuary. Waiting for the arrival of the choir, we stood and talked.

This man immediately related to me the difficulties that had deeply disturbed his community in the past five days. An older woman, a respected saint, had decided to sell her homeplace and move to a nursing facility. Friends assisted her. On the afternoon of her arrival at the new dwelling place, the woman died. The deacon leader told me he planned to visit the woman's family members and friends just after the worship service. Continuing to talk, the man then related an account of a young man in the community who had just learned that he was the victim of a terminal disease. The people in the community were hurting.

Time passed quickly as I listened to the deacon talk. But before I realized it, members of the choir arrived. I abruptly ended the conversation in order to enter the sanctuary with the choir and take my appointed seat on the platform. Once everyone was appropriately positioned, the choir burst into song. Phrases from the text which they presented stuck in my psyche like splinters in the quick of a finger. Loudly they asserted, "Surely the Lord is in this place." Then they referred to hearing the "rustling of angels' wings." The musical piece concluded with a reference to the "glory on each face."

Suddenly I wanted to scream. "Wait. This is not the right piece of music for this moment. These folks are upset. We do not have to hide our hurts or, worse still, ignore them to be acceptable to God. God understands us. It is all right if everything in our lives is not well." I hurriedly scanned the faces of the people in the congregation to identify reactions to what was being sung. I did not see "glory on each face." Not a single look even came close. Actually, most of the people were expressionless. While the choir sang, one couple slipped into the sanctuary late. Three people yawned.

"So this is Christian worship!" I mumbled to myself. "What about the pain of these people? Why does the music not tell them that God understands their grief and anxiety? If that message is not in the music, why does one of the ministers present not speak it? How does it make these people feel to hear that everything is going great—even angels are present—when they are feeling rotten?" Like never before, I could see how worship can seem totally irrelevant.

Sensitivity while planning worship and exercising flexibility in worship can promote genuine helpfulness in worship. But that takes work. Careful preparation for worship is necessary if worship is to be worthy of the nature of God and beneficial in relation to the needs of the worshipers.

Certain principles can be used in planning meaningful worship experiences. First, though, consideration should be given to the basic factors—controllable and uncontrollable, external and internal—that influence worship.

Basic Factors that Influence Worship

Every worship experience is unique. Though all services of worship share things in common, each service or worship is influenced by certain particulars. The congregational worship of God takes place at a specific time in a definable place among particular people. In every instance, the nature of a worship experience is affected significantly by variations in these ingredients. Planners for worship who fail to take into account the uniqueness of a service sabotage its potential as a medium for a meaningful spiritual experience.

Conscientious planning for a worship service requires an informed awareness of the factors which will most affect it. The site of the service is of no little consequence. A similar significance belongs to the time of the event. Finally, understanding the nature and needs of the members of a congregation is crucial.[1]

Location

Public worship is possible almost any place. However, the character of worship is unlikely to be identical in every place. Inevitably, the nature of the place where people convene to worship has an impact to some extent on the spirit, if not the content, of the worship that occurs there.[2]

Neither the order, the mood, nor the media for worship will be the same when people are outdoors standing around a bonfire as when inside seated in a sanctuary traditionally furnished. Similarly, expressions of worship from persons who meet in a hospital chapel will differ from those of individuals who gather in the chapel of a local church. Public worship convened in a cemetery beside an open grave will be much different from that which occurs in a lakeside amphitheater.

When congregational worship takes place inside a building, the architecture of the structure can be an important factor in the kind of service that occurs there. Often an emphasis on informal fellowship between members of the congregation dominates worship in a box-like room with a low ceiling. Conversely, in spacious cathedrals with vaulted arches and stained-glass windows a sense of transcendence pervades the worship experience. Entering an auditorium (by structural design as well as by verbal description) for worship suggests an experience centered around the spoken words of those "up front." Members of the congregation are auditors. By way of contrast, taking a seat in a sanctuary for worship tends to indicate the need for personal involvement in a service that will attempt to use and appeal to all of the senses.

Taking seriously the place of worship means giving attention to practical concerns which can have profound spiritual significance for the worshipers. An acoustical engineer told me an astounding story that makes this point dramatically.

A congregation invited this engineer to study their worship center in order to determine the needs to be met by the installation of a new sound magnification system. During his analysis of that building, my friend discovered an area within it that was practically "dead" acoustically. He determined that persons who sat in the ten or so pews in that part of the worship center heard only distorted sounds at best and most likely missed many sounds completely. The engineer's comment to me was, "Just think, for more than ten years, the people who have gathered for worship in the problem-plagued part of that building have not heard a clear presentation of the gospel."

An ability to see, hear, and feel what is taking place around them is always affected by where people have gathered. Whether individuals have a sense of inclusiveness or isolation, warmth or distance, is partially dependent upon the character of the place in which they meet. When these factors are considered in relation to a congregation's worship of God, seemingly common, practical concerns become important spiritual issues. Logistics and acoustics take on religious significance.

Worship planners do well to review periodically certain questions related to the places in which public worship occurs. Does the nature of the worship place make people self-conscious or God-conscious? Does the setting for worship encourage or hinder congregational participation through singing and readings? Within the worship center, can the prayers of individual members of the congregation be heard by other worshipers without the use of sound magnification? Are all the people in the sanctuary able to see the baptistry and to focus on the activities which take place around the table from which the Lord's Supper is served?

Please do not misunderstand. Place is important. However, difficulties which hinder meaningful worship in a specific place do not completely destroy the possibilities of such worship being experienced there. Adverse factors simply need to be recognized and addressed. After all, in the first century, profound congregational worship took place in the catacombs under Rome. During World War II, many European congregations worshiped while meeting in the bombed-out ruins of former church buildings or while constantly moving to different locations to avoid bombings.

Historical Moment

Another factor that exerts major influence on the substance and spirit of congregational worship is the time in which the worship occurs. The moment of worship significantly determines the needs and expectations, as well as the contributions, which people bring to an occasion for worship.

People gather for worship fully conscious of legal holidays and periods of unusual civil importance. John Carlton enjoyed telling of a minister who structured a worship service around the text for his sermon on Jezebel. At the appointed hour for worship, after taking his seat on the platform, the minister realized that this Sunday was being observed as Mother's Day.

On the Sunday prior to Thanksgiving Day or in a special service of worship on that national holiday, the dominant emphases are apt to be different from those of a Sunday worship experience in which recently deceased family members are remembered as a part of a Memorial Day weekend. A New Year's Eve service of prayers, supplications, and Communion allows worshipers to interact with God in a manner distinctively different from the celebrative spirit that pervades a service of worship on a day designated for commemorations of a nation's liberation and independence.

Important also in worship planning is an awareness of the special periods and days of the Christian year.[3] Historically, congregations of believers in the Free Church tradition have tended to view the Christian calendar with suspicion (often seeing it as a "high-church" phenomenon, fraught with the perils of ritualism). Little to no deference has been given to the basic emphases of the Christian year. That is changing.

For years, congregations have observed Christmas and Easter. More and more worshiping fellowships within the Free Church tradition are discovering the powerful potential in other special emphases during the Christian year. The Christian calendar provides a means of annually reliving the ministry of Christ and keeping in touch with everything that matters in the history of salvation.[4]

I know firsthand the value of a congregation's pilgrimage through the four Sundays of Advent. Not only is the celebration of Christmas greatly enhanced by this journey of worship, the important spiritual gifts of memory, patience, promises, and hope are better understood and exercised. Similarly, corporate worship services which take seriously the various aspects of Jesus' passion increase people's capacity for a God-honoring celebration of Jesus' resurrection. Holy Week services bring into focus dimensions of discipleship that are missed completely by a simple leap from Palm Sunday to Easter. Worship services which take seriously the truths of Maundy Thursday and Good Friday please God because they challenge a greater commitment and a more comprehensive ministry of compassion among the people of God. I have been delighted to see how congregational worship oriented to the Christian festival of Pentecost can sensitize people to the presence, power, and ministry of the Holy Spirit in a manner that is helpful to the community of faith and acceptable in the sight of God.

Reviewing orders of worship from a congregation which I served as pastor, I made an interesting discovery. My pastoral predecessor had been a loyal fan of serial preaching. One September he embarked upon a series of sermons from the Gospel of Matthew. Nearly four months later, on the Sunday prior to Christmas, his homiletical journey brought him to the resurrection narratives.

People came to worship ready to join exuberantly in the singing of "Joy to the World" because of Christ's birth, but they were denied that opportunity because of their pastor's relentless devotion to a preaching plan. Of course, the resurrection narratives deserved attention. Actually, these texts inspire an exultant joy in worship also. But this was not the Sunday for a focus on the resurrection.

Dates on the Christian calendar do (and should) impact decisions about the nature of worship experiences. For example, the mood of worship on Good Friday cannot appropriately be the same as that of worship on the previous Palm Sunday. Emphases and expressions of worship on the first Sunday of Advent are usually much more muted and reflective than those more festive and celebrative ones on the fourth Sunday of Advent, the Lord's Day just prior to Christmas Day.

Calendars do not tell the whole story of the historical moment though. Often events in the news determine the concerns that dominate people's lives at a specific time. Worship planners who ignore this fact jeopardize the possibility of meaningful worship.

Traditionally, the Sunday prior to Thanksgiving Day is a time for praise and expressions of gratitude of God in congregational worship. However, I remember making my way to worship and encountering other worshipers on the Sunday following the assassination of the President of the United States. Heaviness, not happiness, filled people's hearts. Mourning had replaced thanksgiving. Words of celebration fell silent as prayers of intercession were voiced. Had it been otherwise, the worship of God would have been scandalized.

The historical moment is as varied as a crisis in the Middle East, an activation of military forces in a war zone, a critical downturn in the economy, a destructive fire in the community, the tragedy of widespread destruction resulting from a killer tornado, the closing of a major industry in the city causing the loss of hundreds of jobs that affect the church family, or a significant achievement by officials in the local government. Public worship is touched by all such moments.

Christian worship is incarnational. It is patterned after the example of the One in whose name it is convened. Thus, meaningful worship always takes into consideration the historical moment in which it happens.

Spiritual Maturity

Place and time are external, nonpersonal factors that influence public worship. Internal considerations important to worship planning are personal in nature.

The possibilities of a worship service and the quality of what transpires within it are directly related to the spiritual maturity of the people involved as worshipers. A holistic experience of worship is virtually impossible among persons with only a childish (not childlike) faith.

For their work to be effective, planners of worship have to take into account the level of spiritual maturity which exists among the people who will be involved in worship. Certainly growth can occur and experiences of worship can move toward greater fullness. But if a service of worship is based upon a presupposition that worshipers are at one level of spiritual maturity and in reality most are more immature than that, the result is likely to be frustration at best or negative reactions at worst.

Whether the following story is real or apocryphal, I do not know. But the truth involved is real.

At the beginning of the Christmas holidays one year, when Paul Tillich was teaching in New York City, the renowned lecturer went downtown to worship with a small congregation in a storefront church. The pastor was one of Tillich's students. Tillich listened with dismay as the young preacher related the Christmas story to a beleaguered group of uneducated people using the language of the lecture hall. He spoke eloquently of how "the divine transcendent had become immanent." After the service ended, the brilliant teacher, with tears in his eyes, approached his student. Tillich said, "Son, just tell them that God became a man in Jesus of Nazareth." Paul Tillich understood the importance of planning the content of worship while keeping in mind the spiritual maturity of the worshipers.

Piety is a good word to employ in this discussion—a suitable synonym for spirituality. The nature of a person's relationship with God and the capacity of a person for fellowship with God are concerns of piety that impact an experience of corporate worship. Craig Douglas Erickson describes piety as "that quality of openness of God that is itself a gift of the Spirit of God."[5]

People's perceptions of God are of fundamental importance in the development of their worship of God. If people think of God primarily as a Judge, their worship will tend to be somber and penitential in nature. In both words and music, leaders of worship will take aim at correcting the worshipers. A confrontational, at times almost negative, spirit may prevail. If God is viewed as "the man upstairs," or a kind of "heavenly buddy," worship may be very informal, almost casual in nature. Efforts will be made to address God in the same manner in which one would speak to a special friend. Colloquialisms seem more holy than formal expressions. Where the mystery of the Divine Being dominates people's understanding of God, worship is usually filled with awe, and remarks are made with reverence. An overwhelming sense of the majesty of God produces worship experiences that involve stately expressions of adoration offered in genuine humility. Among people who recognize God primarily as the Redeemer, worship tends to be inclusive, energizing, encouraging, and festive.

Most dangerous and threatening to meaningful worship are partial understandings or misunderstandings of God which bear the claims of accuracy and wholeness. For Christian worship to occur, worship must be directed to the God revealed in Jesus Christ.

Piety is a dynamic concept, not a static one. Authentic spirituality contains a constant push toward greater maturity. Meaningful worship reflects this impulse. Conversely, spirituality is stifled and meaningful worship is hindered when growth-oriented changes are resisted by people who declare, "What has been good enough in the past is sufficient for the present. We do not intend to change!" Achieving the heights of worship joyfully requires continued growth spiritually—growth toward a Christ-like piety.

Personal Circumstances

Far more subjective in nature and exceedingly more difficult to recognize, but equally influential on public worship, are the personal circumstances of the worshipers. At issue here are emotions and concerns unique to the people in one congregation alone, attitudes and interests that distinguish one group of worshipers from all other worshipers, even from others in the same neighborhood or town.

Tragedies which rock a church fellowship cannot be neatly set aside for corporate worship. Even if that were possible, such a segmentation of life is inappropriate in an experience that is intended to bring all of life before God. When members of a congregation are preoccupied with the death of one of their leaders, the breakup of a prominent family in their fellowship, a fight between two people who are friends with almost everyone, or a widening split over the church budget, their worship is affected by that reality. In the face of such adversities, worship does not have to be affected adversely. Actually, it can be enhanced. However, that requires thoroughgoing honesty and careful planning. Sincere confessions and prayerful intercessions are always acceptable to God. Each of these acts is a possible medium of worshiping God that can correct and strengthen the spirituality of the people involved.

Of course, personal circumstances can be filled with joy as well as sadness, gratitude as well as grief, success as well as failure. When people meet for worship needing to give voice to happiness, desiring to state declarations of praise, and seeking other ways in which to set before God their joy, leaders of worship best make provisions for these expressions. Otherwise, the experience will be more superficial than real, more fake than authentic. God desires worship laced with honesty.

Personal circumstances, like piety, are more difficult to determine in large congregations than in small ones. An awareness of that reality is important as worship is planned for large congregations. An obvious recognition of, if not provisions for actual expressions of, the wide range of emotions present among worshipers is beneficial. In smaller congregations, though, the spirit and content of an entire worship service can be determined as much by the personal circumstances of the people in it as by any other factor of influence on it. Despite the place and time, if the people who meet for worship need to weep or to rejoice, it is important that opportunities be provided for their tears and laughter to be offered to God as gifts of worship.

Essential Principles of Meaningful Worship

Occasionally I am asked to speak or to write on the subject of how to make worship meaningful. I am troubled by assumptions behind those requests. First is the conviction that generally worship is uninteresting. Second is the suggestion that worship can be made interesting by human ingenuity and creativity. Both ideas are as mistaken as they are common.

I am always pleased to address the topic of meaningful worship. However, I work with the assumption that worship *is* meaningful. To explore meaningful worship is to examine worship. Corporate experiences claimed as worship and complained about because of their lack of meaning are misnomers. Authentic worship is always meaningful worship.

Quests for meaning in worship are best served by discovering how to worship with integrity. Determining the nature of true worship is much more important than exploring the ways humans can bring novelty to worship.

Sources of meaning in worship vary. One person is more inclined toward the worship of God when seated in a Gothic cathedral with the sounds of medieval music reflecting off the thick walls and reverberating against the high ceiling. Another person, maybe a next-door neighbor of the first, is best moved to reverence and praise by gathering with friends out-of-doors and singing familiar gospel choruses around a crackling campfire.

Without presuming to know what is most meaningful in worship for every individual, sketching a general understanding of worship that is meaningful for all people is possible. Worship is worship—whether the site is an ornate sanctuary or a rough-hewn retreat center, whether twenty people are present or two thousand, whether musical accompaniment comes from a magnificent pipe organ or a hand-held harmonica. For worship to take place, adherence to certain principles essential to worship must be evident. All concerns for meaning in worship do well to start with a study of these principles.

Meaningful Worship Centers on God

Worship is for God. Only! The chief aim of worship is to please God—whether by adoration and praise, prayer and proclamation, confessions and offerings, thanksgivings and commitment, or by all of these actions combined. In worship, God is more and more recognized as "the only Fact of existence" and "the one Reality." The conviction grows that "God alone matters."[6]

Only God is worthy of worship. If any person, institution (religious or secular), principle, or program becomes the recipient of worship, the result is idolatry. When God is not the center of worship, worship becomes a blasphemous, horrendous sin. Like all sin, if continued without repentance, idolatry plunges life downward. Historians document the depths of depravity to which people fall when God is replaced as the center of worship and life is oriented to an idol.

Any blatant movement toward idolatry will be condemned and stopped in contemporary Christian congregations. Everyone knows that God alone is to be worshiped. Subtlety is the problem. Inspired by "good" motives, committed to right-intentioned actions, and without any consciousness of the severity of what is happening, people begin to nudge God aside in worship because of their fascination with a particular minister, enthusiasm for a certain program, or interest in an institution. Anytime that participants in a worship service are preoccupied with the personal power of a leader, the talents of a musical contributor, the eloquence of a speaker, or the novelty of a program, true worship is jeopardized. Every aspect of every experience of worship—personal, organizational, and ideological—is to direct all attention to God.

Perhaps the greatest threat to worship in most churches is a tendency to *use* worship. Here again subtlety contributes to the difficulty. Goals are good. Motivations are commendable. No one overtly thinks or speaks about *using* worship, but it happens. Personal priorities sometimes cause it: "I'm looking for some answers"; "I just need to feel good again"; "I'm searching for the kind of peace that will help me calm down"; "I need strength for the week ahead." At other times the source is an institutional incentive: "This service can kick off our attendance campaign"; "By way of our worship, we want to make a noticeable impact on this community"; "Maybe through this worship service we can move people to increase their pledges enough to exceed our goal." Nothing is wrong with any of these individual desires or the accomplishment of any of these individual desires or the accomplishment of any of these institutional purposes. But to establish any one of them as an aim in worship is wrong. Worship is not a means to any personal or institutional end. Worship is only for God.

The substance of the dialogue at the heart of worship is salvation history, the mighty acts of God in the world, not how to feel good or raise a budget. Worship resounds with a recital of God's creative and redemptive actions. Individuals and institutions can find great help in what is declared and dramatized in worship. However, those benefits are due to God's gift of revelation, not to the nature of people's quests. In fact, worship occurs only as self-serving goals are set aside so that all attention can be focused on God.

In a classic piece of religious literature, Rudolph Otto describes God as *mysterium tremendum ac fascinans*—a mystery both terrifying and appealing.[7] Little wonder that sincere worship involves paradoxical actions—a sense of need to step back and take off one's shoes, coupled with a desire to rush forward with open arms; a determination to still all of creation in order not to miss the slightest sound or sight of revelation and a will to start speaking so as to confess everything to God; an emergence of awe which borders on fear and a surge of love that is filled with passion.

Worship begins, continues, and concludes with a recognition of the holiness of God. Ancient Hebrews made no provision for the use of superlatives in their language. Thus, often their response to revelations of the worth of God consisted of conscious repetitions: "Holy, holy, holy"; "Hallelujah, hallelujah, hallelujah." Contemporary terminology also falls short of ascribing to God the adoration due the Divine Being. God is without competitors. Divine redemption has no rivals. Distractions in worship cannot be tolerated. Centering on God is the most fundamental action of life. The pattern of the Hebrews bears duplication. Whether by words, actions, or symbols, God is recognized as Saving Love and addressed with unhindered confessions: Holy! Holy! Holy! Lord God of Hosts.

Meaningful Worship Glorifies Christ

Worship that is Christian glorifies Jesus Christ. Followers of Christ gather in the name of Christ (Col. 3:17). Worship is a form of obedience to the teachings of Christ, and disciples of Christ share as participants in the worship of Christ.[8] Worship is an epiphany of Christ.[9]

Christians congregate for worship having seen the glory of God uniquely revealed in the person of Jesus Christ.[10] In Jesus of Nazareth the invisible, incomprehensible, ineffable, eternal God became visible, comprehensible, audible, and historical.[11] Through the life of Jesus, the God of creation was identified as the God of redemption. Christian worship is the grateful response which persons offer to God because of the total work of Christ in the entirety of human experience.

Jesus stands in the grand tradition of Old Testament worship. He represents the highest reaches of that tradition, fulfills what was incomplete in it, and answers the questions left unanswered by it. Michael Marshall helpfully describes this activity, declaring that Jesus is "the size and shape of Christian worship, drawing together all the conflicting strands of insight from Old Testament worship, refining (though never emasculating or falsely spiritualizing) even the earliest and most primitive urges for worship."[12]

When disciples of Christ join together for the worship of God, what transpires should reflect a commitment to Christ and a sensitivity to the presence of Christ. Worship practices with roots in the Old Testament Scriptures remain important. But all of them—praise, prayers, confession, and proclamation—glorify Christ.

Worship in the primitive community of faith was Christocentric to its core. Believers assembled for worship in the name of Jesus, the risen Lord. Their earliest corporate prayer was the jubilant petition "marana-tha"—"Our Lord, come."[13] Pervasive in the worship of these early believers, and completely without precedent in their previous experiences of divine worship, was a joyful celebration of the presence of the risen, living Christ in their midst.

Jesus' life revealed the nature of God. Thus, no detail concerning the person and ministry of Jesus is inconsequential within the worship of a Christian community. The worship of God facilitates important memories of Christ. Subsequently, these memories of Christ strengthen and enhance in other ways the worship of God.

The basic content of a service of Christian worship is a dramatic presentation of the good news of Christ. What is known about God through the revelation of Jesus profoundly affects the nature of the praise and confession, repentance and commitment offered by Christian worshipers. Likewise, the proclamation which occurs in worship is shaped by implications of the incarnation of God in Christ. Integral to every service of Christian worship is an announcement, not a commandment—"This is what God has done in Jesus Christ," not "This is what you must do to be acceptable to God."[14]

With Jesus at the center of every experience of worship, worshipers are prevented from yielding to the temptation to distort worship by escaping into the realm of the secular apart from the sacred or vice versa. As Christ links together heaven and earth, Christ-centered worship joins the sacred and the secular. The involvements and concerns of this world become the substance of worshipful offerings made to God in Jesus' name. The holiness of God and meanings of redemption discovered in worship inspire and direct ministries offered to the world in Jesus' name by worshipers.

"What about competition?" someone asks. "Doesn't this approach to worship place God and Christ in competition with each other for the reception of the praise of creation?" By no means. God was in Christ. As the Son of God, Jesus participated in the worship of God. All attempts to separate the two Beings must be corrected by a realization of their theological union.

A meaningful Christian worship service harmonies completely the theocentric and Christocentric elements of worship. To glorify Christ is to please God. To submit to God in worship is to focus on Christ and to seek to magnify His Name.

Meaningful Worship Involves People

Christianity is faith which moves individuals to social interaction—nurturing interpersonal fellowships, inspiring corporate gatherings, and causing communal celebrations. Christian worship is a group experience in which every person is expected to participate. Worship is weakened when all members of a congregation are not actively involved.

More is at stake than keeping people interested. Worship is a reenactment of the drama of redemption. All of the redeemed are in the drama. Each time the story of salvation is told in worship, every one of God's people needs to be involved in the presentation. How can worship convey the good news of people's participation in the life of Christ if worship itself does not allow the full participation of all of Christ's disciples? The medium must be consistent with its message.

Christian redemption is for everybody. God loves the world

and desires fellowship with every person in the world through Christ. The praise of God prompted by the reality of redemption is for all of the redeemed. Every person is capable of making an acceptable offering of thanks to God. Life in Christ, the life of faith, knows no elite. Each individual has the same access to communion with Christ as every other individual. Every disciple of Christ is called to proclaim the gospel. No group of individuals can be chosen to herald the good news of Christ in place of all other people. Authentic worship complements and reinforces these theological truths. True worship involves people—a lot of people; every person in a given service.

Worship is not a spectator event. A few persons cannot "put on" a service of worship for other persons. Praise and confession are communal acts. Writing against the backdrop of the corporate nature of early Christianity, Elton Trueblood tags as "the greatest single weakness of the contemporary Christian Church" the lack of involvement on the part of most members and, "what is worse," the fact that they "do not think it strange that they are not" involved.[15] Pointing to the general participation of all believers in New Testament worship (2 Cor. 14:26-33; Col. 3:16), Trueblood questions the credibility of an assumption that God inspires one person to speak fifty-two times a year and other members of a church are never so inspired.[16] Worship has no auditors or observers. "All are involved."[17]

For some reason, predominantly black congregations have grasped this truth and implemented it in corporate worship in a manner uncharacteristic of the worship of white Christians. Generally, in black congregations a partnership exists between worship leaders and all of the people present in worship. Worship is filled with physical movements and oral confessions among everyone present. Even during the delivery of a sermon, a preacher will often say to the congregation, "I need your help." People respond with supportive prayers offered in silence and encouraging comments spoken aloud.

My own memories of numerous experiences of worship with black brothers and sisters in Christ form a rich resource for understanding the dynamic nature of real corporate worship. I recall an occasion on which I was preaching in a black church. A young man suddenly said aloud, "Oh, I needed that! Thank you God." What a tremendous contribution to the proclamation of the gospel—to know from a person's confession, to know even while preaching, that God is using what is being said and done in the cause of divine redemption.

A consensus about worship exists in most black congregations. Everyone has a personal responsibility to be involved in every act of the service. Participation can come by way of a prayer, a specific action, a spoken word, or through all of these. That consensus is biblically based and worthy of widespread emulation.

Worship services in black churches typically contain certain comments and questions voiced by members of the worshiping body: "Praise Jesus"; "Tell it like it is"; "Well? Well!"; "All right"; "That's it"; "Speak the truth"; "Tell us"; "Speak to us, God." That is liturgy. Those comments consist of mutually understandable and acceptable words which every individual in worship can speak and by which the unity of a worshiping community can be formed.

What creates this unity? The answer to that question defines the liturgy. Every community of faith needs commonly understood hymns, words, actions, and symbols through which all members of the fellowship can offer worship to God.

Meaningful Worship Expresses Praise

More on praise? Yes. Has not praise already received enough attention? Impossible.

Praise is "the hallmark of Christian existence," a "litmus test in decisions about whether or not a person's loyalty is to God."[18] The roots of that truth run deep into the theological soil of Old Testament faith. Ancient Hebrews equated praise with life. A major horror associated with Sheol, the realm of the dead, was the inability of persons there to praise God. To be alive is to be praising God. Not to offer praise to God is to be "as good as dead."[19]

Truth about the priority of praise grew to full flower in the New Testament. Praise pervaded the primitive community of faith, giving it an identity and a direction for ministry. God's people, disciples of God's Son, were people filled with praise. Showing forth God's praise to the whole world was most prominent among their responsibilities. But that duty was a pleasure.

Verbs in the past tense can be set aside. Praise remains a (no, *the*) priority for the people of God. What other fellowship in the world assembles for the expressed purpose of praising God? What other body is committed to the constancy of praise regardless of the variables of its context? What other people can retain a spirit of praise in their hearts and speak words of praise from their lips whether going to a nursery or to a cemetery, enduring bondage or relishing freedom, laughing or crying? None! Praise is synonymous with God's people. "The church gains its identity by the act of praise, by celebrating the story of Israel and Jesus."[20] The ministry of the church is service to people in need performed with praise and a gift to God as an offering of praise.

T. S. Eliot's drama *Murder in the Cathedral* tells the story of the murder of Thomas Becket, the archbishop of Canterbury. Naturally, the people in that little English parish were stunned and deeply saddened by the death of their beloved leader. But these people were Christians. This tragedy touched them at the deepest part of their beings and, like no other experience, clarified their true nature. And what was that? What was to be found at the deepest level of their existence? What was the product of their faith? Praise!

As the people grieve over Becket's death, their grief is mingled with praise. A chorus of mourners speaks to God. Their first words are, "We praise Thee, for Thy glory displayed in all the creatures of the earth." Thanksgiving follows. "Even with the hand to the broom, the back bent in laying the fire, the knee bent in cleaning the hearth, we, the scrubbers and sweepers of Canterbury...thank Thee for Thy mercies of blood, for Thy redemption by blood." With those words, the people's attention turns to the blood of the murdered archbishop and to the realization that God can accomplish great good even when working with tragedy. The chorus prays, "O God, we thank Thee Who hast given such blessing to Canterbury."[21]

God created persons to be living instruments of praise. Praise is every individual's major purpose of living. People are truest to their God-given nature when praising God. No wonder offering praise to God is enjoyable and fulfilling.

A particular Sunday stands out in my mind. Worship that morning had been a riot of joyful praise. Handbells rang throughout the sanctuary. Members of the congregation declared their praise in a variety of ways. My sermon was a biblical elaboration, a pastoral commendation, and a personal exclamation of the jubilant Hebrew word *hallelujah*."

Late that evening I went to a local hospital to visit a friend scheduled for serious surgery the next morning. An examination at the end of the last week had discovered a malignancy that had to be removed immediately. The woman and I talked quietly. She had been in the morning worship service. She immediately commented on the positive nature of that experience. Then we discussed her anxieties and fears, concerns for her family, and the resourcefulness of her faith. Finally, I verbalized a prayer. After saying, "Amen," I looked into the woman's face to say, "Good night." She had tears in her eyes, but she was smiling. And just before I turned to leave, my friend said quietly, but with great intensity, "Hallelujah!"

She knew. She understood. The praise so essential to worship in a sanctuary is not silenced by the intimidating sterility of a hospital room, the need for a biopsy, or a scheduled surgery. For Christians, all of life is laced with praise. Certainly, then, an experience of worship without praise is unthinkable.

Meaningful Worship Communicates the Truth of the Bible

The Bible is a worship book; the basic book of worship. The Bible commends the importance of worship, calls us to participate in worship, teaches us about the nature of worship, and gives us resources for use in worship. But more, the content of the Bible is the substance of the truth to be celebrated in, dramatized by, and communicated through worship.

Multiple readings from the Bible can be most beneficial in worship. A disciplined faithfulness to the Bible in proclamation spares worship from the ignoble trivia of nice little talks, editorial opinions, and locker-room type appeals of spiritualized "Go get 'ums." Confessions of "In my estimation" and "I think" give way to the declaration "Thus says the Lord." Worshipers come to understand that human judgments about the Bible or any specific passage in it are not nearly so important as God's judgment about the human situation conveyed through the divine Word.

Scriptural themes should be woven throughout congregational worship. Traditionally in Free Church worship, concerns for the Bible have been associated almost exclusively with preaching. Great emphasis has been placed on the importance of every sermon serving as an act of biblical proclamation. A worthy emphasis to be sure, but the significance of the Bible in worship relates to the entire experience, not to one part of it alone. Every act of worship must be transparent to the message of biblical revelation. Worship, from beginning to end, is to be both a portrait and a conduit of biblical truth.

Without the Bible, worship will cease to be Christian. So will the church. History documents the sad reality that when the church "deserts the community-forming word of the Bible, it ceases to be distinctively Christian and invents new faiths or begins to be absorbed into one or another cultural philosophy, ideology, or community."[22]

The content of the Bible is *Heilsgeschichte,* salvation history. This is history rich in revelations from God, history in which God has spoken and then acted to fulfill what was declared. Worship set in the context of salvation history and resounding with divine disclosures helps worshipers understand their own history and find their personal mission in it.

Interacting with biblical truths, worshipers discover their identity and nature, their gifts and needs. The Genesis narratives about Adam and Eve are exposés of personal pilgrimages. "That's me. That's how I have treated God. What Adam and Eve did in the garden of Eden, I have done in my office." David's mournful confession becomes personal, "I too have sinned. I long for the cleansing that creates a clean heart." A dialogue between Jesus and Nicodemus brings out our own question, "Dare I approach Jesus in broad daylight? I want the new birth, but I don't understand it." Pondering the Gospel accounts of Jesus' journey to the cross, worshipers have a strange sense of seeing their own faces and hearing their own words among the crowds. "We also have sought to push Jesus out of our world." "I have shouted 'hosanna' in one breath and 'crucify' in the next." "God, I need the forgiveness for which Jesus prayed on behalf of His killers." Then come the resurrection stories, and worshipers realize that the living Christ can join our journeys, too.

Worship devoid of the biblical message leaves worshipers without a clue to their identity, lacking an understanding of the plight of a life without God and missing the promise of what life can be with God. No human words or institutional message can substitute for the word of God. Worship in "the community of the Christian church is formed and sustained by the biblical word or it ceases to be Christian."[23]

Meaningful Worship Encourages Faith

"Salvation is the end of worship—but it is the front end!"[24] Generally, in worship people take on the character of the object worshiped. In Christian worship, individuals are shaped in the image of Christ, over the course of time conforming more and more to the character of God. The beginning of that transformation is important. Actually, the moment of the commitment when a person embraces God's salvation is of inestimable significance. But the beginning is not the end. Running the race is as important as getting to the starting blocks. So is pressing toward the finish. Worship celebrates the beginning of every pilgrimage of faith, then offers constant instruction, inspiration, and encouragement in order for faith to grow all along its journey. Worship and faith are inseparable—faith desiring worship, worship encouraging faith, worshipers taking on the character of God.

At the heart of the gospel is the person of Christ. Acceptance of the gospel means commitment to a life-transforming relationship with Christ. Biblical faith is not a set of propositions to be accepted, gripped, defended, proven, and declared. Rather, it is a relationship of trust to be lived. No part of life is exempt from the influence of total fidelity to Christ. Worship nurtures people's faith relationship to Christ, provides insights into how this faith takes form in response to specific challenges, and encourages continued growth toward spiritual maturity.

In worship, *the* story of faith and individual stories of faith are told and retold. Worshipers caught up in contemporary faith-related struggles learn from the experiences of their predecessors. The holy tales of Daniel amid the lions, the three Hebrews who were tossed into a fire, Paul before the Roman authorities, and John on the island of Patmos bring a redemptive touch to the beleaguered lives of believers struggling with major problems in the present. Revelations of the sufficiency of faith in the past reinforce the church's confidence in the promises of faith and assurance about the power of faith today.

Cognizant of the difficulties in analogies, I continue to find value in imagining the dialogue of worship as a kind of ecclesiastical counterpart to the conversations of the pilgrims in Chaucer's *Canterbury Tales*. Sojourners in faith gather for worship to swap stories of their pilgrimages. Congregating for the glory of God, individuals share with each other detailed accounts of the successes and failures of their spiritual experiences. They celebrate together the joy of obedience. In the wake of their sins, they pray for one another, requesting divine forgiveness even as they assure each other of mutual understanding and the certainty of human forgiveness. Every individual's story is set in the context of God's story. Each pilgrim is encouraged in faith by the Word of God and by the words of brothers and sisters in the family of faith who gather for worship in response to the Word of God.

People properly bring to worship not a dogmatic faith to be thrown down like a gauntlet but a humble faith to be set before God with an openness to new insights and growth. Two statements from the New Testament exemplify the spirit of faith most appropriate in worship. Each is worthy of emulation among all worshipers.

First, a father, with the kind of honesty about faith that honors God, says to Jesus, "I believe; help my unbelief" (Mark 9:24). That statement opens the door to God-inspired growth. Worship is an experience in which an individual can confess, "God, my faith is strong in some areas of life, but there are spots in which I behave as an unbeliever. Help me, please." Also in order in worship is the declaration, "I believe, but I long for a faith that is fuller, stronger, and happier."

Second, after observing Jesus in prayer, one of His disciples says to Jesus, "Lord, teach us to pray" (Luke 11:1). What a way to learn to pray! And that is the manner in which faith can grow. Wise persons enter the presence of God for worship not as people who have all of the answers, not as smug believers who hold faith close to their chests, not as dogmatists looking for an experience to toughen the protective shell which surrounds their convictions but as questioners, seekers, and learners. Always acceptable in worship are words like "Lord, teach us about faith." Such a request shows not of a lack of faith but of a desire for more faith. Jesus' disciples already believed in prayer. But they wanted Christ's help in praying. Surely that is the spirit about believing that is best suited for worship.

In reality, apart from worship, people interested in faith seek to accomplish the impossible. Faith arrives, expands, and grows strong only amid devotion to God. Devoid of worship, faith is reduced to a human endeavor doomed to failure. Faith is a divine gift, not a human achievement. In the worship of God, people find the reason for faith, a motivation for growth in faith, wisdom in all applications and expressions of faith, and constant encouragement for "keeping the faith." No wonder the apostle

Paul understood edification to be a major derivative of the worship of God.

Meaningful Worship Promises Redemption

Occasionally I hear people make comments such as, "I always leave worship mad. I feel worse after attending a worship service than I did when it began. Worship depresses me." Each of those statements is a brilliant red flag fully unfurled to signal serious danger.

Worship can cause disturbances in a misdirected life. A vision of the holiness of God often results in a healthy sense of guilt which prods repentance. The realization of a world out of touch with God can produce real sorrow. However, worship does not lock people into these negative perspectives and confine them to despairing emotions. Christian worship trades in promise and elevates hope. If judgment is sounded, the way of deliverance is described. If guilt is inflicted, the possibility of forgiveness is assured. If people are admonished to change and to effect change, they are provided spiritual guidance on what to do and an assurance of the divinely given strength which makes change possible.

When a church gathers for worship, "the proclamation of the divine *agape* is [its] first and fundamental task."[25] Worship resounds with announcements of the revelation of God upon which it is founded and to which it is a response. Clear to any worshiper are the assurances that human problems are occasions for divine deliverance, that sin is no match for grace, that hopelessness cannot be maintained once the gospel is encountered, that nothing in all of creation can separate a person from the love of God revealed in Jesus Christ.

Worship proclaims salvation history and celebrates it. But more, worship participates in salvation history. Worship is a part of God's redemptive action in the world. In worship, God can affect in the present what is remembered as the very best of the past.

Indicatives dominate Christian worship. Here is a sampling: "The kingdom of God is at hand" (Mark 1:15); "The Spirit helps us in our weakness" (Rom. 8:26); "God is faithful, and he will not let you be tempted beyond your strength" (1 Cor. 10:13); "I will not leave you desolate; I will come to you" (John 14:18); "For freedom Christ has set us free" (Gal. 5:1); "He is our peace" (Eph. 2:14); "My God will supply every need" (Phil.

4:19). Wishful thinking? It almost sounds like it. However, these indicatives are not projections of fond human dreams but declarations of the authoritative Word of God.

Imperatives are present in worship: "Repent"; "Believe"; "Go"; and "Do." But the commands never come first. Even as in the Old Testament, "I will be your God" is forever the prelude to an enumeration of requirements for the people of God. In the New Testament gift always precedes demand. The order of the two can be no different in the authentic worship of God.

Of greatest priority in worship is an announcement of what God has done and is doing, not a reprimand for what worshipers have done or a declaration of what each one must do. Right actions among human beings are possible only as a response to divine initiatives. Once a person understands God's provision for redemption, guilt is a blessing, repentance is a joy, and conversation is the realization of life's highest aspirations. That is why even worship in the worst of circumstances takes on the character of a party, a messianic banquet, a festival that will only get better and better throughout eternity.

Meaningful Worship Reflects the Incarnation

"The Word became flesh" (John 1:14). That is the most important statement within Christianity and the most characteristic statement about Christianity. God became a person. To the dismay of individuals who embrace the ancient heresy which divides the physical and spiritual dimensions of life, labeling the spiritual as "good" and the physical as "evil," the writer of the Fourth Gospel uses the term "flesh," the epitome of physical terms, to describe what happened to the Word. The *logos* became *sarx*—precisely the same word which Paul uses in his warnings about immorality (e.g. Gal. 5:19). The ultimate spiritual revelation took form in the controversial medium of flesh.

The incarnation is the foundation of Christianity. Far more than a doctrine, the incarnation provides the motivation and the pattern for all Christian ministries. The divine-human paradox inherent and evident throughout the ministry of Jesus instructs the integration of the spiritual and the material which is essential in a Christian's life. Christianity is the most material-minded of all the world's religions, and Christian worship is incarnational.[26] God was revealed in a specific place and time among particular people. That is the pattern by which the worship of God is to proceed.

In Christian worship, no part of life is inconsequential. Rather, every aspect of life is a potential medium through which an offering to God can be made. Michael Marshall describes the consequence of this reality, "The inevitable result is that since the very beginning of the Church's life, an offering spiritual in its goal has never been ashamed to pick up and shape the raw material that is at hand on the way, bending it exclusively to the glory of the spiritual and unseen God."[27]

Incarnational worship requires that every dimension of a worshiper's personhood be involved in expressions of God. Contemplation and meditation are important acts of worship to be sure. But Christian worship is much, much more than a cerebral exercise. For every individual within a congregation, the whole person is involved—physically, mentally, emotionally, and spiritually. William Temple states this truth beautifully,

> What worship means is the submission of the whole being to the object of worship. It is the opening of the heart to receive the love of God; it is the subjection of the conscience to be directed by him; it is the declaration of need to be fulfilled by him; it is the subjection of desire to be controlled by him. . . . It is the total giving of self.[28]

A person's body is important in worship. In fact, the Hebrew verb most commonly translated "to worship" calls attention to the significance of appropriate physical expressions in the presence of God.[29] In the early church, people always stood to offer congregational prayers to God and knelt to offer specific pleas to God. At times, the hands of worshipers were raised in praise and at other times extended openly to dramatize a reception of divine blessings.[30] Today, a more meaningful involvement of the human body in worship can enhance the quality of people's praise to God as well as prevent the difficulties caused by a wandering mind, so often the subject of people's complaint related to their attentiveness in worship.

In the not too distant past, even among Christians who insist on a bare minimum of forms and rituals in worship, the physical posture of worshipers received a great deal of attention. Congregations will do well to rethink, if not return to, certain precedents such as standing for praise and kneeling for prayer. Protests from some worshipers are predictable, "We stand up too much. It is inconvenient to kneel in a public service."

Explaining the theological significance of these actions is the best response, and a critically needed one.

Persons serious about the worship of God may fuss about "getting up and down" to sing a song or so the "offering" can be taken. Complaints may be sounded if a request for kneeling merely grows out of routine conformity to a tradition. However, if standing in worship is seen as a means of honoring God and kneeling as an act of contrition, a sign of humility, that is different. Such actions should be accompanied be theological understanding. Then if complaints about them continue, so be it. Incarnational worship is honest to the core whether that is for better or worse.

Incarnational worship perpetuates a dialectic of glory and humility. Even as God is transcendent yet immanent, worship must reflect the heights of glory and the humbleness of the simple. Grandeur is appropriate to worship, but so is all that is common. God readily accepts gifts of splendor and simplicity. Jesus is honored by a regal crown or a simple act of extending a cup of water in His name. God can be worshiped by everybody. The ultimate value of a gift to God is determined not by the worth of what is given but by the love for God with which it is given.

Christian worship "contemporizes" the gospel. When worship is incarnational, people are well aware that God is not confined to a past available only by memory or relegated to a future which can be appropriated only by hope. God is now. God is present; God is involved in our lives. Paul speaks for all who experience incarnational worship, "Now is the acceptable time; behold now is the day of salvation" (2 Cor. 6:2).

Meaningful Worship Builds Up the Church

Worship is the primary function of a church. The church is constituted in worship. Every church exists to glorify God. Without worship, a congregation ceases to be a church.

If worship is not the fundamental activity of a church and its unrivaled priority, every aspect of the church's ministry is adversely affected—fellowship, evangelism, ministry. Worship is essential in winning people to Christ. Worship is nonnegotiable if people are involved in ministries in Christ's name. Worship is the foundation of a close-knit fellowship. Worship is the only guarantee that church administration will be devoted to serving God rather than maintaining an organization.

In worship, as at no other time, a church is open to challenge, to change, to renewal, and to growth. Worship is the context in which the Spirit of God moves in the community of faith for correction, reformation, and direction. Without worship the church is at risk. Apart from regular experiences of corporate worship, the church becomes a totally human fellowship in which individuals attempt to do by their own resourcefulness that which is possible only when done by God. J. S. Whale said it well, "The church lives . . . on God's grace itself, mediated by his spirit in corporate worship."[31]

In the thoughts of the apostle Paul, worship is indispensable for the "upbuilding" of the church. The term Paul uses to express this truth, *oikodomein* ("to build up"), is corporate in nature and totally distinctive. "It has nothing to do with a secular, human fellowship, constituted by human beings but a fellowship 'in Christ,' in the Spirit."[32] Corporate worship does something important to the whole body of worshipers, not just to individuals. In reality, reciprocal actions are involved. Worship builds up the church and contributes to the realization of the body of Christ. At the same time, in worship the church is presented as a gift to God, another offering dedicated to the exaltation of Christ.

Small congregations realize a benefit in worship often overlooked by larger, stronger bodies. In corporate worship, one fellowship of believers is able to sense the strength of a worldwide fellowship of believers. Worship is a cosmic experience as well as a local activity. Worshipers realize, *We are not alone. We are a part of a community of faith that spans the globe.* They experience encouragement and inspiration. A new confidence develops and a renewed commitment to fellowship and ministry is declared.

The church exists by and for worship. Authentic worship builds up the church. Imitations and imposters are easy to spot. Corporate activities which fail to make positive contributions to the church are not worship. All that exalts Christ and glorifies God strengthens the family of God which meets and ministers in Christ's name.

Meaningful Worship Instills Vision

Basic to worship is a vision of God. In fact, where there is no vision of God, there is no worship. But the vision of God spawns other visions. When the prophet Isaiah saw the divine glory, immediately he had a clearer vision of himself and eventually a better vision of his world. Realizing his spiritual condition, Isaiah moved quickly to a confession of his sin and an acceptance of God's forgiveness. Seeing his world with all its needs, Isaiah offered himself to be used by God to bring promise amid problems. Such visions and their consequences are not uncommon among people serious about worship.

Worship instills a vision of reality unavailable elsewhere. Many people outside the church will not understand that vision. Worship bears evidence of the transcendent dimension of life—"the rootage of created reality in a creative Reality."[33] Enlightened by worship, people are convinced that the ultimate values in life and the most meaningful directions for life are oriented to the kingdom of God.

Though that vision is a transcendent one, it does not ignore cares of this world. Actually, the vision instilled in people by worship includes a view of the world from the perspective of the incarnation. Individuals and their needs are seen from the point of view of the love of God and the redemptive ministry of Christ. Thus, rather than a worship-instilled vision leading people out of the world, their purity protected from its problems, this vision thrusts people into the world to share the hurts of the brokenhearted, to bind the wounds of the hurting, to offer food to the hungry, and to speak the good news to those ready to give up. The more "spiritual" worship becomes, the more "worldly" will be the ministries born of the vision which develops there.

Worship creates a mind-set of compassion and a life-style of mission. To see God is to know of God's love for the world. To see Christ is to be aware of His identification with the people seeking to cope with the greatest needs. Vision becomes motivation. To love God is to live lovingly in the world. To serve Christ is to serve problem-plagued people in Christ's name.

A meaningful experience of worship often fills people with an "uplifting" vision. Shattered bonds, radical freedoms, and soaring spirits are not uncommon in worship. Do not be mistaken, though. This vision leads people to a life-affirming engagement, not to a life-denying escape. The vision which "lifts people up" soon "sets them down" in the middle of difficulties. Nourished by the God-shaped vision encountered in worship, people expend their energies dealing with the problems of this world confident that in so doing they are serving God.

Liberated worshipers are free for service, free even to fail. A sense of victory prevails despite what appear to be grinding defeats in ministry. When God is involved, failure is only a temporary condition. God's kingdom will come. "God's will *will* be done. Worshipers know this to be true. They "see" it every time they gather for worship.

Meaningful Worship Makes an Offering

If worship does not extract something costly from worshipers, likely it is not very meaningful. In the truest sense of worship, all of life is laid before God as an offering. Every act of worship is an extension of the congregation's offering to God and as an incentive to offer still more.

The epitome of worship is the self-giving of Christ on the cross. No one better captures the meaning of that event than the author of the great kenotic hymn in Philippians 2:5-11. What is the essence of making an offering? Christ answers that question with His actions—He "emptied himself" (v. 7), "he humbled himself and became obedient unto death" (v. 8).

No worshiper can give more. But no one can give less and be a true worshiper. Making an offering is the essence of worship. People give themselves. The church gives itself. Material gifts are important. Yet alone they are inadequate. Augustine gave his congregation a correct understanding of an offering when he said, "That is *you* being placed on the altar, along with your gifts."[34]

Worship requires a corrective for the current craze aimed at "receiving a blessing." Making an offering is the very first act of worship described in the Bible. It will be the last as well and an integral part of every experience of worship until then. Worship does not happen without self-giving.

Spiritual maturity is not exhibited when "getting a blessing" is the primary motivation behind worshiping. Rather, growing toward a likeness to Christ involves going to worship to make an offering. For a person under God, no higher honor exists than being used by God as a blessing to others. But complete self-giving is a prerequisite to service as an instrument of God's blessing.

Giving in worship throws caution to the wind. Calculators are not needed. Restraint is inappropriate. The actions of others are not relevant. Extravagance is birthed by devotion. Henry Scott Holland tells of a bishop's favor for a certain shepherd who had learned "that the candles on the altar were lighted in broad daylight, because they had no utilitarian purpose."[35] That is the spirit of the offering in worship!

We do not give to God because of God's need but because of our love. In this act, measurements are of no worth. Minimums and maximums are irrelevant concerns. Who can put limits on what love should give to God? Everything seems hardly enough. A true offering in worship is not an attempt to meet an expectation or even to satisfy a need. Offerings in worship are expressions of love. Thus, worship centers on the "foolish" gift—lighting candles in daylight, offering to God what God has plenty of already, sacrificially laying down a life that could be invested in other ways with great material benefits.

When participants in worship realize that their contributions to a service are, in fact, gifts to God, the nature of worship experiences is enhanced immensely. No longer can people do just enough to get by, mumble a few words to fill a time slot, and entertain others present. Words and acts in worship are gifts to God. Thus, everything done and said in worship needs to be appropriate to the praise of God and a worthy presentation to God.

Meaningful Worship Nurtures Communion

Worship is a corporate response to God's call for communion. From the first breath of the first Adam, God has desired fellowship with that part of creation shaped in the divine image. But, persistently and incredulously, humanity has rejected the will of the Deity. God did not quit, though. The depth of God's desire for communion with all persons is dramatically defined by the One nailed to a splintery board crudely attached across a shaft of wood sunk deep into a mound of earth just outside the wall around Jerusalem. God would not be stopped. By means of the crucifixion of Christ, God provided once again for the possibility of fellowship with all people. Worship is communion with God. In worship, people enjoy fellowship with the Creator-Redeemer.

Communion with God results in communion between people who enjoy fellowship with God. Worship nurtures that communion. Worship is an integrative experience which encourages unity among worshipers and creates community. Prior to Pentecost, the dominant word used to describe believers was *disciple*, while after Pentecost the most prevalent term was

family oriented ("brother" was used 230 times after Pentecost).[36]
Worship nurtures a family of faith.

Christians cannot reach their full spiritual potential in solitude. Believers need each other. God calls disciples together. The worship of God keeps people together and establishes a bond between them.

Worship is singular in its power to form a solid unity out of great diversity. Like no other experience, worship transcends divisions, spans schisms, and causes people to set aside their opposition to each other. Caught up in the uninhibited praise of God, people find it difficult to maintain competitive factions in a fellowship. Christian unity is a product of Christian worship and the ministry of Christ. Barriers to fellowship and divisive distinctions between believers are destroyed by Christ (Gal. 3:28). Unity is unattainable by any other means. Worship that does not contribute to unity is not the worship embraced by Christianity.

One other dimension of Christian communion takes me far beyond the realm of my understanding. In worship, the people of God experience communion with each other and join the adoration of their predecessors in the faith, the "great...cloud of witnesses" (Heb. 12:1). The author of Revelation describes this congregation as "a great multitude which no man could number, from every nation, from all tribes and peoples and tongues, standing before the throne and before the Lamb,...and crying with a loud voice, 'Salvation belongs to our God who sits upon the throne, and to the Lamb!'" (Rev. 7:9-10).

So wed are worship, communion, and community among the people of God that to remove any one of the three is to compromise, if not to destroy, the other two. The worship of God nurtures communion among the people of God.

Meaningful Worship Evokes an "Amen"

No word dominates Christian worship more than *amen*. Both in the contemporary Christian community and throughout Christian history, "amen" is prevalent.

Etymologically, "amen" comes from the Hebrew term *aman*, typically used as an adverb meaning truly or verily. To say *aman* was to make a positive declaration. To say "amen" is to declare "yes" emphatically.

In the Scriptures, *amen* is a word of theological as well as liturgical significance. Ancient Hebrews described the God of revelation as the "Amen" (Isa. 65:16). God makes and keeps promises. God's nature involves certainty and sovereignty. Similarly, in the New Testament, Jesus is understood as the "Amen." Paul describes Jesus as the eternal "Yes" to all of God's promises (2 Cor. 1:19-20). In relation to all that God has revealed, Jesus is an "Amen"—a verification, evidence of certainty, the embodiment of truth.

To say "amen" in worship means "so be it," "let it be that way," or "yes." Basically, the term is corporate in nature—the expression of a group rather than an individual's word. By speaking aloud an "amen," people can voice agreement with what is being said in a testimony, a litany, or a sermon. At the conclusion of a prayer, an "amen" indicates a community's appropriation of what has been said to God. One person's words become the prayer of an entire community when joined by a congregational "amen." "Amen" is an offering to God, a crucial act of affirmation in Christian worship and of Christian worship.

Meaningful worship evokes a "yes," an "amen," among all of the worshipers. Spoken aloud? That question can spark a debate. Pros and cons are numerous. However, one matter is a certainty. Voicing an "amen" in worship is not a recent informal innovation. Saying "amen" in worship is a biblical act as old as Christianity, an act from which many congregations have departed, probably to the detriment of their worship.

Offering an "amen" in worship involves much more than speaking. The voiced word anticipates the acted word. "Amen" is a total life response to the call of God—a description of the life situation of a Christian as well as a theological conviction and a liturgical expression. Disciples of Christ think "amen," say "amen," and live as an "amen."

To say "amen" to the God of salvation is to live as a changed being, demonstrating personally the possibility of a new creation.

To say "amen" to the God of faith is to journey faithfully as a pilgrim, holding to convictions, asking questions, and translating grace into actions.

To say "amen" to the God of hope is to live as an agent of encouragement, clinging to the vision of redemption and rejoicing in the promise of the future.

To say "amen" to the God of peace is to live as a peacemaker caring not only about the peace with God which leads to heaven but working for the peace on earth which avoids nuclear annihilation.

To say "amen" to the God of compassion is to care about all of creation, seeking to alleviate starvation, working to eradicate prejudice, attempting to effect social reconciliation, facilitating justice, and establishing community.

The "amen" of conviction and devotion sounded in worship is an expression of personal commitment evidenced in life. Saying "amen" is a means of declaring about the Christian life, "I'm for it. Count me in. Here I am Lord. Use me. Send me."

Amen! The word encapsulates the gospel and epitomizes a truly worshipful response. Our God is faithful to us and worthy of faithful worship from us. Amen! Christ is the incarnation of God and the author of redemption. Amen! Our lives are to be testimonies to Christ's truth, expressions of God's will. Amen!

The invitation of the gospel is directly related to this affirmation in worship, the incarnation of Christ to our situation in the world. We are invited, indeed encouraged, not only to say "amen" but to live as an "amen." In relation to God and to all that God wills, our actions as well as our words are "Yes!" "Right!" "So be it." "Amen!" Worship is integral to all of life. All of life is worship.

An Echo of Worship

When Robert Frost, the great American poet, taught at Amherst, school policy required him to give his students a final examination. Reportedly, at the end of the last class meeting of the term, Frost told his students, "Do something appropriate to this course which will please and interest me."

I can easily imagine similar words spoken by God as a part of the divine invitation to worship. Would-be worshipers receive instructions from God, "In this corporate experience, do something appropriate to worship which will please and interest me."

What a challenge! But what a gift! The people of God are given the freedom to find the very best means for expressing their adoration and devotion to God. That is how meaningful worship is formed. Blessed by biblical guidelines and radical freedom, people shape experiences of worship through which they can most humbly open themselves to God and most honestly make themselves known to God. And the end of such worship is as exciting as the beginning. Meaningful worship evokes an "amen" from all of the worshipers. But that is not all.

At the conclusion of well-done worship, worshipers may discern what seems to be an echo of their corporate "amen." More careful attention, though, captures a near-overwhelming realization. The "amen" is not an echo. The "amen" is a declaration from God. Worship has achieved its purpose. God is pleased by the words and actions of the worshipers. God has received our worship with an eternal "so be it," a divine "yes," a heavenly "Amen."

An "amen" sounded in the heavens sets off a virtual explosion of "amens" among people on earth. Like a geyser erupting, shooting high into the air its irrepressible steam—the act which makes it a geyser—worshipers sound forth the unquenchable joy which emerges from the deepest part of their beings—the act which makes us worshipers.

The vision of John on the island of Patmos intersects and enfolds the people of God where ever they gather. Each child of God takes up a position among the creatures who have surrounded the Creator-Redeemer's throne (Rev. 19:4). With words and deeds, through choral expressions and musical instruments, by way of thoughts and emotions, in confessions and commitments, God is worshiped. All of creation is involved in the praise of God.

Worship resounds through the cosmos. Shouts from the earth are hardly distinguishable from words which reverberate through the heavens. All involved know that this is the highest expression of human nature. In worship, life is at its fullest. The gift of worship has been received from God. And with great joy, worship is being offered to God as a gift.

Amen! Hallelujah!
Hallelujah! Amen!

Notes

Introduction

1. James F. White, *Introduction to Christian Worship,* rev. ed. (Nashville: Abingdon Press, 1990), 31.

2. A. S. Herbert, *Worship in Ancient Israel* (Richmond: John Knox Press, 1963), 47.

3. William Temple, *Readings in St. John's Gospel* (London: Macmillan and Company, 1940), 68, cited by John W. Carlton, "Preaching and Worship," *Review and Expositor* (Summer 1965): 319.

4. J. G. Davies, *Worship and Mission* (New York: Association Press, 1967), 72.

5. Ralph P. Martin, *The Worship of God* (Grand Rapids: William B. Eerdmans Publishing Company, 1982), 218.

6. Leo G. Perdue, "Worship in the Old Testament," *Mercer Dictionary of the Bible,* gen. ed., Watson E. Mills (Macon, Ga.: Mercer University Press, 1990), 971.

7. G. Henton Davies, "Worship in the OT," *The Interpreter's Dictionary of the Bible,* ed., George Arthur Buttrick (Nashville: Abingdon Press, 1962), 4:883.

8. Raymond Bailey, "Worship in the New Testament," *Mercer Dictionary of the Bible,* 971.

9. Gerhard Delling, *Worship in the New Testament,* trans., Percy Scott (Philadelphia: Westminster Press, 1962), xii.

10. Oscar Hardman, *A History of Christian Worship* (Nashville: Cokesbury Press, 1954), 114.

11. Free Church worship is often labeled "nonliturgical" worship. Within Free Churches, no forms of worship are considered normative or regulative. Each local congregation determines its order and methods of worship. Free Church "worship demands freedom to reform worship exclusively on the basis of scripture without any compulsion to dilute the purity of reformation by compromise with human traditions." James White calls such worship "liturgical congregationalism." James F. White, *Protestant Worship: Traditions in Transition* (Louisville: Westminster/ John Knox Press, 1989), 80-81.

12. Don E. Saliers, *Worship and Spirituality* (Philadelphia: Westminster Press, 1984), 29. Over a decade ago, William H. Willimon wrote, "Sunday morning worship has changed more in the past ten years than in the past four hundred." *Word, Water, Wine, and Bread: How Worship Has Changed Over the Years* (Valley Forge: Judson Press, 1983), 5.

13. *Word and Table,* rev. ed. (Nashville: Abingdon Press, 1984). 12.

14. Martin, *The Worship of God,* 1.

15. Orlando E. Costas, *The Church and Its Mission: A Shattering Critique from the Third World* (Wheaton: Tyndale House, 1974), 38.

16. Desmond Mpilo Tutu, *Hope and Suffering: Sermons and Speeches,* ed., John Webster (Grand Rapids: William B. Eerdmans Publishing Company, 1984), 84.

17. John MacArthur, Jr., *The Ultimate Priority: On Worship* (Chicago: Moody Press, 1983), 23.

18. William Nicholls, *Jacob's Ladder: The Meaning of Worship* (Richmond: John Knox Press, 1958), 9.

Part I: Priority

1

The Primacy of Worship in the Fellowship of the Church

1. Excellent treatments of the concept of the "priesthood of the believer" can be found in Carlyle Marney, *Priests to Each Other* (Valley Forge: Judson Press, 1974), and Walter B. Shurden, *The Doctrine of the Priesthood of Believers* (Nashville: Convention Press, 1987).

2. John E. Burkhart, *Worship: A Searching Examination of the Liturgical Experiences* (Philadelphia: Westminster Press, 1982), 47.

3. In addition to the practices of late medieval worship and Roman Catholic worship, James F. White identifies nine different liturgical traditions or "families" within Protestant worship. James F. White, *Protestant Worship: Traditions in Transition* (Louisville: Westminster/ John Knox Press, 1989).

4. Stephen F. Winward, *The Reformation of Our Worship* (Richmond: John Knox Press, 1965), 54.

5. C. Welton Gaddy, "The Pastor as Leader of Public Worship," *Faith, Life, and Witness: The Papers of the Study and Research Division of the Baptist World Alliance-1986-1990,* eds., William H. Brackney and Ruby J. Burke (Birmingham: Samford University Press, 1990), 360.

6. William H. Willimon, *The Service of God* (Nashville: Abingdon Press, 1983), 12.

7. Geoffrey Barlow, ed. *Vintage Muggeridge: Religion and Society* (Grand Rapids: William B. Eerdmans Publishing Company, 1985), 159.

8. Orlando E. Costas, *The Church and Its Mission: A Shattering Critique from the Third World* (Wheaton: Tyndale House, 1974), 51.

9. C. S. Lewis, *Letters to Malcolm: Chiefly on Prayer* (New York: Harcourt Brace Jovanovich, 1964), 115.

10. Thomas Oden describes the care of a soul as "a vocation set aside to guide our souls in their journey through life toward fulfillment of their genuine freedom and possibility." The term "soul care" comes from the Latin *cura animarum,* which designated the care of the phenomenon that animates a person. Thomas C. Oden, *Ministry Through Word & Sacrament* (New York: Crossroad, 1989), 5.

Other excellent elaborations of the significance of worship in the care of a soul can be found in William H. Willimon, *Worship as Pastoral Care* (Nashville: Abingdon Press, 1982), and M. Mahan Siler, "Rites of Passage: A Meeting of Worship and Pastoral Care," *Review and Expositor* 65 (Winter 1988): 51-61. See particularly page 31 in *Worship as Pastoral Care* where Willimon demonstrates how worship contributes to each of the functions historically identified as major components of the ministry of pastoral care.

11. Tertullian, *Apology,* 39:1-6, cited in Oden, *Ministry Through Word & Sacrament,* 59.

12. Athanasius, "A Letter to Marcellinus," *Ancient Christian Writers,* eds., J. Quasten, J. C. Plumpe, and W. Burghardt, (New York: Paulist Press, 1946-85), 10:124, cited in Oden, *Ministry Through Word & Sacrament,* 102.

13. Robert E. Webber and Rodney Clapp, *People of the Truth: The Power of the Worshipping Community in the Modern World* (San Francisco: Harper and Row, 1988), 72.

14. Elton Trueblood, *The Company of the Committed* (New York: Harper and Row, 1961), 70.

15. Robert McAfee Brown, *Spirituality and Liberation: Overcoming the Great Fallacy* (Philadelphia: Westminster Press, 1988), 87.

16. J. F. White, *The Worldliness of Worship* (New York: Oxford University Press, 1967), 81.

17. I have discussed the festive and celebrative nature of worship in *God's Clowns: Messengers of the Good News* (San Francisco: Harper and Row, 1990), 114-21.

18. C. Welton Gaddy, *Tuning the Heart: University Sermons* (Macon, Ga.: Mercer University Press, 1990), 29.

19. Victor L. Hunter and Phillip Johnson, *The Human Church in the Presence of Christ* (Macon, Ga.: Mercer University Press, 1985), 169.

20. Charles Wesley, "Love Divine, All Loves Excelling" *The Baptist Hymnal,* ed., Wesley L. Forbis (Nashville: Convention Press, 1991), Hymn 208.

21. Richard John Neuhaus, *Freedom for Ministry: A Critical Affirmation of the Church and Its Mission* (San Francisco: Harper and Row, 1976), 135.

22. Edward A. Sovik, "Images of the Church," *Worship* 41 (March 1967): 134.

23. Paul Waitman Hoon, *The Integrity of Worship: Ecumenical and Pastoral Studies in Liturgical Theology* (Nashville: Abingdon Press, 1971), 29.

24. Neuhaus, *Freedom for Ministry,* 127.

25. Cited in Webber and Clapp, *People of the Truth,* 91.

26. K. E. Kirk, *The Vision of God* (New York: Green and Company, 1931), 445, cited in R. Benjamin Garrison, *Portrait of the Church Warts and All* (New York: Abingdon Press, 1964), 115.

27. Hoon, *The Integrity of Worship,* 59.

28. John Killenger, *Leave It to the Spirit: Freedom and Commitment in the New Liturgy* (New York: Harper and Row, 1971), 22-23.

2

The Centrality of Worship in the Ministry of the Church

1. Paul Waitman Hoon, *The Integrity of Worship: Ecumenical and Pastoral Studies in Liturgical Theology* (Nashville: Abingdon Press, 1971), 36.

2. Michael Marshall, *Renewal in Worship* (Wilton: Morehouse-Barlow, 1985), 11.

3. Hoon, *The Integrity of Worship,* 34.

4. Hoyt L. Hickman, *A Primer for Church Worship* (Nashville: Abingdon Press, 1984), 33-34.

5. Ferdinand Hahn, *The Worship of the Early Church,* trans., David E. Green (Philadelphia: Fortress Press, 1973), 9.

6. William Nicholls, *Jacob's Ladder: The Meaning of Worship* (Richmond: John Knox Press, 1978), 9.

7. Robert E. Webber, *Worship Is a Verb* (Waco, Tex.: Word Books Publisher, 1985), 18.

8. Robert E. Webber and Rodney Clapp, *People of the Truth: The Power of the Worshipping Community in the Modern World* (San Francisco: Harper and Row, 1988), 68.

9. Hans Kung, *Signposts for the Future: Contemporary Issues Facing the Church* (Garden City, N.Y.: Doubleday and Company, 1978), 171.

10. Geoffrey Wainwright, *Doxology: The Praise of God in Worship, Doctrine, and Life* (New York: Oxford University Press, 1980).

11. Frank Stagg, *New Testament Theology* (Nashville: Broadman Press, 1962), 267.

12. Cited in Webber and Clapp, *People of the Truth,* 68.

13. George W. Webber, *The Congregation in Mission: Emerging Structures for the Church in an Urban World* (New York: Abingdon Press, 1964), 93.

14. Victor L. Hunter and Phillip Johnson, *The Human Church in the Presence of Christ* (Macon, Ga.: Mercer University Press, 1985), 156.

15. Orlando E. Costas, *The Church and Its Mission: A Shattering Critique from the Third World* (Wheaton: Tyndale House, 1974), 38.

16. W. M. S. West, "Baptist Church Life Today," *The Pattern of the Church: A Baptist View,* ed., A. Gilmore, (London: Lutterworth Press, 1963), 27.

17. Walter T. Conner, *The Gospel of Redemption* (Nashville: Broadman Press, 1945), 277, cited by Paul A. Richardson, "The Primacy of Worship," *Review and Expositor* 65 (Winter 1988): 9.

18. John W. Carlton, "Preaching and Worship," *Review and Expositor* 62 (Summer 1965): 319.

19. Franklin M. Segler, *Christian Worship: Its Theology and Practice* (Nashville: Broadman Press, 1967), 208.

20. Franklin M. Segler, "Worship Is Church's Most Basic Function," *The Window,* March 22, 1984, (Fort Worth, Tex.: Broadway Baptist Church), 3.

21. John Killenger, *The Centrality of Preaching in the Total Task of the Ministry* (Waco, Tex.: Word Books, 1969), 85-86.

22. Gaines S. Dobbins, *The Church at Worship* (Nashville: Broadman Press, 1962,), 116.

23. Marshall, *Renewal in Worship,* 114.

24. James F. White, *The Worldliness of Worship* (New York: Oxford University Press, 1967), 103.

25. Ibid., 104.

26. Cited in Hoon, *The Integrity of Worship,* 59.

27. The whole of salvation history is presented within the cycle of the Christian year: Easter, Ascension, Pentecost, Trinity (or Kingdomtide), Advent, Christmas, Epiphany, Lent, Passion, Good Friday.

28. Webber, *Worship Is a Verb,* 37.

29. Hoon, *The Integrity of Worship,* 135.

30. White, *The Worldliness of Worship,* 101.

31. Don E. Saliers, *Worship and Spirituality* (Philadelphia: Westminster Press, 1984), 58.

32. Compare Jesus' statement with the text of Deuteronomy 6:5, which He knew well. Jesus adds the words "with all your mind" to the Old Testament text, thus enhancing the comprehensiveness of the human love which belongs to God. People are to love God with every aspect of their beings.

33. Hugh T. McElrath, "We Praise You with Our Minds, O Lord," *The Baptist Hymnal,* ed., Wesley L. Forbis (Nashville: Convention Press, 1991), Hymn 599.

34. Hoon, *The Integrity of Worship,* 29.

35. William H. Willimon, *Worship as Pastoral Care* (Nashville: Abingdon Press, 1982), 122.

36. For an excellent treatment of the educational value of Christian worship during a funeral, see the chapter entitled "Liturgy and Life's Crises: The Funeral," in Willimon, *Worship as Pastoral Care,* 100-21.

37. Ibid., 122-46, for a similar treatment on a wedding. Also helpful are two chapters on marriage in William H. Willimon, *The Service of God: How Worship and Ethics are Related* (Nashville: Abingdon Press, 1983), 158-86.

38. Helpful elaborations of the educational value of baptismal services can be found in Willimon, *The Service of God,* 95-117, and Willimon, *Worship as Pastoral Care,* 147-65. Willimon also provides similar treatments of the Lord's Supper. *The Service of God,* 118-37, and *Worship as Pastoral Care,* 166-94.

39. Craig Douglas Erickson, *Participating in Worship: History, Theory, and Practice* (Louisville: Westminster/John Knox Press, 1989), 19.

40. Donald P. Hustad, *Jubilate! Church Music in the Evangelical Tradition* (Carol Stream, Ill.: Hope Publishing Company, 1981), 78.

41. Webber and Clapp, *People of the Truth,* 102.

42. Catechism is defined as "the basic doctrines of the Christian faith for the study of young or new Christians, often in question-and-answer form." James F. White, *Protestant Worship: Traditions in Transition* (Louisville: Westminster/John Knox Press, 1989), 232.

43. More detailed discussions of my definition of preaching can be found in C. Welton Gaddy, *Proclaim Liberty* (Nashville: Broadman Press, 1975), 68-69, and C. Welton Gaddy, "Preaching and Social Change," *Shooting the Rapids: Effective Ministry in a Changing World,* comp., Fred W. Andrea (Nashville: Broadman Press, 1990), 40-41.

44. In Richard John Neuhaus, *Freedom For Ministry: A Critical Affirmation of the Church and Its Mission* (New York: Harper and Row, 1979), 149.

45. Henry Sloane Coffin says, "The preaching of the Word is a corporate action in which preacher, congregation, and a long line of their predecessors reaching back through the centuries to the original event and corroborating the interpretation given that event in Scripture, cooperate." *Communion Through Preaching* (New York: Charles Scribner's Sons, 1952), 9, cited in Carlton, "Preaching and Worship," 321. In a small but very beneficial book, Martin E. Marty discusses the preaching event from the perspective of the congregation's responsibility to participate in it. Martin E. Marty, *The Word: People Participating in Preaching* (Philadelphia: Fortress Press, 1984).

46. A full discussion of these characteristics of incarnational preaching can be found in a chapter on "The Nation and the Pulpit," in Gaddy, *Proclaim Liberty,* 70-77.

47. John Knox, *The Integrity of Preaching: How Biblical Sermons Meet Modern Needs* (New York: Abingdon Press, 1957), 78.

48. John Carlton makes a plea for avoiding "impromptu preaching," stating that more than one sermon has conformed to Warren G. Harding's description of a speech: "An army of pious phrases marching all over the landscape in search of an idea." Carlton, "Preaching and Worship," 324.

49. In Willimon, *Worship as Pastoral Care,* 93.

50. P. T. Forsyth says, "The sermon is the Word of the gospel returning in confession to the God who gave it. It is addressed to men indeed, but in truth it is offered to God. Addressed to men but offered to God—that is the true genius of preaching." P. T. Forsyth, *Positive Preaching and the Modern Mind* (London: Independent Press, 1957), 66, cited in Carlton, "Preaching and Worship," 325.

51. Knox, *The Integrity of Preaching,* 76.

52. Ibid., 85.

53. Hoon, *The Integrity of Worship,* 110-11, discusses several insights regarding the priority of worship in relation to mission. He cites Dietrich Bonhoeffer's comment: "The first demand...made of those who belong to God's Church is...that they shall be witnesses to Jesus Christ before the world....This testimony before the world can be delivered in a right way only if it springs from a hallowed life in the congregation of God. But a genuine hallowed life in the congregation...at the same time impels a man to testify before the world." (From Dietrich Bonhoeffer, *Ethics,* ed., Eberhard Bethge; trans., Neville Horton Smith (New York: The Macmillan Co., 1955), 69). Hoon also cites Douglas Webster's words, "The end of all our worship is that we should be transformed into Christ's likeness and that he should be formed in us. And the end of the Christian mission is that the kingdoms of this world become the kingdom of our God and of his Christ.... The mission of the people of God is to be so completely his, that they are agents of this transformation." (From Douglas Webster, "The

Mission of the People of God," *Liturgical Renewal in the Christian Churches,* 195.)

54. Saliers, *Worship and Spirituality,* 78.

55. The phrase is from Thomas J. Talley, "The Sacredness of Contemporary Worship," *Worship in the City of Man,* 38, cited in Hoon, *The Integrity of Worship,* 136.

56. Hoon, *The Integrity of Worship,* 136.

57. Saliers, *Worship and Spirituality,* 84.

58. Hoon, *The Integrity of Worship,* 36, cites the work of Gregory Dix which documents how weaknesses in a church's worship adversely affect the effectiveness of that church's mission. Gregory Dix, *The Shape of the Liturgy* (Westminster: Dacre Press, 1945), xii.

59. Saliers, *Worship and Spirituality,* 89.

60. Max Kadushin, *Worship and Ethics: A Study in Rabbinic Judaism* (Evanston: Northwestern University Press, 1964), 6.

61. Robert McAfee Brown, *Spirituality and Liberation: Overcoming the Great Fallacy* (Philadelphia: Westminster Press, 1988), 93.

62. Willimon, *The Service of God,* 34. See also 74 and 203.

63. Hoon, *The Integrity of Worship,* 31.

64. Willimon, *The Service of God,* 15.

65. Emil Brunner, *The Divine Imperative,* trans., Olive Wyon (Philadelphia: Westminster Press, 1947), 536.

66. Willimon, *The Service of God,* 194.

67. Webber and Clapp, *People of the Truth,* 95.

68. Baptismal terminology suggests the importance of morality. Baptism is described as a washing or a cleansing (Willimon, *The Service of God,* 111, posits that the best biblical analogy is a drowning) and as a dying to one way of life followed by a resurrection to a new way of life in which one consistently walks. Don Saliers gathers the biblical imagery related to baptism in a comprehensive manner in Saliers, *Worship and Spirituality,* 67-68. Geoffrey Wainwright declares, "It would be possible to develop a whole Christian ethic from the figures associated with baptism." Wainwright, *Doxology,* 412. The most complete exposition of the ethics of baptism in the New Testament is Paul's statement in Romans 6:1-11.

Jurgen Moltmann writes of the Lord's Supper, "Anyone who celebrates the Lord's Supper in a world of hunger and oppression does so in complete solidarity with the sufferings and hopes of all men, because he believes that the Messiah invites all men to his table and because he hopes that they will all sit at table with him.... Christ's messianic feast makes its participants one with the physically and spiritually hungry all over the world." Jurgen Moltmann, *The Church in the Power of the Spirit: A Contribution to Messianic Ecclesiology,* trans., Margaret Kohl (New York: Harper and Row, 1977), 258.

69. "The greatest single threat to the principalities and powers comes in the worship of God." Hunter and Johnson, *The Human Church in the Presence of Christ,* 155.

70. Willimon, *The Service of God,* 81.

71. T. W. Manson, *Ethics and the Gospel* (New York: Charles Scribner's Sons, 1960), 68.

72. Elmer L. Towns, John N. Vaughn, David J. Seifert, eds., *The Complete Book of Church Growth* (Wheaton, Ill.: Tyndale House, 1981), 187-216. This is not untypical of most church growth publications. Indexes of composites of church growth periodicals reveal a sparsity, if not a total lack, of references to worship.

73. Ibid., 249-50.

74. J. G. Davies, *Worship and Mission* (New York: Association Press, 1967), 51, citing D. Jenkins, *The Strangeness of the Church,* 1956, 35.

75. Oden, *Ministry Through Word & Sacrament,* 188, citing Salvian the Presbyter, *The Four Books of Timothy to the Church,* Bk. 1, sec. 1, *Fathers of the Church,* ed., R. J. Deferrari, Vol. 3 (Washington, D. C.: Catholic University Press, 1947ff), 270.
76. Marshall, *Renewal in Worship,* 116.
77. Oden, *Ministry Through Word & Sacrament,* 184-85.
78. John H. Westerhoff III and John D. Eusden, *The Spiritual Life: Learning East and West* (New York: The Seabury Press, 1982), 119.

Part II: Activity

3

An Order of Worship

1. Oscar Cullmann, *Early Christian Worship* (Philadelphia: Westminster Press, 1953), 20.
2. Cited in Ralph P. Martin, *The Worship of God: Some Theological, Pastoral, and Practical Reflections,* (Grand Rapids, William B. Eerdmans Publishing Company, 1982), 190.
3. C. C. Richardson, "Worship in NT Times, Christian," *The Interpreter's Dictionary of the Bible,* ed., George Arthur Buttrick (Nashville: Abingdon Press, 1962), 4:888-89, and Richard M. Spielmann, *History of Christian Worship* (New York: The Seabury Press, 1966), 28-30.

Allen Cabaniss carefully analyzes the work of Justin Martyr and then compares it with the description of worship found in a letter from Pliny the Younger to the Emperor Trajan (who reigned 98-117) to establish the exact order of Christian liturgy in the second century. Cabaniss's volume includes translations of the original materials from Justin Martyr and Pliny and Younger as well as an extensive bibliography on early Christian worship. Allen Cabaniss, *Pattern in Early Christian Worship* (Macon, Ga.: Mercer University Press, 1989).

4. Cabaniss writes, "If we should, for example, take the New Testament to be an absolute source of Christian liturgy, the very first thing we would have to get rid of is the New Testament itself!" Ibid., 74.

Based on his studies of New Testament worship materials and second-century documents related to liturgy, Cabaniss offers an order of worship "as close to New Testament procedure and content as possible": Baptism precedes the service. (1) The service proper opens with a reading or singing of one or more psalms or hymns. A brief prayer concludes this first section of worship. (2) An Old Testament lesson is read. Then, part of Psalm 119 is read or sung. If not the psalm, a canticle or hymn is sung. (3) A passage from the Epistles, Acts, or Revelation is read. Next comes a recitation of jubilant singing of one of the Hallelujah psalms or *Gloria in Excelsis.* (4) A Gospel lesson is read with solemnity. (5) The congregation recites a profession of faith. (6) A "great prayer" inclusive of adoration, acknowledgement of sin, intercession, supplication, thanksgiving, and communion of the saints is offered by one person with multiple "Amens" from the congregation. Next, everyone speaks the Lord's Prayer together. (7) Bread and wine are blessed and distributed for people to participate in communion. A brief prayer of thanksgiving is spoken. (8) The service ends with a psalm, hymn, or canticle followed by a blessing or some other form of dismissal.

A sermon can be included after (7) or (8) and a "collection" after (5) or (6). The collection is not accompanied by a prayer to prevent glamorization. The sermon is a conversational exposition of a Scripture passage concluded with an exhortation.

5. Ibid., 75-80.

4

Gathering

1. The New Testament word usually translated *church* actually means *assembly.* Hoyt L. Hickman, *A Primer for Church Worship* (Nashville: Abingdon Press, 1984), 41.

2. Dale Moody related to me the strangest "call to worship" I have ever heard. Moody was serving as a guest preacher in the First Baptist Church of a small town in Kentucky. As the service began, a man walked to the pulpit and said, "Take your chew tobacco out, get you a hymnbook, let's sing!"

3. Geoffrey Wainwright, *Doxology: The Praise of God in Worship, Doctrine, and Life* (New York: Oxford University Press, 1980), 32.

4. Craig Douglas Erickson, *Participating in Worship: History, Theory, and Practice* (Louisville: Westminster/John Knox Press, 1989), 201.

5. Ibid., 64.

5

Praising

1. Robert E. Webber and Rodney Clapp, *People of the Truth: The Power of the Worshipping Community in the Modern World* (San Francisco: Harper and Row, 1988), 94.

2. Ralph P. Martin, *The Worship of God: Some Theological, Pastoral, and Practical Reflections* (Grand Rapids, Mich.: William B. Eerdmans Publishing Company, 1984), 29.

3. Robert E. Webber, *Worship Is a Verb* (Waco, Tex.: Word Books, 1985), 136, and Martin, *The Worship of God,* 20.

4. Evelyn Underhill, *Worship* (New York: Crossroad, 1985), 100.

5. Martin, *The Worship of God,* 23.

6. Joachim Neander, "Praise to the Lord, the Almighty," trans., Catherine Winkworth, *The Baptist Hymnal,* ed., Wesley L. Forbis (Nashville: Convention Press, 1991), Hymn 14.

7. Francis of Assisi, "All Creatures of Our God and King," *The Baptist Hymnal,* Hymn 27.

8. Ibid.

6

Listening

1. Craig Douglas Erickson, *Participating in Worship: History, Theory, and Practice* (Louisville: Westminster/John Knox Press, 1989), 51.

2. Evelyn Underhill, *Worship* (New York: Crossroad, 1985), 95.

3. William H. Willimon, *The Bible: A Sustaining Presence in Worship* (Valley Forge: Judson Press, 1981), 15.

4. Geoffrey Wainwright, *Doxology: The Praise of God in Worship, Doctrine, and Life* (New York: Oxford University Press, 1980), 165. On pages 173-75, Wainwright provides an excellent summary of the reasons for and against regular readings from the Old Testament in Christian worship.

7

Praying

1. Cited in William H. Willimon, *Worship as Pastoral Care* (Nashville: Abingdon Press, 1982), 216.

2. Cited in ibid.

3. Cited in Raymond Abba, *Principles of Christian Worship* (New York: Oxford University Press, 1966), 115.

4. Cited in ibid.

8

Confessing

1. Raymond Abba, *Principles of Christian Worship* (New York: Oxford University Press, 1966), 89.

2. Ibid.

3. Cited in Geoffrey Wainwright, *Doxology: The Praise of God in Worship, Doctrine, and Life* (New York: Oxford University Press, 1980), 131.

9

Proclaiming

1. Ralph P. Martin, *The Worship of God: Some Theological, Pastoral, and Practical Reflections* (Grand Rapids: William B. Eerdmans Publishing Company, 1982), 101.

2. James F. White, *Introduction to Christian Worship,* rev. ed. (Nashville: Abingdon Press, 1990), 156.

3. Thor Hall, *The Future Shape of Preaching* (Philadelphia: Fortress Press, 1971), 104.

4. Cited in Raymond Abba, *Principles of Christian Worship* (New York: Oxford University Press, 1966), 64.

5. Merrill R. Abbey, *The Word Interprets Us: Biblical Preaching in the Present Tense* (Nashville: Abingdon Press, 1967), 28, citing Gerhard Ebeling, *Word and Faith* (Philadelphia: Fortress Press, 1963), 330f.

6. Abba, *Principles of Christian Worship,* 64.

7. William H. Willimon, *The Service of God: How Worship and Ethics Are Related* (Nashville: Abingdon Press, 1983), 153.

8. Phillips Brooks, *On Preaching* (New York: The Seabury Press, 1964), 5.

9. William H. Willimon, *With Glad and Generous Hearts: A Personal Look at Sunday Worship* (Nashville: The Upper Room, 1986), 97.

10. Ilion T. Jones, *Principles and Practice of Preaching: A Comprehensive Study of the Art of Sermon Construction* (New York: Abingdon Press, 1961), 43, citing Emerson's *Journal* as quoted in Harold W. Ruopp, "The Christian Century Pulpit," May 1941, 117.

11. James W. Cox, *Preaching: A Comprehensive Approach to the Design and Delivery of Sermons* (San Francisco: Harper and Row 1985), 92.

12. James S. Stewart, *Heralds of God: A Practical Book on Preaching* (New York: Charles Scribner's Sons, 1946), 67.

13. In the "Preface to the English Edition" of the first volume of his *Theological Ethics,* Helmut Thielicke writes, "It became clear to me that in this scholarly undertaking what I was basically trying to do was to lay a new foundation for Christian preaching." Helmut Thielicke, *Theological Ethics: Foundations,* ed., William H. Lazareth (Philadelphia: Fortress Press, 1966), 1:xv.

14. Herbert H. Farmer, *The Servant of the Word* (Philadelphia: Fortress Press, n.d.), 15.

15. In Abba, *Principles of Christian Worship,* 139.

16. Willimon, *The Service of God,* 97; Hoyt L. Hickman, *A Primer for Church Worship* (Nashville: Abingdon Press, 1984), 95; and James F. White, *New Forms of Worship* (Nashville: Abingdon Press, 1971), 155.

17. Frank Stagg, *New Testament Theology* (Nashville: Broadman Press, 1962), 233.

18. The term comes from William H. Willimson's statement, "We must cease promiscuous baptism," in *The Service of God,* 115.

19. White, *New Forms of Worship,* 160.

20. Michael Marshall, *Renewal in Worship* (Wilton: Morehouse-Barlow, 1985), 74.

21. Geoffrey Wainwright, *Doxology: The Praise of God in Worship, Doctrine, and Life* (New York: Oxford University Press, 1980), 412-13.

22. Ibid., 413, and Dale Moody, *The Word of Truth: A Summary of Christian Doctrine Based on Biblical Revelation* (Grand Rapids: William B. Eerdmans Publishing Company, 1981), 313.

23. Martin, *The Worship of God,* 156.

24. Willimon, *The Service of God,* 129.

25. White, *New Forms of Worship,* 164.

26. Ibid., 72.

27. Abba, *Principles of Christian Worship,* 175.

28. Willimon, *With Glad and Generous Hearts,* 142.

29. White, *New Forms of Worship,* 139.

30. Gaines S. Dobbins, *The Church at Worship* (Nashville: Broadman Press, 1962), 85.

31. Abba, *Principles of Christian Worship,* 120.

32. Paul Waitman Hoon, *The Integrity of Worship: Ecumenical and Pastoral Studies in Liturgical Theology* (Nashville: Abingdon Press, 1971), 69.

33. Marshall, *Renewal in Worship,* 130.

34. Robert E. Webber, *Worship Is a Verb* (Waco, Tex.: Word Books Publisher, 1985), 175.

10

Singing

1. Craig Douglas Erickson, *Participating in Worship: History, Theory, and Practice* (Louisville: Westminster/John Knox Press, 1989), 95.

2. Hugh T. McElrath, "Praise and Worship," *Review and Expositor,* 62 (Summer 1965): 294.

3. Allen Cabaniss offers the only serious argument I have seen for an absence of singing in the worship of the early church. Cabaniss recognizes that singing was common among early Christians. But he suggests that this singing was for the sake of instruction, not a part of their liturgy. Allen Cabaniss, *Pattern in Early Christian Worship* (Macon, Ga.: Mercer University Press, 1989), 50.

4. Cited in Ralph P. Martin, *The Worship of God: Some Theological, Pastoral, and Practical Reflections* (Grand Rapids: William B. Eerdmans Publishing Company, 1982), 46.

5. Erickson, *Participating in Worship,* 82-83.

6. See Bernard Schalm, *The Church at Worship* (Grand Rapids: Baker Book House, 1962), 54-55, for arguments against the use of gospel songs in corporate worship. Conversely, a rationale for the use of gospel songs in public worship can be found in Donald P. Hustad, *Jubilate! Church Music in the Evangelical Tradition* (Carol Stream, Ill.: Hope Publishing Company, 1981), 257-61.

7. Winifred Douglas, *Church Music in History and Practice* (New York: Charles Scribner's Sons, 1940), 9f, cited in Michael Marshall, *Renewal in Worship* (Wilton: Morehouse-Barlow, 1985), 66.

11

Offering

1. Paul Waitman Hoon, *The Integrity of Worship: Ecumenical and Pastoral Studies in Liturgical Theology* (Nashville: Abingdon Press, 1971), 231.

2. Ralph P. Martin, *The Worship of God: Some Theological, Pastoral, and Practical Reflections* (Grand Rapids: William B. Eerdmans Publishing Company, 1982), 66.

3. Hoon, *The Integrity of Worship,* 352.

4. J. E. Fison, *The Meaning of the Holy Spirit,* 197, cited in Stephen F. Winward, *The Reformation of Our Worship* (Richmond: John Knox Press, 1965), 52.

5. Donald P. Hustad, *Jubilate! Church Music in the Evangelical Tradition* (Carol Stream, Ill.: Hope Publishing Company, 1981), 284.

6. Will D. Campbell, *Brother to a Dragonfly* (New York: The Seabury Press, 1977), 5.

7. William Nicholls, *Jacob's Ladder: The Meaning of Worship* (Richmond: John Knox Press, 1958), 26. Similarly, Hoon, *The Integrity of Worship,* 348, says, "The liturgy of Jesus Christ, finally, determines the action of worship to be *sacrificial* in the sense that it is the action of man offering himself to God."

8. J. G. Davies, *Worship and Mission* (New York: Association Press, 1967), 138.

12

Departing

1. William H. Willimon, *The Bible: A Sustaining Presence in Worship* (Valley Forge: Judson Press, 1981), 99.

2. Ibid., 103.

3. Ibid., 100.

4. Martin E. Marty, *The Word: People Participating in Preaching* (Philadelphia: Fortress Press, 1984), 104.

Part III: Priority

13

Affirming Variety While Assuring Unity in Worship

1. Ernest A. Payne, *The Fellowship of Believers: Baptist Thought and Practice Yesterday and Today* (London: The Carey Kingsgate Press, Ltd., 1954), 93-93, citing W. H. Burgess, *John Smyth the Se-Baptist,* 170-71.

2. Will D. Campbell, *The Glad River* (New York: Holt, Rinehart, and Winston, 1982), 272-73.

3. Paul Waitman Hoon, *The Integrity of Worship: Ecumenical and Pastoral Studies in Liturgical Theology* (Nashville: Abingdon Press, 1971), 38-39.

4. William H. Willimon, *The Bible: A Sustaining Presence in Worship* (Valley Forge: Judson Press, 1981), 21, discusses the significant seventeenth-century debate on how the Bible properly contributes to and judges worship.

5. Ibid.

6. Stephen F. Winward, *The Reformation of Our Worship* (Richmond: John Knox Press, 1965), 77.

7. Michael Marshall, *Renewal in Worship* (Wilton: Morehouse-Barlow, 1985), 53.

8. William H. Willimon, *Worship as Pastoral Care* (Nashville: Abingdon Press, 1982), 23.

14

Providing Meaningful Worship

1. James White identifies seven such factors and treats them as "categories or worship." James F. White, *Protestant Worship: Traditions in Transition* (Louisville: Westminster/John Knox Press, 1989), 15-21.

2. An excellent discussion of "the language of faith," both historical and analytical in nature, is available in James F. White, _Introduction to Christian Worship,_ rev. ed. (Nashville: Abingdon Press, 1990), 88-121.

3. The Christian year is a calendar developed around the incarnation—from Christ's birth to His expected coming again. The Christian year is composed of two parts. First, this calendar focuses on Christ's birth, earthly ministry, death, and resurrection. The second half of the Christian year involves the time of the church under Christ's lordship and the Holy Spirit's leadership. See Patricia B. Buckland, _Advent to Pentecost: A History of the Christian Year_ (Wilton, Conn.: Morehouse-Barlow Co., 1979).

John Westerhoff III writes, "The church is a story-formed community, a people on pilgrimage through time, through seasons of profane time made holy by the eternal cycle of sacred time. The manner in which we order and use time is the best indicator of what is important to us.... the days we celebrate give meaning and purpose to our lives." John Westerhoff III, _A Pilgrim People: Learning Through the Church Year_ (Minneapolis: The Seabury Press, 1984), 9.

4. White, _Introduction to Christian Worship,_ 72-76. "One of the fundamental aims of liturgy is to help us to relive God's story in such a way that it touches, illumines, and transforms our human story and thereby shapes our lives to serve God's purpose for personal and communal life." Westerhoff, _A Pilgrim People,_ 10.

5. Craig Douglas Erickson, _Participating in Worship: History, Theory, and Practice_ (Louisville: Westminster/John Knox Press, 1989), 3. Erickson also writes, "Participatory worship is founded upon _pietas_ or piety—that personal trust in and reverence for God that inclines the heart to true worship and devotion."

6. Evelyn Underhill, _Worship_ (New York: Crossroad, 1985), 5.

7. Rudolph Otto, _The Idea of the Holy_ (London: Oxford University Press, 1923), cited in Ralph P. Martin, _The Worship of God: Some Theological, Pastoral, and Practical Reflections_ (Grand Rapids: William B. Eerdmans Publishing Company, 1984), 173.

8. William Nicholls, _Jacob's Ladder: The Meaning of Worship_ (Richmond: John Knox Press, 1958), 17.

9. "Eastern churches to this day speak of worship as an _epiphany,_ a manifestation of all that Christ was and is." Don E. Saliers. _Worship and Spirituality_ (Philadelphia: Westminster Press, 1984), 80.

10. Nicholls, _Jacob's Ladder,_ 18.

11. Underhill, _Worship,_ 69.

12. Michael Marshall, _Renewal in Worship_ (Wilton: Morehouse-Barlow, 1985), 20.

13. Underhill, _Worship,_ 219, and Martin, _The Worship of God,_ 197.

14. Underhill, _Worship,_ 68.

15. Elton Trueblood, _The Company of the Committed_ (New York: Harper and Row, Publishers, 1961), 38.

16. Ibid., 31-32.

17. Ibid., 32.

18. Martin, _The Worship of God,_ 23-24.

19. Elizabeth Achtemeier, _Preaching as Theology & Art_ (Nashville: Abingdon Press, 1984), 66.

20. Robert E. Webber and Rodney Clapp, _People of the Truth: The Power of the Worshipping Community in the Modern World_ (San Francisco: Harper and Row, 1988), 95.

21. T. S. Eliot, _Murder in the Cathedral_ (New York: Harcourt, Brace and World, 1963), 87.

22. Elizabeth Achtemeier, _Preaching from the Old Testament_ (Louisville: Westminster/John Knox Press, 1989), 29. Similarly, James White writes, "Without the Scriptures the church would simply be an amorphous conglomeration of people of good will without any identity." James F. White, _New Forms of Worship_ (Nashville: Abingdon Press, 1971), 53.

23. Achtemeier, *Preaching from the Old Testament,* 29.

24. Gaines S. Dobbins, *The Church at Worship* (Nashville: Broadman Press, 1962), 124.

25. Nicholls, *Jacob's Ladder,* 36.

26. Michael Marshall writes, "The principle of the Incarnation is a continuous principle and process throughout the whole history of the Church and should never be more in evidence than in the worship and liturgy of God's people in every age." Marshall, *Renewal in Worship,* 24. Likewise, Paul Hoon writes, "Christian worship first is profoundly incarnational; and the dialectic of the incarnation understood as the whole Event of Jesus Christ, not merely his birth, is to govern all thinking about worship." Paul Waitman Hoon, *The Integrity of Worship: Ecumenical and Pastoral Studies in Liturgical Theology* (Nashville: Abingdon Press, 1971), 122.

27. Marshall, *Renewal in Worship,* 27.

28. Cited in ibid., 31.

29. Stephen F. Winward, *The Reformation of Our Worship,* (Richmond: John Knox Press, 1965), 167.

30. Marshall, *Renewal in Worship,* 35.

31. J. S. Whale, *Christian Doctrine* (Cambridge: The Cambridge University Press, 1952), 152, cited in Franklin M. Segler, *Christian Worship: Its Theology and Practice* (Nashville: Broadman Press, 1967), 209.

32. Martin, *The Worship of God,* 199, citing Ph. Vielhauer, "Oikodome" *Aufsatze zur NT,* band 2 (Munich: Chr. Kaiser Verlag, 1979), 108.

33. Geoffrey Wainwright, *Doxology: The Praise of God in Worship, Doctrine, and Life* (New York: Oxford University Press, 1980), 2.

34. Cited in William H. Willimon, *Worship as Pastoral Care* (Nashville: Abingdon Press, 1982), 71.

35. Cited in Marshall, *Renewal in Worship,* 22.

36. Bernard Schalm, *The Church at Worship* (Grand Rapids: Baker Book House, 1962), 107.

Abbreviated Topical Index